# The Midwestern Pastoral

# THE
# MIDWESTERN
# PASTORAL

Place and Landscape in
Literature of the
American Heartland

WILLIAM BARILLAS

Ohio University Press

Athens

Ohio University Press, Athens, Ohio 45701

www.ohio.edu/oupress

© 2006 by Ohio University Press

Printed in the United States of America

Ohio University Press books are printed on acid-free paper ⊗ ™

14 13 12 11 10 09 08 07 06    5 4 3 2 1

Dust jacket/frontispiece art: *Madison Oaks,* drawing by Dan Beresford

*Library of Congress Cataloging-in-Publication Data*

Barillas, William David.
   The midwestern pastoral : place and landscape in literature of the American heart-
land / William Barillas.
      p. cm.
   Includes bibliographical references and index.
   ISBN 0-8214-1660-X (acid-free paper)
   1. American literature—Middle West—History and criticism. 2. Pastoral literature,
American—History and criticism. 3. Authors, American—Homes and haunts—
Middle West. 4. Place (Philosophy) in literature. 5. Middle West—Intellectual life.
6. Middle West—In literature. 7. Landscape in literature. I. Title.
   PS273.B37 2006
   810.9'3217340977—dc22

2005026992

*Para María,*

*el amor de mi vida*

# Contents

# Preface

This is a book about literary place, focused on writers with strong attachments to particular rural landscapes in the American Midwest. Following a general introduction and a chapter on the historical background of midwestern pastoral ideology and literature, I devote separate chapters to five major writers: Willa Cather, Aldo Leopold, Theodore Roethke, James Wright, and Jim Harrison. Why I choose these five to represent midwestern pastoral writing is a topic that I take up in the introduction. To clarify the relation of these writers to recent trends and to demonstrate the continuing development of midwestern pastoral as a literary tradition, I turn in chapter 7 to three contemporary authors: novelist Jane Smiley, poet Ted Kooser, and essayist Paul Gruchow, whose writings echo and modify themes developed by their predecessors.

My choice of representative authors and my overall perspective on midwestern culture owes something to my own midwestern upbringing and experience. Because midwestern pastoral writers relate to place emotionally as well as aesthetically and intellectually, I find it necessary to anticipate my discussion of their work with a brief personal essay, an approach consistent with established practice in ecocritical scholarship. Books such as John Elder's *Imagining the Earth: Poetry and the Vision of Nature* (1985) and Frederick Turner's *Spirit of Place: The Making of an American Literary Landscape* (1989) are at once pastoral texts and analyses of pastoral literature.[1] Readers interested in the inclusion of first-person narration in scholarly writing will continue with this preface; those preferring to enter directly the argument of this book may move ahead to the introduction.

I grew up near the industrial city of Flint, Michigan, in a typical suburban neighborhood of aluminum-sided houses surrounded by manicured lawns and blue spruces. Meadows and forests, fortunately, remained nearby for me to explore. My rambles most often proceeded south, over our rail fence into an old pasture that had yet to be subdivided. There I would consider my options. I might investigate the edge of the local lake, a flooded gravel pit that had been reconstituted as a swimming club. In fall, when the sunbathers and shrieking children had abandoned the beach, the lake attracted geese, ducks, even an occasional heron. By keeping low as I approached the lake, concealed behind the Queen Anne's lace and late blooming asters, I could glimpse these birds from a distance. A painted turtle might slip from the sandy bank into the water before me, or a largemouth bass silently cruise the drop-off in search of prey.

Usually my walk took me to the woods. That part of Michigan, where water flows to the Flint River and thereby to Saginaw Bay of Lake Huron, lies within a transition zone of forest types. To the south, deciduous trees (oak, hickory, maple, and beech) dominate, whereas northward, thinner, sandier soils support pine-oak forests. I lived where Ohio hardwoods meet the white pines of upper Michigan, where one knows both the fiery exuberance of autumn colors and the scent of evergreens in every season. Walking from that field, across the road marking the township border into a reforested quarter section of white pines (maples and oaks forming an emergent lower canopy), I entered the heart of the local landscape. Trees, including an old oak with massive horizontal limbs and a certain tall, swaying pine, marked the stations of my pilgrimage. In a hidden spruce grove, where skunk cabbages rise in spring, and spotted touch-me-not in autumn, the four cardinal directions and the axis linking heaven and earth converged. As I sat on the exposed roots and soft fallen needles of those trees, the rest of the walk—the hidden spring, the city cemetery with its sweeping vista and Depression-era gravestones—dropped away, along with thoughts of the future and of the past. I was simply there, in the place and in the moment.

Unlike some parts of Michigan, that area is not a tourist destination. The Flint River flows murkily, its sediments contaminated and its banks strewn with broken cinder blocks and twisted rebar on the stretch near my old home, a section that includes the city sewage plant. (Years later, Wright's Ohio River poems would resonate strongly for me.) A five-lane highway borders the eastern edge of the city cemetery, connecting major retail areas to the north and south. Interstate 75 slices through the country only a mile away, a wide ribbon of asphalt running from Miami to Sault Ste. Marie, Michigan (and Ontario). Another road parallels the river upstream to Flint, county seat and birthplace of General Motors.

On free weekends or their annual two-week vacation, people climb into their cars to join the suburban exodus from Detroit seeking respite "up north," as the expression goes, in the last good country of campgrounds, lakes, and summer cottages. The area near my childhood home suffices for houses, a cluster of restaurants near the freeway off-ramp, and a miniature golf emporium, but who wants to "get back to nature" where they live? Who cares for trilliums and mayapples in the corner of a potter's field when they can race recreational vehicles through a state forest or seventy-horsepower motorboats across Houghton Lake? On my walks, I approached the edge of wild nature, but to what avail was a child's momentary dissent from the cult of money and mobility? An absentee landowner cleared the grandest oaks from the woods north of our neighborhood. Developers studded the field with identical condominiums, lawns mown to the edge of the diminished lake. The city neglected the pine forest, planted a half-century earlier in the rigid rows of old-time conservation, until the trees started dying off because they were too close. The forest remains, but in a tangle of fallen timber and bramble left by a timber company contracted to thin the trees. When I return to those woods I seek the spruce grove because no one has "improved" that hidden spot. It is a sad commentary on our stewardship of nature (or lack of it) that the loveliest places are often those that have not been maintained at all, those nooks and bowers that enjoy, for the present anyway, a welcome neglect that allows ecological succession to take its own slow course in restoring the local biota.

Discovery of local history and literature deepened my appreciation of the changes that had shaped the land. I read how repeated glacial advances and retreats formed the hills, carved out the valleys, and deposited the gravel that underlies the soil of southern Michigan. Archeological treatises informed me that soon after the last ice age ended, about ten thousand years ago, the earliest inhabitants, the Paleo-Indians, established a hunting camp on the high north bank of the river a mile from my childhood home. I spent the second grade at Warner School, built on the site shortly after the Civil War. The school has since been converted into a duplex, and the road to Flint runs over much of the site, effectively protecting the old fire rings, burials, and remaining artifacts. People drive over at high speed, but the place remains, made sacred by time if profaned by disregard.

I read of the 1819 Treaty of Saginaw, in which leaders of the Ojibwa nation signed over their land to the United States, and of Alexis de Tocqueville crossing the Flint River on his way from Detroit to Saginaw in 1831. I tried to imagine my home country as he describes it in *Journey to America,* with giant trees forming "an immense and indestructible edifice under whose vaults eternal darkness reigns" (383). Tocqueville viewed the forest with melancholy, anticipating the changes that would follow the arrival of American settlers. Within a generation the old-growth trees had been girdled, felled, and burned in a process the pioneers called "windrowing." While clearing was necessary for farming, the extent to which the pioneers denuded the land was greater than can be explained by the exigencies of survival or even ambition.[2] Like the killing of the area's last bear, an event that occurred within sight of my accustomed walk in the city cemetery, the burning of Michigan's hardwood forest expressed a desire to dominate nature, to bring light and order to what the pioneers perceived as chaos, waste, and danger.

While regretting their destructiveness, I admired the pioneers' energy and much in the culture they transplanted from New York and New England: Greek Revival architecture, Romantic poetry, public schools, and representative government. Not everyone was included in their idea of democracy, not women, blacks, or Native Americans. Their love of nature, sentimental and bucolic, preserved more than a little Puritan fear of darkness and the wild. But their ideals, both republican and Romantic, would bear fruit generations later, when social movements brought reality a little closer to the cherished images of myth.

I also learned about Flint's role in the automotive industry, which has elevated mobility far above place in the American imagination. My maternal grandmother left her parents' farm to sew carriage covers downtown not long before the companies switched to cars. My grandfather, a skilled tradesman, made tools and dies for the production lines. While I honor their work and cherish their memory, my feelings about Flint are decidedly mixed. What D. H. Lawrence said about the United States strikes me as especially true of the place the Ojibwa called Pewanogowing, Place of the Fire Stones: "When you're actually *in* America, America hurts" (60). The gifts of my home country—natural abundance and beauty, as well as a grand prehistory and a democratic heritage—seem to go unappreciated.

My interest in midwestern literature began with writers from Michigan. One of my elementary school teachers read aloud from *The Situation in Flushing* (1965), Edmund G. Love's memoir of my hometown in the early twentieth century.[3] Theodore Roethke presented himself when I was in college. It is hard to describe the initial impact of great poetry about your own watershed (the Flint River, like Roethke's Tittabawasee, is part of the Saginaw drainage, the most extensive in the state). Like Roethke I had stood at the field's edge, watching workers speed home in cars they may have assembled. I perceived in Roethke's lines the very atmosphere of the place: the gray, overcast skies of winter and fall, the profound blue of summer, and the wild shifts in barometric pressure that presage the change of one season into the next. His fields and woods, rivers and ponds, roads and cemeteries were intimately familiar to me. They were the haunts of my youth, the places where I had entered, at once, the world and my imagination. "My true self runs toward a hill," Roethke writes in his last poem. "More! Oh more! / Visible" (*Collected Poems,* 243).

Roethke and the other authors I have chosen to represent the midwestern pastoral tradition reflect my own personal geography: two writers associated with Michigan, one with Ohio, one with Wisconsin, and one with Nebraska tilt the perspective of this book toward Michigan and the Great Lakes. Since, as geographer James Shortridge has observed, the term "Midwest" has become more associated with the Great Plains (91), this apparent bias may disconcert some readers situated west of the Mississippi. (A bartender I met in Nebraska City insisted that Michigan was not part of the Midwest, and she had her doubts about Wisconsin.) The tendency to define the Midwest exclusively in terms of agricultural landscapes and rural experience means that the Great Lakes states, with their heavy industry and large cities, are perceived as less midwestern, or not at all. My "bias," then, may be a critical advantage. In southern Michigan you are never far from either a factory or a cornfield, which may explain why the modern reality of industrialism is never far from my reading of pastoral prose and poetry. Whatever else the Midwest may be, it is part of the American industrial empire, a fact that we (in Nebraska, Michigan, or any other state) ignore at our own peril.

I was startled to find how closely Shortridge's map of "The Midwest as Seen from Michigan" (91) matches one I created, plotting the locations most associated with Cather, Leopold, Roethke, Wright, and Harrison.

Both maps center on the stretch of the Mississippi River where Wisconsin touches on Minnesota, Iowa, and Illinois, the heart of the heartland from a Michigan point of view. Strangely enough, I now live in that area, in La Crosse, Wisconsin. As I write these words, looking out my window to the east, I see Grandad Bluff, the highest in the area, looming almost six hundred feet above the rooftops. La Crosse lies in the Coulee Region, an area of valleys enclosed by high hills that often break into cliffs of exposed sandstone and limestone. The place pleasantly confounds expectations about the Midwest. If the Midwest is flat, this area is anything but. If the midwestern landscape was formed by the ice ages, La Crosse lies within the "driftless" area, which the glaciers largely missed. Like many here I enjoy hiking in the bluffs and bicycling in the extensive wetland that occupies the center of town. The La Crosse River winds through that wetland en route to its mouth at the Mississippi, by the park downtown. I seem to be the only person who swims in the La Crosse, except for Hmong children, the sons and daughters of recent Southeast Asian immigrants.

Perhaps one of those children will grow up to write notable prose or poetry about the place. There is certainly precedent for it, since La Crosse is not without its literary associations. Samuel Clemens and Ernest Hemingway admired this stretch of the Mississippi, particularly the bluffs that parallel the river on both the Minnesota and Wisconsin sides. The homestead of Hamlin Garland, a central figure in American realism and naturalism, can be found a few miles north of La Crosse, near West Salem, Wisconsin. Like the horses grazing in Wright's famous poem "A Blessing," La Crosse is located just off the road to Rochester, Minnesota. The area is well known by Harrison, who includes La Crosse in a list of great destinations in the United States.[4] A character in his novel *Dalva* spends the winter here before heading off to undertake missionary work among the Lakota in 1866; Northridge often climbs Grandad Bluff for an unobstructed view of the western horizon. If these writers perceived the place as charged with meaning and worthy of literary portrayal, it seems likely that future writers will also.

Such is the ground, figurative as well as literal, whereon this book makes its stand. The appeal of pastoral literature derives, in large part, from its insistence on particularities both local and personal. Thoreau comments at the beginning of *Walden* that he required "of every writer, first or last, a simple and sincere account of his own life, and not merely what he has heard of other men's lives" (325). That account having been made, I now turn to those other lives: the writers who have shaped our understanding of the midwestern landscape.

# Acknowledgments

This book won the Midwestern Studies Book Award, sponsored by the Society for the Study of Midwestern Literature (SSML) and Ohio University Press. As the society's representative, Edward Watts directed the review of my manuscript; David Sanders, director of the press, saw it through to publication. I extend to them my sincere gratitude and respect.

I must recognize two fine scholars, now retired from Michigan State University, who favored me with their mentoring and friendship. David D. Anderson, the founder of SSML, offered essential advice and, as editor of society publications, an audience for my work in progress. James I. Mc-Clintock nurtured this project from its earliest origins. His marvelous book *Nature's Kindred Spirits: Aldo Leopold, Joseph Wood Krutch, Edward Abbey, Annie Dillard, and Gary Snyder* (1994) offered a template for the kind of study I have here completed. He and Dr. Anderson have been, and remain, kindred as well as tutelary spirits.

Important help was also provided by colleagues at several institutions, including Michigan State University, Grand Valley State University, Rutgers University, and the University of Wisconsin–La Crosse, and by independent readers. I especially wish to thank Thomas Bailey, Terrell Beck, Roger Bresnahan, Joseph Burroughs, Leslie Fishbein, Milton Ford, Angus Gillespie, Sharon Jessee, Katherine Joslin, Ted Kooser, Stephen Lee, Deborah Popper, Frank Popper, Michael Rockland, and Robert Treu. My thanks also go to Jim Harrison for many kindnesses, including the moving tribute to my late sister, Teresa, in his essay "Eating Close to the Ground." *Et in Arcadia ego.*

Artist Dan Beresford provided the illustration for the dust jacket and the frontispiece. Having spent his early years in Wisconsin and Michigan, Beresford has an eye for midwestern scenes, though he makes his home in Livingston, Montana.

My mother, Caroline, and my late father, Guillermo, encouraged me all along, and my beautiful wife, María, inspired me to complete the manuscript. This book is dedicated to her.

Versions of several passages appeared in *Midamerica* and *Midwestern Miscellany,* published by SSML. A version of chapter 3 appeared as "Aldo Leopold and Midwestern Pastoralism" in *American Studies* 37, no. 2 (Fall 1996): 61–81, © 1996 by the Mid-America American Studies Association and reprinted by permission. Quotation of Jim Harrison's poem "Northern Michigan," from *The Shape of the Journey: New and Collected Poems,* © 1998 by Jim Harrison, is by permission of the author and Copper Canyon Press, P.O. Box 271, Port Townsend, WA 98368–0271. Three short poems from *Braided Creek: A Conversation in Poetry,* © 2003 by Jim Harrison and Ted Kooser, are reprinted by permission of Harrison, Kooser, and Copper Canyon Press. The poem "Milkweed" by James Wright, quoted from *Above the River: The Complete Poems of James Wright,* is from *The Branch Will Not Break* (Wesleyan University Press, 1963), © 1963 by James Wright and reprinted by permission of Wesleyan University Press.

The Midwestern Pastoral

Since to settle somewhere, to inhabit a space, is equivalent to repeating the cosmogony and hence to imitating the work of the gods, it follows that, for religious man, every existential decision to situate himself in space in fact constitutes a religious decision.

—Mircea Eliade, *The Sacred and the Profane*

Conceive if you will the mightiness of that dream, that these fields and places, out here west of Pittsburgh, may become sacred places, that because of this terrible thing, of which we may now become a part, there is hope of hardness and leanness—that we may get to lives of which we may be unashamed.

—Sherwood Anderson, *Mid-American Chants*

# Introduction

What is so strange about a tree alone in an open field?
It is a willow tree. I walk around and around it.
The body is strangely torn, and cannot leave it.
At last I sit down beneath it.

With these lines Robert Bly begins "Hunting Pheasants in a Corn-field," a poem in *Silence in the Snowy Fields* (1962), his first book and one that celebrates the prairie of the poet's native Minnesota and other mid-western American landscapes. The speaker's caution in approaching the willow initially suggests physical awkwardness and feelings of existential absurdity. Hesitation, however, turns to ritual observance, as he circles the tree and comes to dwell in the place just as he dwells on the topic in the poem. The scene is far from idyllic. Late fall has come to Minnesota and the tree has lost its leaves; the scene is quiet ("Only the cornstalks now can make a noise") and rather colorless. The starkness of the season provokes darker meditations on time and mutability: "The sun is cold, burning through the frosty distances of space. / The weeds are frozen to death long ago." One might expect the poet, conventionally, to remind himself of the promise of spring, of the new life that will emerge from the metaphorical death that is winter. Instead, centered in the place, in his body, and in the moment, he embraces the silence, darkness, and cold, finding that he loves "to watch / The sun moving on the chill skin of the branches":

> The mind has shed leaves alone for years.
> It stands apart with small creatures near its roots.
> I am happy in this ancient place,
> A spot easily caught sight of above the corn,
> If I were a young animal ready to turn home at dusk.
>
> (14)

Like a Druid by a sacred oak, or Buddha under the bo, the poet finds enlightenment under a native tree, experiencing a sudden dissolving of ego, a realization of the world's congeniality to human residence. Just as the cornfield feeds the human body, the landscape as a whole, including its characteristic plants and animals, nourishes the human spirit. This epiphany occurs not in a sublime wilderness, but in an agrarian country where the appreciation of subtle topographical variations like this "spot above the corn" requires patience and circumspection. By identifying his consciousness with the local flora and fauna, Bly enters the landscape not only as an observer, but as a participant and resident in an "ancient place": a landscape with a history both natural and human.

Bly's poem introduces a number of themes and motifs in midwestern pastoral, the tradition in twentieth-century American literature that is the subject of this book. The spiritual joy and renewal in nature, the admiration of subtle beauty in domesticated as well as wild environments, and the awareness of landscape as the result of historical change evident in "Hunting Pheasants in a Cornfield" appear in the writings of many midwesterners, both preceding and contemporary with Bly. Five important midwestern pastoralists are Willa Cather, Aldo Leopold, Theodore Roethke, James Wright, and Jim Harrison, each of whom I treat in a separate chapter. In major works of fiction, nonfiction, and poetry, these writers portray specific locations in the north-central part of the United States, conveying through description and narration dimensions of the region's landscape, from the aesthetic and spiritual to the social and ecological. They exemplify a literary tradition of place and rural experience in the Midwest.[1]

My analysis of that tradition follows recent work in American studies on literature and nature. The central conflict in this scholarship, as Law-

rence Buell writes in a useful survey, is political: whether pastoral ideology and art "ought to be looked at as conservative and hegemonic" or
"as a form of dissent from an urbanizing social mainstream" (35). An
older tradition, exemplified by Leo Marx in *The Machine in the Garden:
Technology and the Pastoral Ideal in America* (1964), viewed major writers
such as Thoreau as "social prophets: critics of corruption in the name of
a purer American vision of a society founded on the order of nature"
(Buell, 34). In the last quarter century, that affirmative interpretation has
been challenged by revisionists who read pastoral texts "more in terms of
what they exclude or suppress": a history of environmental abuse, and the
experiences of women, ethnic minorities, and the working class (Buell,
35). From this perspective, literary evocations of landscape serve primarily
symbolic functions, which historically have included rhetorical support
for territorial expansionism, racism, and sexism.

    I hold with critics like Buell who distinguish *versions* of pastoral, which
"has sometimes activated green consciousness, sometimes euphemized
land appropriation" (31). Pastoral, which can be either conservative or
progressive, has changed over time in response to new social and ecological imperatives. The five authors whom I discuss exemplify ethical development in the pastoral literature of one region. Each of the writers
developed a version of pastoral that revises earlier conceptualizations of
the human-nature relation in the Midwest and elsewhere. By modifying
the literary conventions of the pastoral mode, Cather, Leopold, Roethke,
Wright, and Harrison contribute to the "redefinition of pastoral" outlined by ecocritic Glen A. Love:

> The redefinition of pastoral . . . requires that contact with the
> green world be acknowledged as something more than a tempo-
> rary excursion into simplicity. . . . A pastoral for the present and
> the future calls for a better science of nature, a greater under-
> standing of its complexity, a more radical awareness of its primal
> energy and stability, and a more acute questioning of the values
> of the supposedly sophisticated society to which we are bound.
> (210)

In demonstrating their redefinition of pastoral, I am first concerned with
locating these authors in the broader context of midwestern regional
identity. The cultural history that is chapter 1 provides that context. More

than any other part of the United States, the Midwest has been understood in relation to pastoralism, succinctly defined by geographer James R. Shortridge as "the concept of an ideal middle kingdom suspended between uncivilized wilderness and urban-industrial evils." Even names for the region, as Shortridge documents, "revolve around its identification with American pastoralism" (6). The Midwest is the nation's middlescape, its "heartland," a regional label that associates geographical centrality with a defining role in national identity and emotional responses to place. Not only books but paintings, films, and other media have reinforced this image of farms, bucolic woods and streams, and small towns populated by plain-speaking, upright citizens. The Midwest, according to pastoral myth, is what America thinks itself to be.

Just as there are many versions of pastoral writing, there are many varieties of pastoral ideology. By outlining philosophical and political dimensions of midwestern pastoralism, I prepare the way for discussion of each author's interpretation of regional myth and landscape. Midwestern pastoralism flows out of several currents in American thought, including Jeffersonian republicanism as well as utilitarian and Romantic versions of individualism. Since the settlement of the North American interior by Anglo-Americans in the eighteenth and nineteenth centuries, these ideologies have combined as well as competed in creating attitudes about the human estate in nature. They underlie civil society, commerce, and cultural production in the Midwest, including literature from and about the region. Chapter 1, therefore, treats midwestern pastoralism in relation to its component ideologies and pastoral myth in midwestern politics, science, technology, and the arts.

Cather, Leopold, Roethke, Wright, and Harrison espouse versions of the democratic agrarianism of Thomas Jefferson, whose philosophy and public policy established the material terms of midwestern social development. Jeffersonian ideology exalts the yeoman farmer, characterized by Henry Nash Smith as "the heroic figure of the idealized frontier farmer armed with that supreme agrarian weapon, the sacred plow" (138). Closely fitting this regional archetype are Willa Cather's pioneers, strong-willed but compassionate characters who create homes and communities on the Nebraska prairie. The yeoman farmer also appears in Leopold's description of himself at work restoring his Wisconsin farm, in Roethke's greenhouse poems, and in Harrison's novels and poems on rural life.

Even Wright, who does not write about farming or horticulture, uses agrarian motifs, as when he envisions Spanish poems as "seeds" that "scatter out of their wings a quiet farewell, / a greeting to my country" (*Above the River*, 130). Associating cultivation of land with cultivation of self and society, midwestern pastoral writers characterize people in the provinces who are not provincial but generous, tolerant, and cosmopolitan in outlook.

The five authors may also be described as latter-day Romantics. Their close observation of nature as fact and symbol, cultural localism, and concern for children's experience of significant place all derive from nineteenth-century American Romanticism, particularly from the work of Ralph Waldo Emerson, Henry David Thoreau, and Walt Whitman. The basic continuity between these writers and their Romantic precursors is mysticism. Spiritual individualists who perceive divinity in nature, they reject both mainstream Judeo-Christian distancing of nature and spirit and the utilitarian abstraction of land as mere property. They seek and encounter sacred sites in the midwestern landscape, where they approach transcendence and reassessment, as in Bly's poem about his epiphany under a willow tree.

This analysis, however, is complicated by troubling legacies of American history. Jeffersonian and Romantic ideologies provided rhetorical support for nineteenth-century expansionism, expressed in the language of Manifest Destiny. As the chief architect of American expansionism, Jefferson initiated not only land survey and settlement but also policies leading to Indian assimilation, removal, and extermination in the Midwest. In practice, agrarianism also meant the destruction of native ecosystems, from the hardwood forests of the lower Great Lakes to the tall grass prairies to the west. Some Romantics, including Whitman, kept with the Jeffersonian "garden myth" in imagining the North American plains as vacant land in need of development by white Americans. Cather followed Whitman's example, as recent critics have pointed out, in ignoring the presence of Native Americans on the plains and the violence of their displacement. Midwestern pastoralism, from this perspective, is complicit in conquest and in the continuing hegemony of economics over nature and landscape.

Midwestern pastoralists, however, have become increasingly attentive to historical realities and the demands of ecological sustainability. There

is a marked progression from Cather's celebration of pioneers to more recent pastorals that acknowledge the violence and environmental disruption that accompanied the continental growth of the United States. This
contrition for history stems from pastoral's reformist and at times even
radical dimension. While accepting Jeffersonian ideals, including the institution of private property, writers from Cather to Harrison excoriate
the cooptation of those ideals by the dominant utilitarianism of American society. They criticize their own society for its materialism, provincialism, and lack of appreciation for the subtle beauty of midwestern
landscape. Yet they call not for the rejection of pastoral ideology but for
its reform. Their descriptions and narratives of midwestern life illustrate
ways that Jeffersonian, utilitarian, and Romantic values may be modified to fit changing circumstances and the lessons of historiography and
ecological science. The elusive object of their work is a progressive land
stewardship, one that protects cultural and natural diversity in the region.

I consider these particular writers representative for a number of reasons. The first is historical continuity. Their dates of birth, listed below,
form a chronology, as do their dates of first book publication: Cather
(1912), Leopold (1931), Roethke (1942), Wright (1957), and Harrison
(1965). Then there is biographical coincidence. All five had midwestern
childhoods that included formative experiences in rural and semiwild
settings. They all witnessed both constructive and destructive expressions
of agrarianism and felt compelled to describe and explain what they
had seen. Diversity of genre is also a factor; that the group consists of a
novelist, an essayist, two poets, and an author working in all three genres attests to the variety and complexity of midwestern pastoral writing.
Finally, I chose these authors for their thematic coherence: though they
write about different landscapes at different moments in history, they
speak to common issues of individualism, community, and nature. The
development of these concerns becomes plain when we consider the writers first individually and again as a group.

Willa Cather (1873–1947) came to Nebraska as a child in the 1880s,
when European immigrants—Swedes, Czechs, Danes, and others—were
transforming the prairie wilderness into the agricultural heartland of
North America. Cather admired her immigrant neighbors, some of whom
became lifelong friends. Their pride in cultural traditions and courage
in adapting to the plains inspired her first major writings. Cather's Ne-

braska novels, particularly *O Pioneers!* (1913) and *My Ántonia* (1918), are central texts of the Midwestern Renaissance, the region's classic period, which also produced Edgar Lee Masters, Sherwood Anderson, and Sinclair Lewis. While all of these writers exemplify the period, Cather, by wide critical consensus, produced the largest body of first-rate, enduring prose. Furthermore, her Nebraska novels and certain of her short stories represent midwestern pastoral at its most purely Virgilian, Romantic, and Jeffersonian, with all the aesthetic and ethical strengths and deficiencies implied by those terms. While place-centered, antimaterialistic, and respectful of ethnic diversity, Cather's elegies to the passing of the pioneer era raise distressing questions about the relation of pastoral literature and ideology to issues of race, gender, and the legacy of western conquest.

Cather's life span closely coincided with that of Aldo Leopold (1877–1948), by many accounts the most influential figure in twentieth-century ecology. Born and raised in Iowa, Leopold spent his most productive years in Wisconsin, where he worked as a college professor and researcher in conservation science. His book *A Sand County Almanac* (1949), a classic of the American nature essay genre, also fits into the midwestern pastoral tradition by virtue of its subject matter (the restoration of Leopold's Wisconsin farm) and its argument for ethical, aesthetic, and ecological appreciation of undervalued and abused landscapes such as are common in the Midwest. Leopold drew on his midwestern experience, as well as archetypes from regional history and literature, in mediating the perennial American conflict between holistic and materialistic attitudes toward nature. To the dominant Romanticism and Jeffersonianism of midwestern pastoral ideology he brought the corrective wisdom of modern ecological science.

From Aldo Leopold I turn to Theodore Roethke (1908–1963), a major twentieth-century poet who established his reputation with lyrics about his father's greenhouses and the surrounding countryside in Saginaw, Michigan. A master of traditional poetic forms as well as free verse, Roethke became the most widely read and highly regarded of the "middle generation" of American poets, who came to attention midcentury, after the modernist period of T. S. Eliot, Wallace Stevens, and William Carlos Williams. Like Cather, Roethke was drawn to classical models in literature, yet applied his study of European forms to American settings and themes. He combined a mystical apprehension of nature with an exploration of his own troubled psyche, arriving late in his life at an integration of his Michigan origins into a vision of North American landscape that reflects his study of frontier history and the poetry of Walt Whitman.

James Wright (1927–1980), who studied under Roethke at the University of Washington, also related psychic conflict to the experience of place, but went further than Roethke into the historical roots of modern alienation and environmental distress. Calling himself a "jaded pastoralist" (*Above the River,* 328) he wrote poems about his native Martins Ferry, Ohio, and western Minnesota that address "the whole loneliness / Of the Midwest" (*Above the River,* 119), an estrangement from place evident in the destruction not only of landscapes but of people, from Native Americans to the working class in midwestern cities. In poetry of great emotional range and descriptive power, Wright struggled to reconcile pastoral idealism with industrial reality, and Whitman's celebration of bodily experience with modern alienation.

Finally, Jim Harrison (b. 1937), the one living author among the five, has written poetry, fiction, and essays that extend and modify the concerns of the others. Like Roethke, he grew up in Michigan and has written poetry with a spiritual sense of the state's woods, fields, and waters; like Leopold, he appreciates undervalued places and stewardship by private landowners; and like Wright, he traces America's troubled spirit of place to the nation's genocidal destruction of its Native American tribes. Harrison's pastoral fiction, modeled in part on Cather's Nebraska novels, redresses Cather's neglect of the continent's original inhabitants and implicit approval of Manifest Destiny.

While diverse in genre and style, Willa Cather, Aldo Leopold, Theodore Roethke, James Wright, and Jim Harrison share key values: a spiritual sense of place and relation to nature; a respect for the practical means by which individuals create and strive to sustain home and community; and a critical awareness of human history and the destructive influences of ignorance, materialism, and bigotry that threaten both natural and human diversity in the region. All of the authors grew up in the Midwest, and while, as we will see, only Leopold and Harrison opted to reside there permanently, all five loved and sought to understand better their places of origin, writing major fiction, poetry, and essays about those locations. In expressing the beauty of midwestern landscapes and the possibility of positive human residence, they promote aesthetic, religious, and political ideals derived from common sources, especially Romantic literature and Jeffersonian democracy. They reveal awareness of their artistic and philosophical heritage—ancient, modern, and regional— indirectly through thematic and symbolic resonances, and directly through allusion and quotation. But they view tradition critically, questioning the assumptions of midwestern pastoralism as they know it through personal experience and from the region's history and literature. Of a mind to reform their region's cultural ideology, they celebrate an attachment to land that is spiritual as well as practical, based on historical and ecological knowledge as well as personal experience. They love and admire midwestern landscapes but would transform cultural perceptions of nature that facilitate ignorance and abuse of the region's biodiversity.

This book is interdisciplinary, in the American studies tradition. Where appropriate, I engage in close textual analysis and note trends in critical response to the authors under discussion. Yet my consideration of midwestern pastoral owes as much to recent studies in cultural geography, environmental history, and mythology as to traditional literary criticism. My task is essentially bioregional: to relate these writers to their local geographies and to explain the terms by which they counter the placelessness, despair, and abstraction of much mainstream literature and literary theory. For them, the aim of writing is not merely intellectual, aesthetic, or even spiritual, but democratic and ecological. Romantic individualists each and all, Cather, Leopold, Roethke, Wright, and Harrison also depict and promote commitment to local communities, human and natural. In such depiction and such commitment lies their topophilia— their love for, their understanding of, their sense of place in the American Midwest.[2]

## one

# Midwestern Pastoralism

We shall never achieve harmony with land, any more than
we shall achieve absolute justice or liberty for people. In
these higher aspirations, the important thing is not to
achieve, but to strive.

—Aldo Leopold, *A Sand County Almanac*

The five writers who concern me emerge not only from literary tradition, but also from a specific geography and history that shaped their
ideas about the human estate in nature. This chapter examines the significance of the Midwest in American culture and the long-standing
association of the region with pastoral values and imagery. Pastoralism
in midwestern arts, sciences, and politics is the context in which I read
the literary pastoral of Cather, Leopold, Roethke, Wright, and Harrison.

This is by no means a straightforward proposition, given the prob-
lematic history of "pastoral," "regional," and "midwestern" as descriptive
terms in critical and popular discourses. I begin therefore by comment-
ing on these concepts as they have been understood (or misunderstood)
by critics of midwestern writers. In defining pastoralism, I refer to the
controversy in recent American studies scholarship over its political significance. The suspicion with which revisionist critics view pastoral correlates with older prejudices against regionalism and ideas about a "sense
of place." I also connect this critical background to the perceptual insta-
bility of midwestern cultural identity. Persistent stereotypes of the Midwest

as American (representing an essentialized U.S. national identity), the Midwest as provincial, and the Midwest as flat and undifferentiated should be addressed before I offer an affirmative definition of the region and its unique cultural traditions.

## Pastoral Theory, Regionalism, and Midwestern Literature

Pastoral writing has deep historical roots. Ancient poets, among them the Greek Theocritus and the Roman Virgil, established many of the conventions still associated with pastoral, which first implies the characterization of intelligent and resourceful farmers, shepherds, and other country people, and description of landscapes, plants, animals, and natural phenomena such as weather and seasonal changes. Pastoral often entails a contrast between urban and rural life, usually but not exclusively in favor of rurality, to which special virtue is attributed; and a tone of nostalgia or "regret over the loss of an idyllic condition: childhood, a perfect love, an idealized farm, a promised land, the innocence of Eden" (Cooley, 3). While this nostalgic tendency can lend itself to sentimentality and a false idealization of life in nature, the best pastoral writing acknowledges social complexities and conflicts inherent in the individual's striving for a meaningful life.

Virgil, for example, portrayed in the first of his *Eclogues* a dialogue between two shepherds, one who has happily retained his land and another who has been dispossessed by the government in Rome. In *The Machine in the Garden,* Leo Marx cites this eclogue as an example of "complex pastoral," which tends to "qualify, or call into question, or bring irony to bear against the illusion of peace and harmony in a green pasture," rather than oversimplify rural life (25). American writers of complex pastoral in Marx's estimation include Thoreau, Frost, and other canonical figures who emphasize the tenuousness of rustic felicity in an industrialized society. Through the self-conscious use and modification of pastoral conventions, writers of complex pastoral depict the experience of nature in a manner that emphasizes social forces such as war, technology, and urbanization as well the vagaries of love and loss in the lives of individuals.

Literary critics, as I note in the introduction, have recently subjected pastoral to extensive reevaluation. Some deliver sweeping indictments, as when Sara Farris concludes her essay on Cather's *O Pioneers!* and two contemporary novels by asserting that "conquest will always make pastoral a destructive, even *self*-destructive endeavor" (46). While I reserve commentary on Cather for the next chapter, and on Jane Smiley's *A Thousand Acres* (1991), Farris's third text, for the last, it is worthwhile to point out the absolutism of "always." The implication that narratives of people in nature can be signifiers *only* of hegemony of humans over nature, rich over poor, whites over people of color, and men over women is unnecessarily reductive. The very contrast that Farris draws between writers like Cather and Smiley assumes that the pastoral mode has changed over time, developing new ethical responses to society and ecology.

In *The Environmental Imagination: Thoreau, Nature Writing, and the Formation of American Culture* (1995), Lawrence Buell offers a compelling response to pastoral revisionism. Buell succinctly reviews American pastoral scholarship from D. H. Lawrence to recent feminist and historicist rereadings, characterizing "a shift from the hermeneutics of empathy . . . to a hermeneutics of skepticism" (36). While acknowledging the justice of canonical revision and ideological deconstruction, Buell links pastoral revisionism with a long-standing skepticism among literary theorists about the mimetic or representational power of language. How, the argument goes, can texts "purport to represent environments in the first place when, after all, a text is obviously one thing and the world another[?]" (82). This "philosophical antireferentialism," according to Buell, "underrepresents the claims of the environment on humanity by banishing it from the realms of discourse except as something absent" (102). It characterizes all major critical theories, which have consistently "marginalized literature's referential dimension by privileging structure, text(uality), ideology, or some other conceptual matrix":

> New critical formalism did so by insisting that the artifact was its own world, a heterocosm. Structuralism and poststructuralism broke down the barrier between literary and nonliterary, not however to rejoin literary discourse to the world but to conflate all verbal artifacts within a more spacious domain of textuality. . . . New historicism . . . set text within context. But it did so in terms of the text's status as a species of cultural production or ideological work. [It] seemed to render merely epiphenomenal the responsiveness of literature to the natural world. (86)

Pastoral stands at an especial disadvantage in every case, given the urban locus of the theoretical enterprise. Seen from afar, by those removed from daily experience of woods and fields, nature is easily constructed as mere setting or ideological construct. Its symbolic significance may be far more apparent than its transhuman reality.

The skepticism of modern literary theory toward pastoral draws from the cosmopolitan aesthetic of high modernism, which valorizes time over place, abstraction over the concrete, form over content, culture over nature, city over province, the machine over the garden.[1] There is philosophical continuity between T. S. Eliot's declaration in *Four Quartets* that "[h]ome is where one starts from. / Here and there do not matter" (*Collected Poems,* 189) and critic Leonard Lutwack's call for an "accommodation with placelessness," based on the supposition that the "maturation of an individual is not possible without the successive abandonment of places" (236). This variety of modernism holds as sentimental and futile any effort to sustain traditional values for nature and local communities because, according to two much abused truisms derived from W. H. Auden and Thomas Wolfe, "poetry makes nothing happen" and "you can't go home again."[2] Lest they undermine the cultural hegemony of the metropolis, literary pastoralism and regionalism have been conflated with nostalgia and conservatism. "Regret over the loss of places is not a theme that literature can continue profitably," Lutwack insists, ostensibly echoing the tough-mindedness of urbane readers (237).

An example of such criticism as it has dealt with midwestern pastoral is Kathy Callaway's 1983 article on *This Journey* (1982), James Wright's posthumous volume of poetry. After elucidating Wright's book in terms of a European "iconography" (in particular, the Roman past of the poet's beloved Italy), Callaway dismisses "poetry of place," a phrase that Wright himself found useful, in a revealing manner:

> Poetry of place? Not in the sense of regionalism with which
> it's usually applied. "Regionalism" has no meaning in poetry.
> Regional poems are local messages, and the label of "regional
> poet" applied to writers of the stature and complexity of James
> Wright . . . is insulting and incorrect. What's more it ignores a
> fact we've been ignoring ever since that fact became uncomfort-
> able: that major American writers are still being nourished by

something not American. . . . Among poets and their serious
readers there is no room for xenophobia—a special danger in
circles that like to talk about regionalism. (403–4)

In the considerable body of scholarship on Wright, it would be difficult
to find a reference to him as a "regional poet." Regionalism has been
discussed as an *aspect* of his poetry, in which localism of imagery and
idiom complements and even validates his broad range of cultural reference. In accusing those who "like to talk about regionalism" of being
reductive, Callaway is herself reductive; she denies the importance of a
writer to his human community (in Wright's case, his hometown of
Martins Ferry, Ohio). "Supposed poets of place like James Wright," she
writes, "seem to have located their dynamos wherever they felt it, on
terra firma that Martins Ferry . . . would never have understood—past
a literal reading of the iconography, which looked like a moral, and
wasn't. Those readers and fellow-poets who hoped to use Wright and
other 'poets of place' to shore up their own spiritual uneasiness are going
to have to let him go" (404). This is doctrinaire modernism, right down
to the allusion to Eliot's *The Waste Land:* "these fragments I have shored
up against my ruin" (*Collected Poems,* 69). Callaway's attitude is cosmopolitan, formalist, and elitist ("Martins Ferry . . . would never have understood"), her senses of place and time Eurocentric and linear. Claiming a
culturally subservient role for Americans, who in her view "so love and
envy" Europeans (as midwesterners, apparently, envy easterners), she argues for Wright's poems as "examples of the American's only way of having any history, of taking part in the larger, slower pageant of peoples"
(405). Wright does indeed take part in that pageant, as shown by his long
and fruitful meditation on Roman poetry and landscape. Yet his primary
way of having a history, like other writers of place and landscape, was
by transforming local particulars into symbolically rich, thematically universal art. His relationship with the great traditions was one of joyful
participation, not fawning admiration; a neo-Romantic, he would have
agreed with Emerson's assertion that the ancients made their places
"venerable in the imagination . . . by sticking fast where they were, like
an axis in the earth" (*Essays,* 277). Place as a philosophical concept is in-
clusive rather than exclusive; as Wright told interviewer Dave Smith, "I'm
not saying that the value of poetry depends on writing about a place or

not writing about a place, only that there is . . . a poetry of place. It appeals to me very much" (*Collected Prose,* 195).

A special danger in circles that denigrate regionalism is aestheticism, a limited sense of "art for art's sake." Wendell Berry, whose forthrightness on many issues springs from a defense of local culture, speaks against a "Territory of artistic primacy or autonomy, in which it is assumed that no value is inherent in subjects but that value is conferred upon objects by the art and the attention of the artist" (*What Are People For?* 82). This "Territory" is coterminous with Callaway's "terra firma" and the "common ground" that Mark Sanders seeks to establish in the anthology and study of four important Nebraska poets he edited with J. V. Brummels. "Not one of these poets," Sanders insists, "will be remembered by where he lived; not one of these poems will be remembered by where it was created. I would rather think the worth of the poem is due to its intrinsic qualities, the stuff in the verse. . . . The common ground is the immutable perception of each poet, that drive to *see* and *explain* in terms that *create* the image of *knowing*" (15). No one denies the importance of close textual reading in literary study; as the New Critics properly admonished, scholars should respect the form of texts, and give the text itself the first and last say. Similarly, symbolist approaches such as Callaway's provide essential insights into the mediation of human perceptions by cultural constructs. Yet these readings risk abnegation of art's ethical function, including its role in creating responsibility and love for nature and place. As Berry argues, reaffirming the localism of modernist rebel William Carlos Williams and anticipating the work of future ecocritics, the "test of imagination, ultimately, is not the territory of art or the territory of the mind, but the territory underfoot. . . . To assume that the context of literature is 'the literary world' is . . . simply wrong. That its real habitat is the household and the community—that it can and does affect, even in practical ways, the life of a place—may not be recognized by most theorists and critics for a while yet. But they will finally come to it, because finally they will have to. And when they do, they will renew the study of literature and restore it to importance" (*What Are People For?* 83–84).

At the heart of modernist-derived attitudes about pastoral literature is confusion (perhaps at times willful) between regionalism and provincialism. Provincialism connotes local chauvinism, contempt for other places and cultures, racism, sexism, homophobia—a whole host of prejudices.

Regionalism, as understood by writers concerned with the mutual influence of place and humanity, is another thing entirely. Berry defines it as *"local life aware of itself.* It would tend to substitute for the myths and stereotypes of a region a particular knowledge of the *place* one lives in and intends to *continue* living in." Far from bigotry or xenophobia, such regionalism combines local wisdom with universal knowledge, and as such is necessarily multicultural and interdisciplinary in theory and practice. Berry cites "Thoreau's knowledge of the Orient" and the "influence of Villon and Chaucer and Fabre" on William Carlos Williams (*A Continuous Harmony,* 67). As for midwestern pastoralists, one might note Cather's defense of immigrants against assimilationist pressures; Leopold's marriage to Estelle Bergere, a Nueva Mexicana; Roethke's close study of Yeats; and the profound impact of Spanish and Latin American poetry on Wright and Harrison. Beyond literature, distinct references to Japanese design in early homes by Frank Lloyd Wright and his followers in the midwestern prairie school of architecture exemplify the spirit of cosmopolitan regionalism. Such respectful encounters with other cultures enable artists to understand the home place and to create original and autochthonous work, at once regional and international in derivation and scope.

Provincialism, the lack of appreciation of any location or culture but one's own, may be found in all places, including cities. Cosmopolitanism itself can be the ultimate provincialism, "an urban attitude toward nature" that Paul Shepard describes as "insular, cultivated, ignorant, dilettante, and sophisticated" (64). Midwestern culture bears the brunt of such an attitude among some coastals who view the continental interior as a hinterland, its people as "flyovers" (so named because corporate and media elites fly over them while commuting between New York and Los Angeles), and its culture as "regional" in a condescending sense. Harrison, whose writing has won acceptance from the literary establishment (largely due to his wide popularity and growing international reputation), rejects the phrase "regional literature," but as it is misused in metropolitan centers. "In the view of those on the Eastern seaboard," Harrison suggested in his interview with Jim Fergus, "everything which is not amorphous, anything that has any peculiarities of geography, is considered regional fiction, whereas if it's from New York, it's evidently supposed to be mainstream. . . . Years ago it struck me that the Upper East

Side of New York was constitutionally the most provincial place I'd ever been" (64). Harrison testifies to lingering perceptions of midwestern inferiority: the region's culture overwhelmed by metropolitan influences, its landscapes paling in comparison to the continent's ocean coasts and mountain ranges, its literature of limited significance. These deeply rooted stereotypes require an accounting if they are to be supplanted by particular knowledge of place, landscape, and regional culture. In the next section of this chapter, therefore, I turn to the sources of midwestern identity in history and cultural myth.

## The Midwest and the United States

Popular understanding of the Midwest begins (and too often ends) with the notion that it is the most "American" part of the United States: less a distinct region than the nation's heartland, the essence of Americanism. This sublation of regional identity for national representativeness may be traced to the nineteenth-century origins of midwestern society. Historians Andrew R. L. Cayton and Peter S. Onuf argue for a fundamental link between perceptions of the Midwest and the rise of commercial capitalism. "Unlike New England or the South or the Southwest," they note, "the Midwest had no prior existence—as a European community—before this great transformation. The rise of middle-class values and the institutions of capitalism were synonymous with the rise of the Midwest" (117–18). The Midwest came of age with the nation, beginning with the agrarian era and proceeding through the Civil War, industrialization, and the rise of powerful urban centers. During the late nineteenth and early twentieth centuries, Chicago and other midwestern cities dominated the nation's economy through industrial production as well as the handling of agricultural commodities. Political influence followed economic predominance; the Midwest produced most of the nation's presidents from Lincoln (Illinois) to Harding (Ohio). The arts also flourished, as midwestern architecture, then writing, and finally painting entered major phases in the half century between 1890 and 1940. This period, as geographer James R. Shortridge demonstrates, saw the "ascendancy of the term Middle West as the label for a vast section of the American interior" and the elevation of the Midwest as "the standard by which to judge the rest of the nation" (27).

While suggesting a certain confidence, the notion of the Midwest as America also betrays a weak sense of regional identity. Midwesterners refer to themselves as "Americans," and, as Shortridge points out, "tend to waver between neutrality and outright defensiveness" when it comes to their native region (2). Regional history is little known in the Midwest, and regional arts are rarely emphasized by cultural institutions. Instead, people generally turn to electronic media from Los Angeles and New York City for entertainment and information. They think of the Midwest as a good place to live but vacation elsewhere if they can afford it. Its period of preeminence long since past, the Midwest today is positioned in colonial relation to distant centers of political, economic, and cultural influence. "The very name 'Middle West,'" historian Jon C. Teaford concludes, "implie[s] the dual sense of centrality and isolation characterizing the region" (254).

The principal drawback of midwestern nationalism is that it concedes the region's strengths to the nation while ascribing its weaknesses only to the Midwest. Collective memory overlooks the establishment of Anglo-American culture in the continental interior, leaping from the American Revolution to the Industrial Revolution, from the Appalachian Mountains to the Rockies. We have a clearer vision of Lewis and Clark reaching the Pacific than of William Clark's brother George Rogers Clark taking the British fort at Vincennes, in what is now Indiana, during the American Revolution. We remember Squanto and Chief Joseph more than Tecumseh and Black Hawk. Abraham Lincoln, Henry Ford, and Frank Lloyd Wright are American icons, but their midwestern identities are typically understated. The United States, with its heartland somewhere in Iowa or Missouri, is heralded as democratic, modern, full of open spaces signifying freedom and opportunity, while the Midwest, as John Madison points out, is dismissed as "provincial and unsophisticated, pragmatic and materialistic, bland and boring" (4).

Midwestern landscapes have been similarly overlooked and stereotyped. The relative level of midwestern topography is so obvious that geographer John Frazier Hart begins his noted essay on the region with the simplest possible declarative: "The Middle West is flat" (258). Hart naturally qualifies his opening sentence, but popular perceptions fall short of his finer distinctions. The average view of the Midwest is as seen driving seventy miles an hour down an interstate highway, or flying over in a jet, noting how the Cartesian survey grid creates a patchwork of perfectly rectangular fields. In the parlance of farmers, midwestern land is "good"; that is, easily cultivated, graded, built on, altered beyond recognition. Characterizations of midwestern land as "beautiful" are harder to come by. Even Lucien Stryk, who edited two influential anthologies of midwestern poetry, writes that "no one who has seen other parts of this country will claim that the midwest compares in natural beauty with, say, the Pacific northwest or New England" (xv). This notion, what might be called the tourist aesthetic, is an inheritance from the Romantic era: the privileging of mountain and maritime landscapes as fit scenes of contemplation and spiritual transport. Such landscapes do not characterize the Midwest, a region more picturesque than sublime, more pastoral than ruggedly wild. Except for weather (the Midwest is famous for blizzards, floods, and tornadoes), nature is generally modest and beneficent in the American interior plains. Subtle in its aesthetic appeal, the Midwest generally lacks, as Harrison writes of Michigan's Upper Peninsula, "the drama and differentiation favored by the garden-variety nature buff" (*Just before Dark,* 263).

Assessments of midwestern language, both spoken and written, correlate to the geographical perceptions just outlined. Midwestern speech, like the region's culture, is taken as a national average; midwesterners, unlike New Yorkers, New Englanders, and especially southerners, are said to have no accent. News anchors on the national television networks, wherever they hail from, generally speak as though they were from the upper Midwest; Dan Rather, from Texas, learned to sound like Tom Brokaw, a native of South Dakota. Timothy C. Frazer points out in *"Heartland" English: Variation and Transition in the American Midwest* (1993) that there is no "monolithic English variety throughout the vast heartland" and that what is referred to as a "Midwestern" or "General American" dialect is "really Inland Northern," a derivative of western New England and upstate New York speech that "predominates only in Michigan, Wisconsin, and Minnesota, in northern Illinois, Indiana, Ohio, and Iowa, and in enclaves elsewhere" (1–2). Variations of southern speech, vernacular black English, and other dialects are also found in the greater Midwest. Yet popular imagination holds fast to the notion that midwestern speech is uniformly clear, forthright, and *flat,* like the land.

The same analogy appears in studies of midwestern literature. Ronald Weber, for example, echoes assessments of midwestern landscapes in his characterization of the region's literature "by a certain modesty or reserve in the figures it presents and the action it delineates . . . an essentially homely quality that shies away from the extremes of human experience. On the whole, it finds itself most at ease with stories of plain people in a plain environment living plain lives—a people not inclined to excesses of language or action, their dramas . . . enacted within limited emotional and spiritual ranges"(13). Plain-speaking people from the plains: there is a certain truth to the characterization. As evidence, Weber cites the central role played by midwesterners in the development of literary realism, with its emphasis on transparency and verisimilitude. The work of William Dean Howells (born, like James Wright, in Martins Ferry, Ohio) to write and promote fiction "devoid of effectism and devoted to what he called a poetry of the plainest fact helps clarify a main current in midwestern writing" from Hamlin Garland to Saul Bellow. Even in resistance to Howells's agenda, midwestern writers have continued his emphasis on life as lived and language as spoken. Weber sees the "exposure of the hidden and the unpleasant" undertaken by Sherwood Anderson and Sinclair Lewis as a "variation on Howellsian realism" (15). Similarly, Ernest Hemingway's prose reflects midwestern experience and speech; along with modernist experimentalism and his journalistic apprenticeship in Kansas City, the northern inland dialect that Hemingway spoke as a youth in Illinois and Michigan certainly contributed to his characteristically spare and declarative style.

The plainness of midwestern writing, however, easily lends itself to stereotype. Weber comes close when he qualifies his opinion of the period between 1890 and 1930, when "imaginative writing by Midwesterners and about the Midwest dominated, or very nearly so, American letters. . . . First of all," Weber notes, "the Midwestern day in the sun was of relatively brief duration. . . . Secondly, if the Midwestern ascendancy was not particularly long lasting neither did it run particularly deep. It produced only a few works of unquestioned importance—works important for aesthetic reasons rather than social or historical reasons." The assessment seems fair, though most revealing is the topographical metaphor Weber uses to characterize an era that began with Hamlin Garland's early fiction, published in the 1890s, and concluded with Sinclair

Lewis's acceptance of the Nobel Prize for Literature in 1930, the first awarded to an American: "As a regional movement it seems to exist in imaginative vitality . . . in a middle range between the lofty peaks of New England and Southern literary achievement" (4). Weber's image links aesthetics of landscape and literature that have proven disadvantageous to the Midwest: preferences for drama, heightened contrast, and extremities of experience and prospect.

Weber's estimation of midwestern literature is itself very midwestern (he is professor emeritus of American studies at Notre Dame, in South Bend, Indiana). First, his quantification of what is ultimately a qualitative matter (the aesthetic worth of literature) partakes of the utilitarian aspect of midwestern character. Second, the care he takes not to claim too much for the region exemplifies midwestern cultural self-effacement. Intellectuals in the Midwest dread accusations of boosterism, a term associated with the small-town clannishness that Sinclair Lewis personifies in the title character of his novel *Babbitt* (1922). No open-minded, worldly person wishes to be a Babbitt; the name itself has entered the lexicon as a synonym for bourgeois smugness and materialism. Poet Ted Kooser of Nebraska raises this specter in his statement that "most of the talk about regionalism and sense of place is little more than boosterism. The people doing all of the talking are trying to defend their own writing and that of their friends. The defense is usually a lot better than the writing" (qtd. in Sanders and Brummels, 102). Kooser may be right in some cases, just as Weber's qualification has a certain validity. It is also true, however, as Harrison wryly puts it, that "[a]rt is not a sack race" ("Jim Harrison," 135). Faulkner need not be elevated at Anderson's expense; Thoreau's greatness does not depend on comparison of his stature with that of Leopold. The work of each writer is its own best measure, and we need not rank them on some scale of relative merit. It is enough to acknowledge with Weber that regional literatures are not isolated or monolithic, that "the Midwest—every region—turns fuzzy on its borders, merging along with its writers into the claims of other regions, other traditions" (5).

The location of the Midwest depends on whom you ask, and from whence they hail. In 1980 Shortridge undertook a survey of college students around the United States that resulted in quantitative data, including maps, revealing widely varying definitions of the region. Nebraskans, for example, see their own state as the heart of the heartland. They tend not to think of Great Lakes states like Michigan as midwestern. People in Michigan, in turn, are equivocal in their regional identification; while most include their state in the Midwest, they locate the region's center on the Mississippi River, somewhere near Davenport, Iowa (the setting of one of Michigan-born Harrison's best poems, "The Davenport Lunar Eclipse"). Shortridge's survey illustrates how the conflict between pastoral myth and urban reality in the Midwest has led to changes in perceptual geography:

> As urbanization and industrialization brought profound changes to the economic and social life of the Great Lakes and Ohio Valley areas. . . . There were two choices: either modify the rural image of the Middle West to conform to the new reality of the area, or shift the regional core westward to the Great Plains, where rural society still prevailed. Cognitive maps and economic, popular, and cultural associations for the Middle West suggest that Americans elected the latter course.

Americans, in other words, have not yet modified myth to meet changing realities. To return to Leo Marx's terminology, we have not reconciled the machine and the garden, but have maintained a certain falsehood in our pastoralism, a sentimentality that belies social and environmental complexities. The first, rejected option that Shortridge mentions is for scholars and artists to pursue: to "modify the rural image of the Middle West to conform to the new reality of the area" (92).

To claim the Midwest as a reality, as a distinct place with a usable past, requires defiance of a long tradition of intellectual attenuation, disparagement, and dismissal of the region's identity. The danger does exist, as Weber and others have noted, that regional distinctions will fade as the forces of mass culture make for an increasingly homogenized and placeless world. Yet the land is not going anywhere, and writers still need to contend with geography and social environments. The projection of what is best in midwestern culture into an uncertain future requires the avoidance of both regional self-effacement and parochial self-promotion. Geographer Raymond D. Gastil makes this very point about American studies:

> As long as artists or businessmen in the regional centers of the
> country see success as achievable only outside their region, there
> will be no great regional cultures. On the other hand, as long as
> those who remain in the "boondocks" see their task as the glorifi-
> cation of whatever characteristics their regions happen to possess,
> they will build little that is lasting. . . . In summary, *one* approach
> to a cultural analysis of the United States is a regional approach
> that goes beyond assumptions of general uniformity. (45)

In that spirit, the argument of this chapter moves from critical complexities to an affirmative definition of midwestern identity in relation to the
pastoral ideal and pastoral literature.

## Midwestern Pastoral Ideology

Although cities and industry dominate large sections of the modern Midwest, the region retains its association with fruitful fields and quiet small
towns. This imagery appears in popular culture as well as the fine arts.
Films like *Hoosiers* (1986) and *Field of Dreams* (1989) and songs by Indiana rock and roller John Cougar Mellencamp about "American kids
growing up in the Heartland" derive their appeal from their idealization
of the rural Midwest. So too with Grant Wood's *American Gothic* (1930),
the most recognized painting in American art: an iconic image of a
stern-faced man and woman standing before a small white house in an
Iowa town. Ambiguous in its portrayal of small-town, white midwesterners—like Sinclair Lewis's novel *Main Street* (1920) and other classics of
midwestern literature—Wood's painting conveys as much affection for as
censure of its subjects. It honors midwestern, middle-class, middlebrow
sensibilities even while suggesting their psychological and social limitations. In portraying the society and landscape of the Midwest, these films,
songs, paintings, and books draw on archetypal figures and narratives associated with the region and its defining ideology: the pastoral vision of
a peaceful agrarian kingdom between (and away from) the extremes of
eastern urban sophistication and the moral license of unsettled western
frontiers. That ideology, referred to here as midwestern pastoralism, represents a confluence of many currents of thought, first among these being
the dimension of republican ideology referred to as Jeffersonianism.

*Jeffersonian Legacies*

Pastoralism in the United States is closely associated with the thought and public policy of Thomas Jefferson, who implemented plans for land survey and settlement to benefit small landowners in the American interior. Drawing on the poetry of Virgil as well as eighteenth-century political philosophy (particularly that of John Locke), Jefferson envisioned a republic of independent farmers spreading out across the North American continent.[3] Like Hector St. Jean de Crèvecoeur and other contemporaries, Jefferson thought of rural life as an ideal balance between primitive and urban conditions. "Those who labor in the earth are the chosen people of God," he declares in *Notes on Virginia* (1787), "if ever he had a chosen people, whose breasts he has made his peculiar deposit for substantial and genuine virtue" (*Writings,* 290). That famous statement characterizes the archetype of the yeoman farmer, which would in time become associated less with the United States as a whole than with the Midwest.

In discussing the yeoman farmer image, scholars distinguish pastoralism, as a philosophical ideal, from agrarianism, as an economic system. "The difference," Marx asserts in *The Machine in the Garden,* "is the relative importance of economic factors implied by each term":

> To call Jefferson an agrarian is to imply that his argument rests, at bottom, upon a commitment to an agricultural economy. But in Query XIX [of *Notes on Virginia*] he manifestly is repudiating the importance of economic criteria in evaluating the relative merits of various forms of society. Although the true agrarians of his day . . . had demonstrated the superior efficiency of large-scale agriculture, Jefferson continues to advocate the small, family-sized farm. . . . He is devoted to agriculture largely as a means of preserving rural manners, that is, "rural virtue." (126)

Jefferson's vision, then, was pastoral; an ethical, aesthetic preference rather than an economic principle underlay the yeoman farmer archetype. Marx's analysis rests on conclusions drawn by Richard Hofstadter, who wrote in *The Age of Reform* (1962) that the yeoman farmer's "well-being was not merely physical, it was moral; it was not merely personal, it was the central source of civic virtue; it was not merely secular but religious, for God had made the land and called man to cultivate it" (25). As a model republican and moral exemplar, the yeoman farmer stood in Jefferson's estimation as the worthy beneficiary of favorable public policy. Government, Jefferson wrote in 1785, should provide "by every possible means that as few as possible shall be without a little portion of land [because] small landholders are the most precious part of a state" (qtd. in Johnson, 39).

For the benefit of his ideal yeoman citizen, Jefferson drafted the Land Ordinance of 1784, which suggested the division of the Northwest Territory (the present states of Ohio, Indiana, Michigan, Illinois, and Wisconsin) into ten new states. The subsequent Ordinance of 1785 established a Cartesian survey system of intersecting lines and square subdivisions, a nonvarying grid from which rectangular sections could be parceled and sold. Finally, the Northwest Ordinance of 1787 provided for the temporary governance and admission to the Union of three to five new states as warranted by increased white male population. The ordinance also prohibited slavery, guaranteed the freedom of religion, and provided for public education. Under these successive ordinances, which resulted in large part from Jefferson's leadership, the Northwest Territory became the first planned settlement of a large region in history, the manner of its settlement and development being largely determined before a single legal American settler entered the area. Democratic institutions in the Midwest originate with this founding document, approved by the same Congress that ratified the U.S. Constitution.[4]

The most tangible evidence of Jeffersonian ideology on the American landscape is the survey system established by the Land Ordinance of 1785. The immense size of the Northwest Territory (and later, the Louisiana Purchase during Jefferson's presidency) required a more systematic establishment of land tenure than the traditional "metes and bounds," which defined properties in relation to streams, ridges, even individual trees and rocks. Each new state would be bisected by a base line running east and west and a prime meridian running north and south. Lines parallel the base and meridian at one-mile intervals. The basic political unit is the township, a square area six miles to the side. The township is further divided into thirty-six sections a mile square, each section of 640 acres typically broken by quarters into rectangular 160-, 80-, or 40-acre parcels (the last being the origin of expressions such as "forty acres and a mule" and "the back forty"). To this day most midwestern roads run between sections, marking the landscape with straight lines easily visible from the air or on satellite photographs. This eminently practical arrangement is "a physical manifestation of a universal order that appealed to both Puritan theology and Enlightenment rationalism" (Opie, 8). It allows precise coordinate description of any piece of real estate, providing for American democracy on Jefferson's terms: agricultural and utilitarian.

Objections to the grid survey rest on practical as well as aesthetic and ecological grounds. The survey is entirely unnatural, imposing as it does a rigid geometry across widely varying terrain. Hills, rivers, marshes, and all other topographical particularities are ignored for the sake of predictability. Jefferson's grid, as agricultural historian John Opie observes, is "indiscriminate. It might cut a farm on good soil off from needed water on a neighbor's claim across the section line. Or it might divide a valuable grove of trees into three rectangular woodlots; none could survive independently, and so the grove disappeared in a decade" (xviii). The grid also complicates travel. Direct travel is possible between two points only if one happens to be directly south or west of the other. If not, the route will zigzag any number of times. Regardless of steep grades or any other obstruction, the section road relentlessly slices through the countryside.

The effect of the grid on midwestern attitudes about nature has been profound. Describing what he believes to be a weak sense of place among Iowans, Michael Martone cites the survey grid as a formative influence. The Midwest, he writes, "began as a highly abstract work of the imagination and lingers so today. The power of the grid that overlays it often prevents us from seeing the place itself. It has been characterized from its inception in two dimensions only, flattened by fiat" (5). The Jeffersonian imposition of the square configures land into space—impersonal, interchangeable, and profane—rather than place—intimate, unique, even sacred.

An example of the Jeffersonian grid survey portrayed in this light appears in the memoirs of historian Bruce Catton, best known for award-winning books about the Civil War. Catton recalls the felling of "a noble tree" in his native Benzonia, Michigan, a local landmark and "the only tree in the whole township that dated back to the original forest." A local official saw that the tree stood on a section line, where the survey grid dictated a road should run. It did not matter that the terrain was such that a road would never be put through. The tree was cut and left to rot, its "destruction [satisfying] something in the soul (if that is the word for it) of the man who felled it" (118–19).

This abstraction of land derives not only from Enlightenment rationalism, with its linear and progressive bent, but from the long-standing western desacralization of nature. Christianity traditionally asserts a transcendent God who is separate from his creation. Nature is fallen, animals do not have souls, and places are sacred only if so declared by designated authorities, as with temples, cemeteries, and monuments. Most readers of environmental literature are familiar with the argument, notably formulated in Lynn White Jr.'s 1967 essay "The Historical Roots of Our Ecological Crisis," that Judeo-Christian anthropocentrism has contributed significantly to the commodification and abuse of nature. While ecologically minded Christians object to such assertions, arguing instead for the religious sanctioning of wise stewardship, the fact remains that Anglo-Americans since the Puritans have cited biblical authority in destroying wilderness and appropriating Indian land. Puritan rhetoric, with a gloss of Enlightenment rationalism, appears in the writings of political leaders and pioneers of the Northwest Territory, including Jeffersonians like William Henry Harrison, first territorial governor of Indiana. Harrison asked, "Is one of the fairest portions of the globe to remain in a state of nature, the haunt of a few wretched savages, when it seems destined by the Creator to give support to a large population and to be the seat of civilization, of science, and of true religion?" (qtd. in Weinberg, 79). Almost as if answering Harrison, Lewis Cass (a military associate of Harrison's who later served as territorial governor of Michigan, as secretary of war under President Jackson, and as a U.S. senator) wrote that "there can be no doubt that the Creator intended the earth should be reclaimed from a state of nature and cultivated" (qtd. in Nash, 31). Harrison's justification of land seizure simultaneously denigrated Indian land use and religion; the Indians to him were superstitious "savages" who had no right to land that they neither plowed nor enclosed. Pastoral ideology, as conceived by those who conquered the American interior, combined Jeffersonian natural rights philosophy with biblical sanction. The popular term for this version of pastoralism was Manifest Destiny, "a dogma of supreme self-assurance and ambition—

that America's incorporation of all adjacent lands was the virtually inevitable fulfillment of a moral mission delegated to the nation by Providence itself" (Weinberg, 1–2).

Jefferson, in his attitude toward the Indians, was his usual contradictory self, the same Virginia squire who could provide, in the Declaration of Independence, the intellectual basis of American civil liberty, yet build his fortune on the forced labor of slaves. While he considered African Americans inferior to whites, Jefferson idealized Indians as noble savages: figures of inherent virtue for their proximity to nature, of picturesque tragedy for their inevitable decline before the advance of civilization. He likened Indians' oratory to that of ancient Rome and cited their ancient relics and earthworks as evidence of their inherent intelligence. With education and a change of environment, Jefferson reasoned, Indians could prosper under American rule. He even proposed intermarriage between Indians and whites, an idea he abhorred in regard to blacks and whites. Through cultural, economic, and biological assimilation, Indians would become good yeoman citizens in the American republic as Jefferson imagined it.

As president, Jefferson exerted some effort in this regard. He spoke of making farmers of the Shawnee, Potawatomi, and other midwestern tribes, stressing in his second inaugural address a moral obligation "to teach them agriculture and the domestic arts; to encourage them to that industry which alone can enable them to maintain their place in existence" (*Writings*, 520). He promised as much on several occasions, as before an 1802 assembly of Miamis and Potawatomis in Washington: "We shall, with great pleasure, see your people become disposed to cultivate the earth, to raise herds of useful animals, and to spin and weave, for their food and clothing. These resources are certain; they will never disappoint you: while those of hunting may fail, and expose your women and children to the miseries of hunger and cold. We will with pleasure furnish you with implements for the most necessary arts, and with persons who may instruct you how to make use of them" (qtd. in Goetzmann, 121). Such largesse, of course, was predicated on Indian land cessions, which Jefferson hoped to obtain through the legal mechanism of treaties, which often included provisions for helping midwestern tribes make the transition to full-time agriculture. The United States, Jefferson believed, should demonstrate that a nation could prosper and grow peacefully and rationally. American treatment of its native people would be an important measure of the success of that mission, the establishment of a pastoral republic in the American interior.[5]

Indian inclusion in the pastoral "empire of liberty" would have required fair negotiations, consistent technical support, and enforcement of settled boundaries. The Jeffersonians, however, did not possess the moral or political resolve to deal such justice. The nineteenth-century frontier saw a pattern of alternating altruism and violence, what historian Richard White calls "the American combination of Jefferson's imperial benevolence and backcountry Indian hating," a "vision of the future that promised [Indians] only alternative routes to obliteration" (502). Events following Jefferson's presidency, including salient moments in midwestern history such as the Shawnee War, the Black Hawk War, the Indian Removal Act, the Minnesota Sioux uprising, and the massacre at Wounded Knee, should be understood in this light. Tribes faced the loss of their lands and traditions whether or not they attempted to assimilate into the agrarian economy. Despite official rhetoric invoking higher ideals of republicanism and Christian charity, and "whatever the desires of the government to maintain the good reputation of the nation, the frontiersmen were more interested in the Indian giving up his land than learning to farm it" (Horsman, 173).

Their population and land base severely diminished, Native Americans have been ill served by pastoral ideology. According to the myth, Euro-American culture would "tame the wild" by transforming wilderness into an agrarian "garden of the world" by civilizing the noble savage. This complex of high ideals, greed, and alternating admiration and denigration of Native Americans lies at the heart of the troubled American spirit of place, contradicting the notion of America as innocent and without history. Jim Harrison writes in one of his angrier moments that "it was greed that discovered the country, greed that propelled the westward movement, greed that shipped the blacks, greed that murdered the Indians" ( *Just before Dark,* 263). Native American cultures, despite that greed and the dubious benevolence of a complicit government, have survived by means of traditions telling a story of the land very different from that projected by Jeffersonian pastoralism.

Ironically, while nineteenth-century Americans thought of Indians as nomads, agriculture was in fact highly developed among midwestern tribes. The importance of cultivation varied according to cultural group. The Shawnee of the Ohio River valley, for example, were seminomadic hunters for whom farming served as a basis for social interaction in the summer months. Other groups, like the Potawatomi and Winnebago in the region around southern Lake Michigan, lived in stable villages based on corn, squash, and beans. On the tall and midgrass prairies, Siouian tribes, such as the Iowa, Missouri, and Kansa, traveled seasonally in pursuit of buffalo and other animals while maintaining crops and long-term residence in river lowlands. Further back in time, seven hundred years before the arrival of Europeans, the people known by archeologists as Mississippians established Cahokia, a highly civilized city-state based on an economy of surplus corn. The remnants of this city—great buildings of earth geometrically arranged across the Mississippi River from present-day St. Louis—invite comparison with our Jeffersonian legacy. The Mississippians, historian Roger G. Kennedy points out, might have impressed Jefferson, had he known more about their accomplishment:

> They were capable, it appears, of mighty exertions in a common purpose, and of architecture having that quality of pertinacity which Jefferson so passionately desired for his young republic.
>
> Here were no dull, drilled, and doltish peasantry, laboring under the lash. Instead, we may imagine them as American's first free and independent yeomen, living on their own modest farms, striding the forest and prairie after game, neither drawn to bright city lights nor abasing themselves to a primogenitrous, entailed local gentry.

The Cahokians were, in Kennedy's provocative term, "Proto-Jeffersonians" (275–76). Considering the settling of the Midwest to be a great failed opportunity, Kennedy suggests that we may do better only if we understand our history on the land. "The time has come," he concludes, "for another mighty effort to fulfill the highest aspirations of the Founders in the central valley of North America, where they glimpsed the possibility of a work of redemption" (5). That effort, as pastoral writers have come to appreciate, must include an honest accounting for the legacies of conquest in the American heartland.

### Midwestern Pastoralism and Forms of American Individualism

In addition to Jeffersonian and Judeo-Christian social thought, versions of individualism constitute basic elements of midwestern pastoralism. Social philosophers have long identified individualism as the overarching American ideology. Alexis de Tocqueville, the French civil servant who investigated American society in the 1830s, defined individualism as the "calm and considered feeling which disposes each citizen to isolate himself . . . and withdraw into the circle of family and friends . . . [leaving] the greater society to look after itself" (*Democracy*, 506). The popular phrase for the myth of freedom and middle-class success is the "American dream," usually thought of in terms of the nuclear family and home ownership. Over the course of history, the favored site of American desire and ambition has shifted from the farm to the city, and then to the suburb, from agriculture to industry and perhaps today into conceptual spaces of electronic communications and trade. Consistent throughout these changes is the American emphasis on private life, with property and freedom of expression as two central concerns.

Building on Tocqueville's analysis, sociologist Robert Bellah differentiates two types of individualism, the utilitarian and the expressive. Each is conveyed mythologically, through archetypal narratives and figures. Utilitarian individualism, personified by the likes of Benjamin Franklin—patriot, inventor, and "archetypal poor boy who made good"—stresses work and economic freedom (32). Assuming that social order results from resourcefulness and self-reliance, utilitarianism directs itself to technology and the management of time and space. Expressive or Romantic individualism, on the other hand, equates success not with material acquisition, efficiency, or social status, but with a "life rich in experience, open to all kinds of people, luxuriating in the sensual as well as the intellectual, above all a life of strong feeling" (34). Such a disposition, embodied by Walt Whitman and other artistic innovators of the nineteenth century, rejects the narrower sense of self, rational and materialistic, inspired by utilitarianism. While the utilitarian associates goodness with usefulness, the Romantic ranks beauty, emotion, and psychological growth above utility as absolute values. To generalize, the utilitarian, who imagines a mechanistic universe, is practical and materialistic; the Romantic, who sees nature organically, is intuitive and idealistic. The utilitarian plans, then picks up tools and constructs; the Romantic turns to nature, then dreams and creates.

While evident everywhere in the United States, these forms of individualism have manifested themselves in the Midwest in distinctive ways. There is a midwestern variety of utilitarianism, particular to the social and geographical conditions of the region's history. It exists in a dialectic with midwestern Romanticism, which has both challenged and reinforced utilitarian values. Both ideologies have been embodied mythologically in archetypal figures and narratives that appear with regularity in popular culture and midwestern arts. Consideration of these belief systems at work will reveal midwestern pastoralism to be a coherent, if ever-changing, worldview.

### Midwestern Utilitarianism

A number of scholars define the Midwest in relation to utilitarian individualism. "Hard work is the quality that distinguishes Midwesterners," claims geographer John H. Garland, who cites the Protestant work ethic of the region's pioneers as a formative influence (12). Nineteenth-century settlement of northern Ohio, Indiana, Illinois, and southern Michigan and Wisconsin was dominated by New Englanders and New Yorkers, people for whom work, property, and commerce amounted to a moral creed. Hart describes them as "materialists, not escapists. They did not flee to the wilderness to get away from society, they came to the frontier to secure the blessings of the good life for themselves and for their posterity" (265). Those blessings—representative government and public education, as well as farms and towns developed after eastern models—came about through work, the first value in midwestern utilitarianism. Hart posits seven core assumptions in this worldview, which he refers to as the "family farm ideology":

1) [H]ard work is a virtue;
2) anyone who works hard can make good;
3) anyone who fails to make good is lazy;
4) a man's true worth can be determined by his income;
5) a self-made man is better than one to the manor born;
6) a family is responsible for its own economic security; and
7) the best government is the least government. (272)

These beliefs, basic to midwestern society, are expressed by the emphasis on applied science and economics in state universities, for which the Morrill Act of 1862 provided federal support. The beliefs fueled the agrarian revolt of the 1890s, when the resentment of farmers against banks, railroads, manufacturers, and middlemen led to the formation of the Populist Party and the political ascendancy of the "Great Commoner," William Jennings Bryan of Nebraska. They were employed by industrialists like Henry Ford, who denied that industrialization had diminished individual opportunity and responsibility. They appear every four years at election time in the pandering of presidential candidates who rhapsodize about heartland virtue. As ideological support for the economic ambition of the middle class, midwestern utilitarianism asserts independence and resourcefulness as civic as well as personal virtues. It amounts, in Lewis Atherton's trenchant phrase, to a "cult of the immediately useful and practical" (116).[6]

Utilitarian values characterize cultural archetypes associated with midwestern social development. A symbolic link between agrarianism and the Industrial Revolution in the Midwest is the archetypal tinkerer, the solitary inventor or mechanic who became a hero in the late nineteenth century and who persists in popular culture to this day. The tinkerer archetype derives not only from the wider tradition of American utilitarianism, symbolized by the likes of Franklin, but from the work ethic and egalitarianism of midwestern family farm ideology. Like the yeoman farmer, the midwestern tinkerer emerges from humble beginnings to achieve, through productive solitude, an objective that will benefit not only himself but society as a whole. No professor or pedant, the tinkerer represents applied rather than pure science, useful technology to serve the greater good. The most celebrated tinkerers, Thomas Edison, Henry Ford, and Wilbur and Orville Wright, were all born and raised within 250 miles of one another in rural Ohio and Michigan communities. In the popular mind, these men represented "practicality, know-how, and the mystique of hard work conquering nature" (Polley, 366). They were "pioneers" crossing technological "frontiers" of electric light, mechanical land transportation, and lighter-than-air flight. Although their innovations actually depended on coordinated team efforts and the financial support of investors, the myth persists of solitary geniuses in barns, garages, and tool shops revolutionizing society through their inspiration and perspiration.

The midwestern tinkerer archetype appears with some frequency in literature and popular culture. Anderson's novel *Poor White* (1920), for example, narrates the transformation of a Missouri ne'er-do-well, modeled after Samuel Clemens's Huckleberry Finn, into a much admired (and misunderstood) inventor of farm machinery. Anderson's theme is the social and psychological cost of the Industrial Revolution to the people of a small Ohio town in the late 1800s. More recently, in a satirical and light-hearted vein, has come *Home Improvement,* one of the most popular television programs of the 1990s. Set in a suburb of Detroit, the show stars comedian Tim Allen (from Birmingham, Michigan) as the host of a television fix-it-yourself program who constantly overestimates his own mechanical aptitude, to humorous effect. Allen emphasized his character's regional identity by wearing shirts emblazoned with the names of Michigan colleges and professional sports teams. Finally, the film *Twister* (1996) portrays young scientists chasing tornadoes across midwestern plains. They seek to perfect a device to measure wind velocity and movement, information that may lead to a more effective storm warning system. This implausible disaster flick is a revealing study in cultural symbolism. Its pastoral settings (filmed in Kansas and Oklahoma), sentimental view of midwestern small towns and farms, and faith in technology remind us of continuities between agrarian and industrial values in the Midwest. As Reynold M. Wik points out in *Henry Ford and Grass-Roots America* (1972), "The average American farmer thought he was an inventor of sorts. After all, his tradition had been one of utilitarianism. Frontiersmen had improvised to survive, and early settlers had shown an affection for machinery" (59–60). The resourceful storm chaser in *Twister,* tinkering with his invention or sifting dry soil in his hands while contemplating weather patterns, is a descendant of the independent yeoman with plow in hand and eyes to the clouds.

Another midwestern utilitarian archetype is the "booster," typically portrayed as a provincial and conformist small-town businessman. While many midwestern writers of the region's classic period developed characters after the type, the booster is most associated with one writer: Sinclair Lewis, the first American to win the Nobel Prize for Literature. Lewis's most popular and well-regarded book, *Main Street,* follows Carol Kennicott, a young college graduate who tries to bring artistic culture and civic pride to Gopher Prairie, a fictional version of Sauk Centre,

Minnesota, Lewis's hometown. With characteristic hyperbole Lewis describes Carol's neighbors as a "savorless people, gulping tasteless food . . . listening to mechanical music, saying mechanical things about the excellence of Ford automobiles, and viewing themselves as the greatest race in the world" (265). They are, in other words, thorough utilitarians, philistines who value money and social status above all else. Lewis identifies the type in *Babbitt,* a name that has entered the American lexicon. A Babbitt, according to *Webster's Dictionary,* is "a business or professional man who conforms unthinkingly to prevailing middle-class standards." Those standards—honesty, optimism, and thrift on one hand, and self-righteousness, provinciality, and materialism on the other—are evident everywhere in American life. But the booster is strongly associated with the Midwest, partly because of Lewis's writing, but more importantly because modern business culture emerged during the era of midwestern economic and cultural leadership.

A proprietary view of nature is implicit in midwestern utilitarianism, which used the metaphor of cultivation to justify not only the seizure of Indian lands but the heedless exploitation of soil, water, trees, minerals, and other natural resources so plentiful as to seem limitless. To Tocqueville, who traveled from New York to Michigan in 1831, it seemed that the "wonders of inanimate nature leave Americans cold. . . . They do not see the marvelous forests surrounding them until they begin to fall beneath the ax. What they see is something different. The American people see themselves marching through wildernesses, drying up marshes, diverting rivers, peopling the wilds, and subduing nature" (*Democracy,* 485). This attitude is familiar to anyone who has seen midwestern marshes replaced by golf courses, groves bulldozed for suburban tract houses, and farmland sacrificed for fast-food outlets and automobile dealerships. The impulse, however couched in rhetoric about "wise use" and "balancing of interests," is consistent with nineteenth-century progressivism and industrial development. As Leopold observes, in his characteristically colloquial manner, "our bigger-and-better society is now like a hypochondriac, so obsessed with its own economic health as to have lost the capacity to remain healthy. The whole world is so greedy for more bathtubs that it has lost the stability necessary to build them, or even to turn off the tap" (*Sand County,* ix).

Utilitarianism, however, need not imply parsimony, greed, or aesthetic insensitivity; it can suggest pioneer fortitude and even an ascetic grace.

Such are the principles called on by Scott Russell Sanders, contemporary Indiana bioregionalist, in reclaiming the Protestant work ethic from "cynical bosses and politicians":

> As I understand it, a regard for the necessity and virtue of work has nothing to do with productivity or taxes, and everything to do with fulfilling one's humanity. As I have seen it embodied in the lives not only of grandparents but of parents and neighbors and friends, this ethic arises from a belief that the creation is a sacred gift, and that by working we express our gratitude and celebrate our powers. To honor that gift, we should live simply, honestly, conservingly, saving money and patching clothes and fixing what breaks, sharing what we have. (*Writing*, 95)

It is this sort of utilitarianism that Cather celebrates in her Nebraska farmers, that Leopold conveys in his metaphor of the "land mechanism," that Roethke and Harrison admire in their horticulturalist fathers, that Wright observed among the working class of Martins Ferry, Ohio. It is also expressed in a version of Grant Wood's *American Gothic* depicting the parents of Berry Gordy Jr., founder of Detroit's Motown Record Corporation, the most successful black-owned business in American history.[7] This unexpected tribute indicates the extent to which faith in education, industriousness, and organization has provided a cultural vocabulary for midwesterners of all races. Like Jeffersonian ideology, of which it is a major component, utilitarianism ideally serves human freedom and a practical grounding in the landscape. The hegemonic, imperial variety, by contrast, makes a fetish of property and power, lending itself to a false pastoralism that neglects cities and allows rural landscapes to fall under miles of pavement and bad architecture.

### Romanticism and the Midwestern Landscape

Resistance against excessive utilitarianism has been couched in the language and imagery of Romanticism ever since the first American settlers entered the Midwest in the early nineteenth century. In fact, the Romantic movement in the East coincided with migration into northern Ohio, Indiana, Illinois, and southern Michigan and Wisconsin. New Englanders and New Yorkers dominated the early development of that

area, then known as the "Northwest." Establishing farms, towns, busi-
nesses, schools, and governmental institutions after eastern models, the
more educated among them also brought books by William Cullen
Bryant, Emerson, and other Romantic writers. Ideas about nature and
the individual contained in this literature tempered to some degree the
culture's dominant arrogance toward the land, suggesting that nature
had aesthetic, spiritual, and cultural value transcendent of its instrumen-
tality as resource and property.

The Romantic movement found its apotheosis in Ralph Waldo Emerson. Since the West of Emerson's day, what we now call the Midwest, was
something of a greater New England, the poet and philosopher spoke to
the region's Yankee transplants, indirectly through his writings and directly on the many lecture tours that took him to Cincinnati, St. Louis,
and other midwestern cities. He was, as biographer Robert D. Richardson notes, "one of the very few literary lecturers from the East to remain
a steady lyceum attraction in Ohio for twenty years" (420). This popularity as a speaker anticipated the deep influence of Emerson's writing
on later midwestern writers. Since Cather and subsequent midwestern
pastoralists modeled their responses to nature in great part after Emerson's, a synopsis of his thinking about nature, the individual, and society
is in order.

Emerson's first major work, *Nature* (1836), probably the most influential American writing on the topic, touches on several themes essential to
the present discussion. Central to Emerson's vision is the Romantic archetype of the solitary individual in nature, kindred to the yeoman farmer as
a symbol of natural virtue and self-reliance. But where Jefferson's favored
farmer-citizen sees nature through the lenses of materialism and rational
self-interest, the lone Romantic values nature's beauty and spiritual significance above its utility. Nature to Emerson is an aesthetic "integrity
of impression made by manifold natural objects . . . which distinguishes
the stick of timber of the wood-cutter, from the tree of the poet" (*Essays,*
9). He accepts instrumentalist claims on nature as resource and property,
but insists "that this mercenary benefit is one which has respect to [a]
higher good" aesthetic and spiritual in character (*Essays,* 13).

Considering the division of land in rural New England, for example,
Emerson notes that though "Miller owns this field, Locke that, and Man-
ning the woodland beyond . . . none of them owns the landscape" (*Es-*

*says,* 9). The Anglo-Saxon names by which Emerson personifies American farmers reflect the utilitarian basis of agrarian ideology. The first, derived from the processing of grain, and the last, which is distinctly anthropomorphic, suggest the task-centeredness of those who "man" the landscape. Emerson's allusion to John Locke recalls the thesis of rationalism for which Romanticism is the necessary antithesis. Much as Jefferson, in the Declaration of Independence, crucially altered Locke's three basic rights from "life, liberty, and property" to "life, liberty, and the pursuit of happiness," Emerson locates that happiness in an aesthetic and mystical sublimation of ownership. "There is," he concludes, "a property in the horizon which no man has but he whose eye can integrate all the parts, that is the poet. This is the best part of these men's farms, yet to this their warranty-deeds give no title" (*Essays,* 9).

Emerson, then, accepts the republican relation of democracy and property (what he calls "commodity"), but in surveying the relation of person to place adjusts the utilitarian compass to indicate a true north of natural beauty and intrinsic value. Emerson's pastoral vision is philosophically idealistic; like Plato and the eighteenth-century Swedish scientist and mystic Emanuel Swedenborg, he believes that the physical creation symbolizes an intangible higher reality. "Nature is the symbol of spirit," so that trees, rocks, and rivers correspond to an immaterial realm of pure mind. Following Emerson's metaphor of nature as language, we read "particular natural facts" as "symbols of particular spiritual facts" (*Essays,* 20). Our reading may begin empirically but proceeds on the basis of intuition and faith. Emerson's "original relation to the universe" requires individuals to go beyond experience as mediated by authorities and traditions and immerse themselves in nature both physically and psychically.

Such receptivity precedes moments of transcendence, as when Emerson discovers "perpetual youth" in the woods and on a "bare common." The essay's most famous passage reminds us that the experience of sublimity does not require mountains or the ocean, but can occur in the most prosaic of landscapes: "Standing on the bare ground,—my head bathed by the blithe air, and uplifted into infinite space,—all mean egotism vanishes. I become a transparent eye-ball; I am nothing; I see all; the currents of the Universal Being circulate through me; I am part or particle of God" (*Essays,* 10).

For all its implications, the passage needs to be appreciated for its spiritual geography. Emerson's is the archetypal Romantic epiphany of place, a mythic narrative of arrival ubiquitous in American nature writing, including the work of midwestern pastoralists. The experience enacts the heroic cycle described by Joseph Campbell as a universal pattern of separation, initiation, and return, a journey both inner and outer, of mind as well as body. "The effect of the successful adventure of the hero," according to Campbell, "is the unlocking and release again of the flow of life into the body of the world." The life-affirming energy emerges "from an invisible source, the point of entry being the center of the symbolic circle of the universe" (40). This is the sacred place, envisioned in mythology as a world navel, a tree of life (as in Robert Bly's poem about the willow in Minnesota), or an *axis mundi* around which the world turns and at which the cardinal directions converge. The Romantic sublime correlates in this crucial instance with Buddhism and Native American religions, which teach that through ritual and meditation one may transcend "mean egotism" to reach a greater selfhood that encompasses the local environment. Emerson's heroic "quest," as Bly comments, is to "marry nature for vision, rather than possession. His aim is not to live more but to see more" (*Winged Life*, 4).

The Romantic sublime must, of course, be read for its cultural and political implications. Emerson's "original relation to the universe" entailed not only spiritual individualism, but also a nationalistic assertion of American cultural distinctiveness. If artists and intellectuals drew their substance and style from conditions unique to the New World, they might inspire republican America to avoid European oligarchy and overrefinement. Europe had ancient traditions in the arts and sciences and great cities teeming with cultural activity. But the United States had nature in abundance, with wild, undeveloped expanses that distinguished the young nation from Europe. Romantic nationalists, as Roderick Nash demonstrates, "argued that far from being a liability, wilderness was actually an American asset" that "by the middle decades of the nineteenth century . . . was recognized as a cultural and moral resource and a basis for national self-esteem" (67). An artistic expansiveness and claiming of American landscape as subject matter coincided with the western movement of settlers into newly acquired territories.

A number of Romantic writers from New York and New England traveled to the Great Lakes and prairie states and subsequently wrote about their experiences. Novels by Caroline Kirkland, including *A New Home—Who'll Follow?* (1839), describe the Michigan wilderness, as does Margaret Fuller's *Summer on the Lakes, in 1843* (1844), a nonfiction account of travel by steamship on the Great Lakes. Kirkland and Fuller not only describe midwestern landscapes but also critique frontier society, which they perceive as overly utilitarian and lacking in aesthetic sensitivity. Poets such as William Cullen Bryant and Walt Whitman, on the other hand, tend to praise rather than admonish, to model aesthetic and spiritual responses to nature rather than contrast such sensitivity with rampant materialism. They assert American cultural nationalism by naming and describing midcontinental American landscapes they had journeyed to see. Because their poetic styles and careers differed to the extreme, Bryant and Whitman are rarely discussed in tandem. Bryant achieved early popularity and respect as a writer of blank verse and rhymed lyrics, whereas Whitman, who became the "national poet" he intended to be only after his death, was an avatar of free verse. They shared much, however, as poets and as men. Both worked in New York as journalists; both wrote poetry addressed to the American public, consciously speaking to readers in familiar and, at times, oracular modes. Both found in the midwestern prairie a poetic symbol of American expansionism, a garden image that they used to express optimism about the United States as a republic of nature.

Bryant's poem "The Prairies," conceived during a trip to Illinois in 1832, is the reverie of a solitary Romantic on the frontier, a meditation on the prairie's natural beauty, human history, and imminent transformation into a populous agricultural region. The poem's title differentiates a midwestern landscape by naming it, a gesture Bryant repeats in the first lines:

> These are the gardens of the Desert, these
> The unshorn fields, boundless and beautiful,
> For which the speech of England has no name—
> The Prairies.

Bryant's naming is an act of aesthetic appropriation, a claiming of the prairie as an American scene and poetic subject. That a new word (derived from the French for "meadow") is needed for the place suggests the necessity of new modes of poetic description. Bryant's immediate task, therefore, is to transform that "boundless," supposedly undifferentiated space into meaningful *place* by noting variety and life in the vista: the play of sun and shade, for example, and "the prairie-hawk that, poised on high, / Flaps his broad wings, yet moves not." As a Romantic, Bryant is compelled to observe not only beauty in the place, but also sacredness. Just as he based "A Forest Hymn" on the extended metaphor of forests as cathedrals, so Bryant sees the prairie as a

> [f]itting floor
> For this magnificent temple of the sky—
> With flowers whose glory and whose multitude
> Rival the constellations!
>
> (162)

Gardens, temples, and the heavenly firmament: these are the images by which the poet transforms the new land into the substance of myth.

"The Prairies" conveys the familiar myth of American innocence, an image of an Edenic republic with every white male cast as Adam in the garden. This myth counteracted the European aesthetic ideal of "association," which valued landscapes according to their connection to historical events and legend. Ruins of Roman temples, for example, endowed Rome with the picturesque quality that endeared it to poets and painters. American Romantics like Bryant were sensitive to the charge that American landscapes lacked the associative power so evident in Europe. Illinois solved the dilemma by offering Bryant Romantic ruins, in the shape of prehistoric earthworks, as well as supposedly untouched wilderness.

The poem's long second stanza focuses on these earthworks, many of which still exist in the Mississippi valley. No mere piles of dirt, the mounds were the first enduring works of architecture in what is now the United States. Kennedy describes them as "great in size, precision, and complexity . . . planned and built . . . under the direction of a priesthood of astronomer-engineer-architects" (276). Bryant may have viewed Monks Mound at Cahokia, a pyramid greater in extent than that at Gizeh, Egypt. For Bryant, the mounds were memento mori, sublime reminders of life's ephemerality and the passing of empires; they resemble in this regard the ancient Greek marbles in the British Museum, which struck John Keats as evidence of the "rude / Wasting of old Time" (1,136). The

Illinois mounds told Bryant that America did in fact have a history that poets and artists could draw on for inspiration.

The history that he imagines, however, is a fabrication in the service of Manifest Destiny. Seeing the region as a "desert" or "verdant waste" in need of reclamation by white settlement, Bryant deftly avoids evidence to the contrary. Although the role of Indian wildfires in prairie ecology was obvious even to many pioneers, he claims, "Man hath no part in all this glorious work" (162). Archeologists were beginning to recognize that the ancestors of contemporary Indians, not ancient Israelites or Egyptians, had built the mounds, but Bryant insists that a "race, that long has passed away, / Built them." He even suggests that the Indians were later invaders who had overthrown the old civilization. "The redman came—," Bryant imagines, "roaming hunter-tribes, warlike and fierce, / And the mound-builders vanished from the earth" (163). He proceeds to a fictive narrative of the sacking of a city; the only survivor is adopted by "the rude conquerors" but is forever haunted by the memory "[o]f his first love, and her sweet little ones, / Butchered, amid their shrieks, with all his race" (164).

Bryant's fictional genocide is a curious projection of the brutality Americans were actually visiting on the mound builders' descendants. While Bryant admired the Illinois prairie in 1832, soldiers were hunting down the region's native people. The Sauk leader Black Hawk had defied federal orders by leading his people back to their ancestral lands in Illinois from temporary residence in Iowa. A war ensued, which for Black Hawk's people turned into a flight from state militia and federal troops, ending in the so-called Battle of Bad Axe, on the Mississippi River south of present-day La Crosse, Wisconsin. The battle was actually a massacre, in which at least three hundred Sauk men, women, and children were killed by white soldiers, cannon-wielding steamboaters, and Sioux warriors allied to the American cause. Black Hawk himself was captured and placed in military custody.[8]

Black Hawk and the Sauks are conspicuously absent from Bryant's poem, removed from his poetic and human sympathies. His poem bestows the sanction of divine providence on Jacksonian policies of conquest and removal, assuring us that "[r]aces of living things, glorious in strength," arise and "perish, as the quickening breath of God / Fills them, or is withdrawn." Given current events, Bryant felt obliged to contemporize this fiction with the astonishing falsehood that "[t]he red-man, too, / Has left the blooming wilds he ranged so long, / And, nearer to the Rocky Mountains, sought / A wilder hunting-ground" (164). The noble savage must be a nomad, if the fiction is to cohere; Bryant must ignore Sauk village life and horticulture. Relegating Native Americans to natural history, he must speak of their displacement in the same breath with which he notes the absence of beaver and buffalo. Bryant thus lyricizes the self-serving rhetoric of the Jacksonians, who "thrust the Indians aside," as Kennedy remarks, "by means which might lie easier on the conscience if those displaced were thought to have neither history, art nor religion worthy of the respect of the displacers" (223). History for Bryant will begin when Illinois is settled, the "deserts" are pastoralized, and the air is filled with "the laugh of children, the soft voice / Of maidens, and the sweet and solemn hymn / Of Sabbath worshippers" (164–65). "The Prairies" advances a distorted pastoralism, casting American history in a gentle morning light despite the violence concurrent with Bryant's visit to Illinois.

Like Bryant, Walt Whitman responded in nationalistic as well as aesthetic terms to the American prairie. Grass, after all, is the central metaphor of his life's work, the much-revised *Leaves of Grass*. A "uniform hieroglyphic" (31), grass signifies for Whitman the immortality of the soul and democratic harmony between individuals and the community. When he finally saw the prairie, while touring Missouri and Kansas by train in 1879, Whitman reacted with astonishment: "I thought my eyes had never looked on scenes of greater pastoral beauty" (852). Countering the current fashion for scenic sublimity—"Yosemite, Niagara falls, the upper Yellowstone and the like"—Whitman decided that the "Prairies and Plains, while less stunning at first sight, last longer, fill the esthetic sense fuller, precede all the rest, and make North America's characteristic landscape. . . . Even their simplest statistics are sublime" (864–65). This subtle sublimity, in Whitman's view, would result in great literature, which as an ardent nationalist he believed necessary to American greatness. Thus he foresaw the prairies "fused in the alembic of a perfect poem, or other esthetic work, entirely western, fresh and limitless—altogether our own, without a trace or taste of Europe's soil, reminiscence, technical letter or spirit" (863).

Whitman deferred such regional cultural expression, however, counseling patience to Americans who yearned for cultural accomplishment to match the nation's growing economic power. While promoting him-self as national poet and prophet, Whitman took care to praise the en-ergies behind conquest and development—in short, to flatter his audi-ence. To a reporter for a St. Louis paper who asked about the prospects for "a distinctively American literature," he responded that "our work at present is to lay the foundations of a great nation in products, in agri-culture, [and] in commerce." Referring to midwestern states by name and to the region as "the seat and field of these very facts and ideas," he concluded that "materialistic prosperity in all its varied forms, with those other points that I mentioned, are first to be attended to. When those have their results and get settled, then a literature worthy of us will begin to be defined" (867–68). Pioneer utilitarianism, in other words, literally needed to clear the ground for a Romantic celebration of place.

The great poet of Manifest Destiny, Whitman celebrated western con-quest with an unmatched stridency. His poem "The Prairie States," for example, echoes predictions made by politicians and boosters that trade and technology would transform the Mississippi valley into an empire of "populous millions, cities and farms, / With iron interlaced" (524). The better-known "Pioneers! O Pioneers!" which gave Willa Cather the title for her first major novel, encourages the subjugation of the American landscape by a "[c]entral inland race . . . from Missouri, with the conti-nental blood intervein'ed." To this supremacist rhetoric Whitman adds a note of male domination: "We the rivers stemming, vexing we and pierc-ing deep the mines within, / We the surface broad surveying, we the vir-gin soil upheaving, / Pioneers! O Pioneers!" (372). Such imagery of vio-lence and sexual penetration betrays Whitman as a writer of his time. While admired for his democratic inclusiveness, Whitman was limited in his sympathies by the day's popular notions about race, gender, and na-ture's instrumental value.

Such poems lend credence to descriptions of American Romanticism as a front for imperialist rapacity. Yet to make such descriptions defini-tive requires that we ignore the movement's countervailing message, as if Whitman were a mere apologist for empire, an American Kipling spout-ing racism and hegemony at every turn. Whitman also warned that "largeness of nature or the nation [is] monstrous without a correspond-ing largeness and generosity of the spirit of the citizen" (6). This is the Whitman still loved by readers of both genders, and by people of every ethnicity, social class, region, religion, and sexual orientation.[9] It is also worthwhile remembering that while Bryant and Whitman ignored the plight of North America's first peoples, Emerson publicly censured president Martin Van Buren for Cherokee removal (Richardson, 278), and that Thoreau saw the natives of Maine not as noble savages but as people from whom he had much to learn. Romantic naturism did in fact serve empire, but not exclusively. What continues to commend Romanticism to American writers and artists is its core message of receptivity and compassion, summed up in the preface to the 1855 edition of *Leaves of Grass,* in which Whitman urges his readers to "[l]ove the earth and the sun and the animals" and to "despise riches" (11).

To regionalize the dialectic of utilitarian and Romantic individualism, I will consider two key figures in the period of midwestern economic and cultural ascendancy: Henry Ford and Frank Lloyd Wright. The resemblances between the men are striking. Both spent their formative years on farms: Ford in southeastern Michigan, Wright in central Wisconsin. Both headed to the nearest major city to apprentice in technical fields: Ford to Detroit and a career in mechanics, Wright to Chicago, where he secured the patronage of the great architect Louis Sullivan. Both men embodied the tinkerer archetype: Ford obviously so, Wright by dint of his lifelong experimentation with new methods, materials, and architectural forms. They both preferred rural to urban life, expressing on many occasions antipathy to cities that matched even Jefferson's fulminations. Both read Emerson and were equally devoted to his credo of self-reliance and originality.

Ford and Wright, however, diverged in the lessons they took from nineteenth-century midwestern agrarianism. Ford assumed anti-intellectualism, fear of bankers and debt, disdain for innovative art and literature, and, not least of all, anti-Semitism. As Wik demonstrates, Ford became a folk hero because he epitomized "values dear to the hearts of the average American. . . . [H]is outlook reflected the midwestern agrarian mind" (8, 10). The apostle of the assembly line can be characterized as a utilitarian absolutist, the epitome of Hart's pessimistic assessment of midwestern character as pecuniaristic, materialistic, self-assured, functionalist, technologic, competent, simplistic, up to the minute, and xenophobic (280). Rejoinders attributed to Ford fit him to the type: as to a choice of colors for the Model T, Ford said the customer could "have a car of any color he wants . . . provided it's black." As for cultural pursuits, he declared, "History is more or less bunk" and "Literature is all right, but it doesn't mean much" (qtd. in Polley, 367–68).

Ford's version of pastoral ideology, while progressive enough to embrace soybeans and organic farming, entailed the patterning of society and nature after the machine. Industrialization, Ford believed, would not enslave people, but free them. He claimed a nobler purpose for the automobile, one that he promoted in well-publicized camping trips with friends like Edison and naturalist John Burroughs. The automobile, Ford insisted, brought people closer to nature. "Unless we better understand the mechanical portion of life," Ford announced on the first page of his 1922 autobiography, "we cannot have the time to enjoy the trees, and the birds, and the flowers, and the green fields" (1). He quoted himself from an advertisement supposedly placed in 1909, when his words would have been visionary: "I will build a motor car for the great multitude. It will be large enough for the family but small enough for the individual to run and care for. It will be constructed of the best materials, by the best men to be hired, after the simplest designs that modern engineering can devise. But it will be so low in price that no man making a good salary will be unable to own one—and enjoy with his family the blessings of hours of pleasure in God's great open spaces" (73). While echoing Emerson as to communion with nature, Ford admits no reservations about the machine in the garden. Mechanization in his estimation is an absolute good: rational, linear, and quantifiable.[10]

Wright, on the other hand, was inspired by Emerson and Thoreau to contemplate an architecture that would turn from European models to embrace the forms and conditions of American landscape. He developed a practice and philosophy, stemming from the work of Sullivan, called *organic architecture*. Organic architecture entailed integration of building to site, continuity between interior and exterior, application of forms borrowed from nature in both structure and ornament, and use of local materials. "A building," Wright wrote in 1908, "should appear to grow easily from its site and be shaped to harmonize with its surroundings if Nature is manifest there, and if not try to make it as quiet, substantial and organic as She would have been were the opportunity Hers" (87). Wright often repeated Sullivan's dictum that "form follows function"—which, far from advocating a cold functionalism, meant that design needed to begin from the inside, considering the occupants' practical and spiritual needs for space, light, and comfort. In advising clients and other architects to "break the box," Wright expressed the essence of his organic philosophy, which rejected not only the outdated enclosures and decorative excesses of Victorian construction, but also the rigid linearity typifying utilitarian design, from Jefferson's survey grid to Ford's massive industrial complex on the River Rouge near Detroit.

Organic principles governed the prairie house, Wright's first original architectural style. Working from his first home and studio in Oak Park, Illinois, Wright created houses with open floor plans and a horizontal emphasis derived from the gentle topography of his native region. "We of the Middle West are living on the prairie," he wrote at the time. "The prairie has a beauty of its own, and we should recognize and accentuate this natural beauty, its quiet level. Hence, gently sloping roofs, low proportions, quiet skylines, suppressed heavyset chimneys and sheltering overhangs, low terraces and out-reaching walls sequestering private gardens" (87). The description fits the many homes built from Wright's plans, including masterworks like the Robie House in Chicago and the Dana-Thomas House in Springfield, Illinois, and more modest houses across the Midwest by Wright and by his followers. The prairie house, which combines nineteenth-century Romantic ideas about nature with modern efficiency and clarity of line, remains a distinctively midwestern artistic statement. It embodies the same landscape aesthetic of subtle beauty that midwestern writers exhibit in pastoral literature of similar spirit and intent.

The ultimate prairie house is Taliesin, Wright's home and studio near Spring Green, Wisconsin. Built of local stone, lumber, and plaster on the brow of a hill overlooking the Wisconsin River, in the lush, pastoral valley settled by Wright's maternal ancestors, Taliesin so clearly expresses Jeffersonian ideals that comparisons of the residence to Jefferson's Virginia home have become a convention among historians of architecture. James F. O'Gorman, for one, makes a persuasive case for Taliesin as the midwestern Monticello:

> Like Jefferson's perpetual "putting up, and pulling down" at
> Monticello, Wright was continually altering and expanding
> Taliesin out of necessity or desire. Like Monticello, Taliesin is

not merely rural, it is anti-urban. Like Monticello, the house
at Taliesin was conceptually one-storied, with its wings wrapped
around its hillside site just below the summit. . . . Like Monticello, the interior of Taliesin joined its surroundings through tall
openings leading onto terraces overlooking the rolling terrain.
Like Monticello, Taliesin is not a mere building but an entire
environment in which man, architecture, and nature form a
harmonious whole. There is at Taliesin Wright's summing up of
the role of man in nature that stems ultimately from the age of
romanticism. (152)

It was at Taliesin that Wright trained his apprentices, a Jeffersonian experiment in practical and cultural education that continues to this day.
It was there that he created designs for hundreds of striking homes and
large projects, including Broadacre City, a plan for urban development
in which homes, factories, shops, and public open space would be distrib-
uted within sections of the grid survey, which a century after Jefferson
might prove amenable to modification. While a new generation of architects known as the international school constructed cold glass and
steel boxes on the presumption that buildings in the Machine Age ought
to resemble machines, Wright, always the Emersonian nonconformist, per-
sisted in designing from organic principles and metaphors: tree branches
in the cantilevers of Fallingwater and the Johnson Wax tower, for instance, and the snail's shell in the spiral of the Guggenheim Museum.
These late accomplishments projected the ideals of Taliesin from their
local circumstances in Wright's native Wisconsin to the nation and world
at large.

   Awareness of Wright's countermodernism, and of midwestern cultural
history in general, reveals literature's place in a larger conversation about
history, politics, and nature. It lends clarity even to seemingly casual ref-
erences in the works of the authors here considered. The appearance in
*My Ántonia,* for example, of Cather's hometown of Red Cloud as the fic-
tional Black Hawk brings to the surface an entire subtext of Native
American history. Leopold summons that same history in his essay "A
Prairie Birthday," about a long-lived native plant in a country cemetery:
"It may have been older than the oldest tombstone, which dated 1850.
Perhaps it watched the fugitive Black Hawk retreat from the Madison

lakes to the Wisconsin River; it stood on the route of that famous march"
(*Sand County,* 45). In his "Eclogue at Nash's Grove," James Wright also
searches for native plant life in a midwestern cemetery, where he medi-
tates on nature and property. Like Thoreau, who speculates that Flint's
Pond near Concord, Massachusetts, had been named after some "skin-
flint, who loved better the reflecting surface of a dollar" than the lake
which bears his name (478), Wright disapproves of place names valoriz-
ing property owners. "No doubt the name [Nash's Grove] belonged to
some soft-eyed, sympathetic / Son of a bitch banker who stamped a
Norwegian / Out of his money, this green place" (*Above the River,* 201).
Wright's mentor Roethke, in one of the journal entries collected in *Straw
for the Fire* (1972), asserts Romantic organicism against the mechanistic
inclinations of modernism, insisting that an "ode to an icebox is possible,
since it contains fruit and meat" (239). Then there is the character in
Harrison's novel *Dalva* (1988) who observes that "[t]hree hundred Sioux,
mostly women and children, were butchered at Wounded Knee while,
back in the Midwest, Henry Ford was tinkering with the idea of spare
parts for his first auto. For those of us who are adults, most of our grandparents were alive in 1890!" (125). Harrison and his precursors reveal
their ideological underpinnings at every turn, in metaphors and assertions drawn from the vocabulary of American individualism and democracy in their midwestern incarnations. These writers continually remind
us of our living relationship to history, both social and natural, and of
the need for conscious examination of myths and archetypes.

## Last Clarifications

I have outlined the ideological bases of midwestern pastoral in order to
anticipate key themes and rhetorical strategies in Cather, Leopold,
Roethke, Wright, and Harrison. Restrictions of space preclude more
than passing reference to ways in which pastoralism has shaped the Midwest. A full-length cultural history would deal more substantively with
women's experience and writing, as well as that of African Americans,
Latinos/Latinas, and other groups; the conquest and settlement of the
Northwest Territory; the often disastrous extention of agrarianism westward onto the Great Plains (and beyond); urbanization and industrialization; and the cooptation of pastoral myth by industrial agribusiness.

Midwestern historiography and social thought bear analysis in relation to pastoral ideology; I have in mind Frederick Jackson Turner and Thorstein Veblen, as well as notable contemporaries such as William Cronon, a leading environmental historian who teaches at the University of Wisconsin, and Eric Freyfogle, professor of property law at the University of Illinois.[11] The early development of ecological science has a midwestern dimension in the careers of Henry C. Cowles and Frederic Clements, who based their influential theories on studies, respectively, of Lake Michigan dunes and Nebraska grasslands.[12] Twentieth-century midwesterners who struggled with the mixed legacy of Jeffersonianism on the land include prophets of sustainable agriculture like Louis Bromfield, landscape architects such as Horace Cleveland, and visual artists including the "midwestern triumverate" of the 1930s, Thomas Hart Benton, Grant Wood, and John Steuart Curry. Continuities between these and other trends and personages await another book, another scholar.

A complete history of pastoral ideology in midwestern literature is also lacking (though scholars like Weber, Robert Thacker, Diane Dufva Quantic, and Edward Watts have laid the groundwork).[13] Such a study would necessarily deal with dissenting views found in Native American writing, beginning perhaps with *Black Hawk: An Autobiography* (1832) and proceeding to the novels of Louise Erdrich. It would treat nineteenth-century fiction, poetry, and memoirs of settlement, with special emphasis on the vigorous literary scene based in Cincinnati before the Civil War (described by Watts as colonial in outlook), before taking on the development of realism and naturalism first by local color writers such as Edward Eggleston and then by the likes of Hamlin Garland. Thereafter would follow pastoral themes in the work of Edgar Lee Masters, Lewis, and other writers of the midwestern ascendancy, as well as subsequent authors of rural and perhaps even urban experience in the Midwest.

A final distinction ought to be made, one generally overlooked by scholars of midwestern literature, between regionalism and pastoralism. The conflation of the two is understandable, particularly in regard to authors of the midwestern ascendancy. Cather and Anderson wrote novels and stories that can be profitably read in either light. Writers of a more realist bent, such as Garland, Masters, and Lewis, also express affection for midwestern landscapes in language drawn from Romantic sources. Even Garland, whose stories about late nineteenth-century farmers are landmarks of literary naturalism, is receptive to natural beauty. In the preface to *Main-Travelled Roads* (1891), he admits that the "main-travelled road" of the title, which symbolizes the unjustly hard lot of rural workers, "does sometimes cross a rich meadow where the songs of the larks and bobolinks and blackbirds are tangled. . . . [I]t may lead past a bend in the river where the water laughs eternally over its shadows" (vi). Lewis, for his part, despite his relentless deflation of bourgeois hypocrisy and pioneer myth, treats one dimension of the Midwest without irony: the countryside. When Carol walks outside town in *Main Street,* she finds "the dignity and greatness which had failed her in Main Street" (58):

> She followed a furrow between low wheat blades and a field of rye which showed silver lights as it flowed before the wind. She found a pasture by the lake. So sprinkled was the pasture with rag-baby blossoms and the cottony herb of Indian tobacco that it spread out like a rare old Persian carpet of cream and rose and delicate green. Under her feet the rough grass made a pleasant crunching. Sweet winds blew from the sunny lake beside her, and small waves sputtered on the meadowy shore. She leaped a tiny creek bowered in pussy-willow buds. She was nearing a frivolous grove of birch and poplar and wild plum trees. (145–46)

Such passages are not decorative asides. Affection for the Midwest and concern for its future underlie Lewis's satire, as well as Garland's naturalism and Masters's exposé of small-town psychology. What Robert Narveson asserts about Masters holds true of the others: "Far from repudiating the American pastoral myth, Masters made it central in his thought; but he was aware that the agrarian ideal differed from the actual condition of life in his times" (58).

The fundamental impulse of Garland, Masters, and Lewis, however, is anti-Romantic, tending first to iconoclastic truth telling. They debunk the notion of rural virtue, uncovering grasping materialism, anti-intellectualism, and xenophobia among the people who, according to Jefferson, ought to exemplify democratic integrity. The authors of the midwestern classic period do not generally espouse transcendentalist views of nature and spirit (Cather and Anderson being notable exceptions). And, however acute their critique of midwestern life, the canonical midwestern writers were short on prescriptions for social change. They avoided politics for the most part; most of them, full of misgivings about the Midwest, left the region for good. Cather lived in New York; Anderson spent his later years in Virginia; Lewis died in Rome. "The notable literature of the Midwest," as Scott Russell Sanders observes in *Writing from the Center* (1995), referring to major early twentieth-century writers, "is largely absentee . . . a literature of exile" (25, 50).

While midwestern regionalism tends toward social realism, pastoral literature retains a stronger Romantic spirit. Contemporary pastoralists like Sanders and Harrison are philosophical idealists, intuiting a spiritual essence within nature, which the regionalists often portray as indifferent or even antagonistic to human concerns. The pastoralists' view of human nature is also more optimistic and less deterministic than that of the classic midwestern regionalists. They emphasize imagination and the individual's need for direct contact with wild nature, a desire that they may problematize with lessons of history and ecology but about which they are never cynical or dismissive. In contrast to Garland, a key figure in early realism and naturalism; Masters, an early modernist; and Lewis, a satirical social realist, the pastoralists are neo-Romantic and countermodernist. They value the individual's interpretation of experience as much as and sometimes more than "objective" views associated with realism and regionalism. Their writings, rather than forming a literature of exile, constitute what Sanders calls "a literature of inhabitation . . . of recovery and reconciliation" (*Writing,* 50).

Recognition of the difference between midwestern pastoralism and regionalism does not negate continuities between the two. Cather, as I discuss in chapter 2, first wrote about rural Nebraska with a cynicism reminiscent of Garland and Clemens. Leopold often alludes to Lewis, and Wright's poetic portraits of people in Depression-era Ohio descend in part from Masters's epitaphs for the denizens of Spoon River. Midwestern pastoralists, furthermore, derive much of their cultural analysis from the classic regionalists. When they disparage greed and provincialism, remind midwesterners of their democratic inheritance, or illustrate individualism's ideological strengths and weaknesses, these writers are continuing cultural work encouraged by their regionalist forebears. And when pastoral writers dwell on picturesque qualities in rural landscapes—quieter, less dramatic beauty resulting from subtle irregularities and the juxtaposition of human and natural elements—they are in accord with Masters, Lewis, and other regionalist writers and artists. This perception of sublimity in unassuming locations resonates with contemporary writers and readers because the forces arrayed against that beauty—materialism, provincialism, and anti-intellectualism—are as strong as ever. Anticipating the discussion of five authors that follows, lines from John Frederick Nims's 1947 poem "Midwest" convey the first crucial lesson about the region's landscape:

> What is beautiful is friendly and underfoot,
> Not flaunted like theater curtains in our faces.
> No peak or jungle obscures the blue sky;
> Our land rides smoothly in the softest eye.

two

# Willa
# Cather

Improvement makes strait [*sic*] roads; but the crooked roads
without Improvement are roads of Genius.

—William Blake, *The Marriage of Heaven and Hell*

The experience of landscape and place pervades the writing of Willa
Cather, from her early stories to her late novels. Although she was born
in Virginia and lived most of her adult life in eastern cities, Cather is most
closely identified with the tallgrass prairie of southeastern Nebraska, the
setting of many of her best fictions. Cather's family moved to Nebraska
in 1883, when the region was still in its frontier period. Having previously
known only the forested, hilly terrain of Virginia, nine-year-old Willa
initially felt homesick and lonely in the "Divide," as the country between
the Republican and Blue rivers was known. What she later described as
"a kind of erasure of personality" in the vast and seemingly barren plains
motivated her to befriend her immigrant neighbors, particularly Scandi-
navians and Czechs, who then greatly outnumbered American-born settlers in Nebraska. These foreign-born pioneers, Cather recalled, "made
up for what I missed in the country. I particularly liked the old women;
they understood my homesickness and were kind to me" (*Kingdom of
Art*, 448). Cather came to view these pioneers as heroic creators of the
midwestern cultural landscape. Comparing western expansion to artistic

creation, Cather wrote that the European immigrants "spread across our bronze prairies like the daubs of color on a painter's palette . . . [bringing] with them something that this neutral new world needed even more than the immigrants needed land" ("Nebraska," 237). Their synthesis of Old World traditions and acquired knowledge of an American environment inspired Cather's own creative endeavor: an American regional literature with European roots, a literature about imaginative, industrious people who relate spiritually as well as practically to their adopted landscape.

Cather's Nebraska stories and novels are prototypes of the midwestern pastoral: Virgilian in conventions of plot and characterization; Romantic in their nature mysticism and autobiographical basis; and Jeffersonian in their esteem for small landowners and supportive local communities. In the quarter century following Cather's death in 1947, literary critics emphasized the formal dimensions of these works, including the author's use of classical models. In the early 1970s, revisionist critics started to foreground issues of gender, ethnicity, and imperialism. Feminist critics have examined sexual ambiguities related to Cather's apparent lesbianism, while historicist critics have tested the extent of her multicultural sympathies. These readings have uncovered discrepancies between pastoral myth in Cather and the documented reality of plains history. While citing and extending these formalist, psychosexual, and historical analyses, the present chapter argues for Cather as a self-conscious pastoralist, one who questioned the ideological underpinnings of Romantic and Jeffersonian pastoralism. Her fictions anticipate the deeper critique of social assumptions and practices undertaken by later midwestern pastoral writers.

Cather's initial impulse when it came to writing about Nebraska was, in fact, anti-Romantic and naturalistic. Her early stories about pioneer life, written while she worked as a journalist in Pittsburgh and New York, resemble Hamlin Garland's in spirit; little about them evokes Virgil, Whitman, or any other of her subsequent literary models. Cather then viewed the prairie, in Bruce P. Baker's phrase, as a "cultural desert, a setting often hostile to those of artistic bent, a place indifferent if not actively hostile to man's creative spirit" (12). Typical of this period is "A Wagner Matinée" (1904), in which a woman revisits her native Boston after thirty years of toil on a Nebraska farm. Once a music teacher, the narrator's Aunt Georgiana has been broken physically and spiritually by her experience, and the opportunity to attend the opera only magnifies her sense of loss. Her nephew, the story's narrator, emphasizes the pathos of her life by contrasting the music's beauty with the Nebraska frontier of his youth:

> The first number . . . broke a silence of thirty years; the inconceivable silence of the plains. . . . I saw again the tall, naked house on the prairie, black and grim as a wooden fortress; the black pond where I had learned to swim, its margin pitted with sundried cattle tracks; the rain gullied clay banks about the naked house, the four dwarf ash seedlings where the dishcloths were always hung to dry before the kitchen door. The world there was the flat world of the ancients; to the east a cornfield that stretched to daybreak; to the west, a corral that reached to sunset; between, the conquests of peace, dearer bought than those of war. (*Stories*, 493)

There is a heroic quality to Aunt Georgiana, who sacrificed herself for the betterment of others, including the story's narrator. But the story's dominant impression is of her exile from art and beauty. In "A Wagner Matinée"—as well as in "On the Divide" (1896), "The Sculptor's Funeral" (1905), and other early stories—Cather portrays the prairie as bleak and barren, and society there as crudely utilitarian and inimical to art. Aesthetic values, associated with eastern refinement and European high culture, found little nourishment in Cather's home country as she then imagined it. These stories anticipate the scathing portrayals of small midwestern towns that made Edgar Lee Masters and Sinclair Lewis famous.

Of singular importance to Cather's development as a writer of place was her friendship with Sarah Orne Jewett, begun in 1908 and sustained until the older author's death the following year. Cather had long admired Jewett's work, particularly *The Country of the Pointed Firs* (1896), a collection of stories about life in coastal Maine that remains a classic of heightened regionalism. Jewett recognized Cather's gift but warned that her journalistic career was impeding her development as a writer of fiction. In the preface to a later edition of her first novel, *Alexander's Bridge* (1912), Cather remembers Jewett advising her that "one day you will write about your own country. In the meantime, get all you can. One must know the world *so well* before one can know the parish" (*Stories,* 942). The advice resembles that given by Sherwood Anderson to William Faulkner, by William Carlos Williams to Theodore Roethke, and many other American writers to their younger counterparts. All suggested that study, work, and travel be considered preparation for imaginative return to one's place of origin, to the people and language one knows best. This cosmopolitan localism is an inheritance from the Romantics, as Sharon O'Brien acknowledges in her biography of Cather. Referring to Jewett's advice, O'Brien observes that "Jewett was passing on to Cather the goal Emerson thought the American writer should pursue: to find transcendent meaning in the everyday materials of American life, as Whitman did in *Leaves of Grass*" (345). Cather fulfilled and surpassed Jewett's hopes for her; she was soon writing about Nebraska with a new compassion and complexity, combining naturalistic candor with a Romantic sense of place.

Cather's new feeling for the prairie country appears in "The Enchanted Bluff" (1909), a story about a group of boys in a Nebraska town who share adventures along the local river. One night by a streamside campfire they stare at the stars and discuss the Aztecs, the Mound Builders, Columbus, and Coronado. When the conversation turns to the places they want to see, one boy tells of an ancient Indian cliff dwelling atop a granite outcropping in New Mexico. Legend has it that a storm destroyed the stairs to the dwelling, preventing the men of the village from climbing back up after the hunt. A group of enemy warriors happened by and killed them all. The women and children, stranded in the village atop the bluff, starved to death.

Stirred by this story, the boys resolve one day to find the Enchanted Bluff and to investigate the legend. None of them do. One dies young; two become tailors; another grows up to be "a stockbroker in Kansas City" who goes "nowhere that his red touring-car cannot carry him"; yet another lives a drab life as a storekeeper. It is this last friend whom the narrator visits at the story's end, as they sit in front of the local school reviving "the romance of the lone red rock and the extinct people" (*Stories,* 72–73).

The central irony of "The Enchanted Bluff" is that while the boys are "sworn to the spirit of the stream" and are "friends mainly because of the river," their imaginations divert them to long-ago times and far-away places (65). One boy's "dearest possessions" are "some little pill-bottles that purported to contain grains of wheat from the Holy Land, water from the Jordan and the Dead Sea, and earth from the Mount of Olives" (66). Like ancient Indian ruins and stories about European explorers, these items possess the Romantic appeal of the remote and exotic. They add a sense of timelessness and wonder to life in the town, which the boys otherwise consider dull and insignificant. As one of them says, "I guess the stars don't keep any close tally on Sandtown folks" (68). Yet Cather characterizes the boys' time along the river as the adventure they will one day assume to have missed. The romance that they project on "dull things from a Baptist missionary who peddled them" and on the Enchanted Bluff is in fact present all along in their local landscape (66).

Cather reinforces the irony by devoting the story's first four paragraphs to detailed place description. The river, "brown and sluggish, like any other of the half-dozen streams that water the Nebraska corn lands," flows past "bald clay bluffs," "scrub-oaks with thick trunks," and "little sandy coves and beaches where slim cottonwoods and willow saplings flickered." This apparently mundane landscape harbors the wildness that has been extirpated elsewhere for "windmills and corn fields and big pastures," where "there was nothing wilful or unmanageable in the landscape." Unlike the prosaic country around them, the island where the boys build their fire is "a little new bit of world, beautifully ridged with ripple marks, and strewn with the tiny skeletons of turtles and fish, all as white and dry as if they had been expertly cured." Seeking refuge from the grasping social world of the village, the boys take care "not to mar the freshness of the place, although [they] often swam out to it on summer evenings and lay on the sand to rest" (64–65). It is a sacred site, albeit one that the boys take for granted. In demonstrating the aesthetic and spiritual value of a nonsublime landscape, "The Enchanted Bluff" modifies Romantic landscape aesthetics to fit the subtle appeal of a midwestern place.

"The Enchanted Bluff" established motifs and settings of subsequent importance in Cather's fiction. The early death of one character anticipates the tragic dimension of *O Pioneers!* and *My Ántonia,* in which happiness is fleeting and physical and emotional suffering and loss never far away. Cather's interest in the Southwest provided settings for *The Song of the Lark* (1915), *The Professor's House* (1925), and *Death Comes for the Archbishop* (1927). The first two novels follow "The Enchanted Bluff" in using the ancient architecture of the Anasazi to lend associative value to American landscape. Coronado, who may have reached Nebraska in the early sixteenth century, is also alluded to in *My Ántonia,* a novel that follows "The Enchanted Bluff" in employing a male narrator. As featured in "The Enchanted Bluff" and subsequent writings, these devices reinforce Cather's ironic contrast between an abundant, subtly beautiful landscape and the increasing utilitarianism of American society. The pastoral mode provided Cather the means to discern cosmopolitan regionalism from the unimaginative, crass provincialism she believed hampered cultural development in the United States.

Cather's first major novel, *O Pioneers!* established her Nebraska in the geography of world literature. By combining two separate stories, Cather created what she called a "two-part pastoral" (qtd. by Sergeant, 11). One part, about a Swedish pioneer woman who turns wilderness into productive farmland, constitutes pastoral epic. The other, about star-crossed lovers, is a pastoral tragedy. That Cather modeled the book on classical pastorals, especially Virgil's *Eclogues* and *Georgics,* has been well established by literary critics. Comparing Cather's characters and situations to Virgil's, John Randall (among others) describes *O Pioneers!* as "good pastoral," which does not sentimentalize or oversimplify life, but makes issues like death, time, and love "stand out by clearing away all the adventitious accretions that clutter things in more complicated and sophisticated city life" (78). "Good" (or to use Leo Marx's term, "complex") pastoral concerns itself not only with descriptions of nature, but with social conflict and the individual's striving for a meaningful life. In the case of Cather's prairie pioneers, tragedy looms in the unpredictability of weather and economic trends, as well as in the fortunes of love and health. Death, as Renaissance painters inscribed on their pastoral scenes, exists also in Arcadia; the Arcadia of Cather's Nebraska is no exception.

Appropriate to its epic theme of struggle against a hostile environment, *O Pioneers!* begins in winter, when the prairie is depressingly cold and colorless. The year is 1883, when frontier conditions prevail, and "the little town of Hanover, anchored on a windy Nebraska tableland, was trying not to be blown away." Like Aunt Georgiana's farm in "A Wagner Matinée," Hanover and surrounding farms need spatial ordering and aesthetic improvement. The town consists of a "cluster of low drab buildings huddled on the gray prairie, under a gray sky" (139). Homesteads are similarly "few and far apart; here and there a windmill gaunt against the sky, a sod house crouching in a hollow." Cather personifies this "stern frozen country" (144) as "a wild thing that had its ugly moods. . . . Its Genius was unfriendly to man" (147). This "Genius" invokes Roman folklore, in which places are inhabited by tutelary spirits that can help or hinder, and must therefore be appeased. The local spirit of wild Nebraska does its best "to overwhelm the little beginnings of human society that struggled in its sombre wastes" (144). As the adversary in this epic struggle, the wild prairie is an "enigma" to be solved, not an opponent to be conquered.

Alexandra Bergson, the novel's central character, is the person to solve the enigma. Cather establishes Alexandra's strength of character early in the narrative when her dying father gives her, rather than his wife or sons, responsibility for the farm and family. Bergson's supreme wish is for his family to stay on the land and to succeed where he failed. After years of crop failures and natural disasters, his sole accomplishment is the completion of payments on his land (a typical farm of the prairie Midwest: a full section of 640 acres). Bergson's two older sons, Lou and Oscar, are hard workers but lack imagination and foresight. Mrs. Bergson contributes significantly to the household, but is of a rather nostalgic mind; having "never quite forgiven John Bergson for bringing her to the end of the earth," she wishes only "to be let alone to reconstruct her old life in so far as that was possible" (152). Among her family, only Alexandra has the courage, patience, and intelligence to make the prairie bloom, to transform it from what Cather considers undifferentiated space to significant place.

Alexandra possesses what Cather, as a Romantic, valued most: imagination. "A pioneer should have imagination," Cather observes, "should be able to enjoy the idea of things more than the things themselves" (161). Just such an idealist, Alexandra succeeds not by imposing order on the landscape, but by imagining its possibilities as an artist surveys the canvas. Her greatest virtue is her *interestedness*. Valuing companionship above material wealth, she pays her workers—Swedish men and young women of various ethnicities—generously, treating them as persons rather than personnel. She delights in the diverse customs of her Czech, French, and Scandinavian neighbors, and maintains Swedish customs and language in her own household. Above all, she loves the local landscape. Cather tells us that "Alexandra's house is the big out-of-doors, and . . . it is in the soil that she expresses herself best" (178).

The sentiment echoes Whitman, certainly, but Alexandra's sense of place also reflects her Swedish heritage. Like her father, who "knew every ridge and draw and gully between him and the horizon" (147), Alexandra has an intimate knowledge of her land. Cather lyrically conveys the depth of Alexandra's feeling for places like the "low, sheltered swale, surrounded by a mulberry hedge" where "fruit trees [stand] knee-deep in timothy grass" (178). Though Cather does not use the term, Alexandra acts on the Swedish principle of *allemansrättan,* defined by ethnologists as the right of all people to "wander freely—even over private property—and glory in the solitude and perfect stillness" (Belt, 22). Aesthetic appreciation of land, associated in the American tradition with Romanticism, is also tied to the maintenance of ethnic customs. In an increasingly regularized landscape, its fields plowed fence row to fence row, its people under ever greater pressure to speak English and conform to mainstream standards of conduct, Alexandra stands for natural and social diversity. Family heirlooms, Alexandra's preservation of a former neighbor's sod house, and the welcome of her home as "an asylum for old-time people" all characterize this crucial link between people and place (184).

Whereas Alexandra represents Jeffersonian community and Romantic love of nature, her brothers Lou and Oscar come to stand for untempered utilitarianism. As young men they are industrious but unimaginative. "They did not mind hard work," Cather says, "but they hated experiments and could never see the use of taking pains" (160). In this they are utterly unlike Alexandra, a resourceful "yeoman" who seeks to learn from others how best to manage the land. During a drought (one that actually caused farm failures on a massive scale on the Great Plains between 1885 and 1887), they become desperate and want to sell their land. Because they reluctantly accede to Alexandra's plans, they stay and prosper. But they oppose her every innovation, from the cultivation of new crops to the adoption of silo technology. Their stubbornness reflects a deep-seated conformity, a desire to avoid standing out among their neighbors. "Everyone will say we are crazy," Lou says in response to Alexandra's plan to remortgage the land. "It must be crazy, or everybody would be doing it" (172).

Once established with homes and families, Lou and Oscar become worse than unimaginative. In contrast to Alexandra, they are now "bigoted and self-satisfied" provincials: anti-intellectual, materialistic, assimilationist, and sexist. They resent their brother Emil's college education and "every change in his speech, in his dress, in his point of view. . . . All his interests they treated as affectations" (253). They abandon family customs and the Swedish language, striving to be as inconspicuously "American" as possible. Furthermore, they demean Alexandra's management ("Good advice is all right, but it don't get the weeds out of the corn") and argue that her share of the family estate belongs to them as the male heirs (220). Not that they care for the property as land, as a place; they simply want to enhance their material and social standing.

Like Alexandra's tolerance and sense of place, her brothers' stubbornness derives from their Swedish heritage as well as from American individualism. Swedish ethnologists note a strong tendency to conformity in their culture, one that goes by the name *lagom*. *Lagom* entails appropriateness, inconspicuousness, and moderation in all things. As Don Belt notes, *lagom* "colors all sides of Swedish life—the home, the workplace, the schools. And while it makes for an orderly society, some Swedes fear that the lagom ethic . . . discourages the best and the brightest" (22). It certainly frustrates Emil, Alexandra, and Alexandra's future husband, Carl Linstrum, each of whom comes into conflict with Lou and Oscar. Ironically, Lou and Oscar's repudiation of their own Swedish heritage is in itself very Swedish. Adherence to *lagom* requires that they conform to the dominant utilitarianism of late nineteenth-century Nebraska, which scoffs at Old World customs and nonpecuniary sensibilities, whether aesthetic, spiritual, or communal.

One character whose nonconformity threatens the Bergson brothers' rigid proprieties is Ivar, an eccentric old Norwegian who initially lives on a beautiful but unproductive piece of land full of hummocks and ridges. Ivar practices "a peculiar religion of his own" at odds with mainstream Christianity. An ascetic, he goes barefoot most of the year, wears his hair long, and lives in a house dug into a hillside. He also exhibits a Franciscan love of nature: a vegetarian, he doctors his neighbors' animals and scatters grain for the wild birds attracted to his pond. "He best expressed his preference for his wild homestead," Cather tells us, "by saying that his Bible seemed truer to him there. If one stood in the doorway of his cave, and looked off at the rough land . . . one understood what Ivar meant" (156). Alexandra, Emil, and Carl so place themselves, and can sympathize with Ivar. Lou and Oscar, however, express contempt in their physical stance; they remain *outside* the door to Ivar's neatly kept cave house. Characteristically, they think of the ducks only as game to shoot and dismiss Ivar's advice about animal husbandry.

Although Ivar shares Alexandra's love of nature, he lacks her Jeffersonian foresight. When he loses his farm through mismanagement, Alexandra takes him into her household as a trusted friend and advisor. Lou and Oscar, of course, take a dimmer view of the old man. They see him as potentially dangerous and want Alexandra to have him committed. With Alexandra, who vows to protect him, Ivar shares his fears and an accurate assessment of provincial intolerance: "The way here is for all to do alike. I am despised because I do not wear shoes, because I do not cut my hair, and because I have visions. At home, in the old country, there were many like me, who had been touched by God, or who had seen things in the graveyard at night and were different afterward. We thought nothing of it, and let them alone. But here, if a man is different in his feet or in his head, they put him in the asylum" (182). The conflict between Alexandra and her brothers over Ivar hinges on divergent ideas about place. Ivar, like Alexandra, retains Old World beliefs about the inherent spirituality of landscape, from graveyards to gardens. His thoughts never stray far from the natural processes of life and death that provide not only material sustenance, but also occasion for joy and contemplation. Again, cultural diversity and natural diversity are under siege in a society that treats people and nature as instruments and seeks to impose uniformity on both.

Yet another conflict between Alexandra and her boorish brothers serves to develop pastoral motifs and ethical dilemmas: their disagreement over her relationship with Carl Linstrum. Carl's family leaves the Divide in 1887, during the same drought that so discourages Lou and Oscar. While Alexandra manages her family's success, Carl works but fails as an engraver in Chicago, returning years later to visit Alexandra before trying his luck in the goldfields of Alaska. When Carl arrives one summer day in 1899, he receives a warm welcome from Alexandra, but only suspiciousness from Lou and Oscar, who feel smug and superior in their material well-being. When Carl's visit extends to a month, they surmise Alexandra's hopes of marriage, which jeopardize their presumptuous claim to her share of the estate. There follows the quarrel in which Alexandra reminds her brothers that they owe their wealth to her good sense and perseverance, and that she has the right to dispose of her property as she sees fit. Lou and Oscar's covetousness opens a permanent breach between them and Alexandra, who is crushed to find their relationship reduced to utilitarian issues. "The authority you can exert by law is the only influence you will ever have over me again," she concludes. "I think I would rather not have lived to find out what I have to-day" (221).

Carl's reaction to Lou and Oscar's opposition reveals his inability to defy social norms, in this case the stricture against a poor man marrying a wealthy woman. Alexandra desires companionship from Carl, not money or social standing. But Carl cannot accept her offer, feeling himself a failure in both expressive and utilitarian terms. Looking at Alexandra's land, he confesses his inadequacy as an artist: "I would never have believed it could be done. I'm disappointed in my own eye, in my imagination" (190). Alexandra is the true artist of the two; as Carl observes, "I've been away engraving other men's pictures, and you've stayed at home and made your own" (194). His lack of financial security similarly weighs down his self-estimation, resulting in his decision not to marry Alexandra unless he has money of his own. "Measured by your standards here," he tells Alexandra, "I'm a failure. I couldn't buy even one of your cornfields. I've enjoyed a great many things, but I've got nothing to show for it all" (197).

Alexandra, however, takes exception to Carl's self-negation. "But you show for it yourself, Carl," she insists. "I'd rather have had your freedom than my land." Her retort starts a dialogue about the advantages and disadvantages of a mobile, unattached life and those of a settled existence. Their conversation is in keeping with the conventional pastoral comparison of urban with rural experience. Each environment harbors particular forms of loneliness—placelessness and anonymity in the city, isolation from wider cultural currents in the country. Having recently retreated from Chicago and New York, Carl sees city life with jaundiced eyes. "Freedom so often means that one isn't needed anywhere," he tells Alexandra: "Here you are an individual, you have a background of your own, you would be missed. But off there in the cities there are thousands of rolling stones like me. We are all alike; we have no ties, we know nobody, we own nothing. When one of us dies, they scarcely know where to bury him. . . . We have no house, no place, no people of our own." But Alexandra, who has been so often frustrated by provincial pettiness, reminds Carl how country life can stultify the spirit: "We grow hard and heavy here. We don't move lightly and easily as you do, and our minds get stiff. If the world were no wider than my cornfields, if there were not something beside this, I wouldn't feel that it was much worth while to work." Alexandra mentions Carrie Jensen, the sister of one of her hired men, who became depressed and suicidal because of the slow pace of life on the Divide. A trip to visit relations in Iowa restored Carrie's spirits by reminding her that the world is made up of many places, the Divide being significant among them in its own way. Alexandra, too, would benefit from the experience of travel, so that like Carrie she can become "contented to live and work in a world that's so big and interesting" because "it's what goes on in the world that reconciles [her]" (197–98).

*O Pioneers!* concludes with world and parish reconciled in a manner recalling the advice of Sarah Orne Jewett, to whom Cather appropriately dedicated the novel. In the end, when Carl has again returned to Nebraska after the murder of Alexandra's beloved younger brother, Emil, and his lover, Marie, Alexandra is presented with the opportunity to broaden her horizons, to travel with Carl to Alaska. This they plan to do, and to marry, with the understanding that they will return to the farm, where even after loneliness and tragedy there is "great peace . . . and freedom." Alexandra's first devotion is to the land, and Carl must give up his wanderlust, if not become a creature of place, to be her husband. "We come and go," Alexandra tells Carl, "but the land is always here. And the people who love it and understand it are the people who own it—for a little while" (289)

Love and property: these are the themes that have caused the most controversy in Cather scholarship since the 1970s, when feminist critics first took on gender, sexuality, race, and ideology in Cather's work. While some feminists admire Cather's characterization of intelligent and independent women like Alexandra Bergson, others identify Cather with hegemony, male power, and sexual frustration. The second group includes Blanche H. Gelfant, whose 1971 essay on *My Ántonia* was foundational to the new revisionism. Gelfant reads *My Ántonia,* "long considered a representatively American novel, not only for its beauty of art and for its affirmation of history, but also . . . for its negations and evasions" (97). Those evasions include race, violence, and an "inherent thematic demand to show physical passion as disastrous." While she focuses on *My Ántonia,* Gelfant mentions characters in other novels who in her opinion possess "a strong intuitive aversion to sex which they reveal furtively through enigmatic gestures" (80). She points out that in *O Pioneers!* Alexandra takes a cold shower after fantasizing about a mysterious lover, and Emil and Marie consummate their forbidden love only to be murdered the same day by Marie's husband. The novel sublimates sexuality into art, which in pastoral means the ordering of landscape for agriculture. Cather attributes voluptuousness not to Alexandra but to "the beauty and fruitfulness" of her fields and "something individual about the great farm" (178). *O Pioneers!* may take its title from Whitman, and much of its feeling for nature and the pioneer experience, but it is far removed from Whitman's erotic celebration of the "body electric."

Although Cather's treatment of sexuality diverges from Whitman's, her idealization of American expansion onto the Great Plains correlates significantly with his example. In terms of feelings for place and nature inspired by the Romantic poets, the key scene in *O Pioneers!* occurs during the period of drought when farmers are leaving the Divide. Returning from what amounts to a research trip to the river country, Alexandra tells Emil of her new resolve to keep the land. Approaching their farm in their horse-drawn wagon, Alexandra realizes how deeply she loves her adopted home landscape. She experiences a transcendental epiphany of place:

> Her face was so radiant that [Emil] felt shy about asking her. For the first time, perhaps, since that land emerged from the waters of geologic ages, a human face was set toward it with love and yearning. It seemed beautiful to her, rich and strong and glorious. Her eyes drank in the breadth of it, until her tears blinded her. Then the Genius of the Divide, the great, free spirit which breathes across it, must have bent lower than it ever bent to a human will before. The history of every country begins in the heart of a man or a woman. (170)

It is a beautiful moment, one that recalls Emerson's "transparent eye-ball" experience and more than one passage in Whitman's "Song of Myself." In narrating her character's achievement of a wider, more generous selfhood, Cather has rewritten the pioneer myth to privilege place over process, sympathy over domination. The climax of the epic aspect of *O Pioneers!* this passage counters male-centered and utilitarian biases in American pastoral. As O'Brien writes, Cather has removed "the misogyny from the Adamic myth as well as the valorization of the isolated, self-reliant individual; by inscribing herself in the land, Alexandra writes her community's story as well as her own" (433).

Alexandra's epiphany, however, raises troubling dimensions of the Adamic myth that Cather does not resolve or even challenge. The problem is simple: Alexandra's is not the first "human face . . . set toward [the land] with love and yearning"; Nebraska's history did not begin with Swedish farmers. Cather not only ignores ten thousand years of Native American inhabitation of the plains, she also turns her back on recent history. The violent displacement of the Pawnee, Ponca, and other Nebraska tribes does not appear in *O Pioneers!* though the novel's narrative timeline (1883–1900) overlaps with the Plains War (1862–1890). That disturbing reality interfered with the story Cather wanted to tell, one of a peaceful pastoralization of an unsettled region, the transformation of "The Wild Land" to "Neighboring Fields," as she titled the novel's first two parts. Though *O Pioneers!* differs from "Pioneers! O Pioneers!" in offering, as O'Brien observes, "another vision of the taming of the land, one erasing the polarities and hierarchies in the Whitman poem: male/female, culture/nature, subject/object" (440), it perpetuates Whitman's elision of Native Americans from the American landscape.

The phrasing of Alexandra's epiphany reveals authorial uncertainty. "For the first time, *perhaps* . . . a human face was set toward [the land] with love and yearning" (emphasis added). The word "perhaps" carries a great moral weight; it betrays Cather's suppressed conscience, which must have suggested the falsity of the sentence. This equivocation is all the more poignant in light of events concurrent to the plot of *O Pioneers!* The Bergsons homesteaded in 1872, the same year that the great buffalo slaughter began on the plains. By the time the novel opens in 1883, commercial hunters had driven the American bison to the brink of extinction, destroying the resource that had sustained Plains Indians for centuries.

Most tellingly, Alexandra's epiphany on the Divide apparently occurs in 1887, the year that the U.S. Congress passed the Dawes Act, which would drastically reduce tribal land holdings in the name of "civilizing" the Indians. In its historical context as well as its lyricism, Alexandra's transcendental experience resembles nothing so much as William Cullen Bryant's "The Prairies." Like Bryant in that poem, Cather imagines her protagonist as the first to appreciate the prairie. Like Bryant, whose visit to Illinois coincided with the Black Hawk War of 1832, Cather ignores contemporary events of great consequence for Native Americans. Both portray the midwestern prairie as a cultural tabula rasa on which the pioneers wrote a pastoral text of peace and harmony with nature.

It is important to balance this kind of historical rereading against an author's moral strengths. While recognizing Cather's failings, we can still admire characters like Alexandra, who embodies an alternative to mainstream attitudes of provincialism, materialism, and sexism. We can sympathize with immigrant pioneers *and* with Native Americans, and learn from both lessons that apply to our own conflicted sense of place in North America.[1]

This kind of negative capability is called for in considering *My Ántonia,* the novel by Cather that has received the most critical reassessment. Gelfant's groundbreaking 1971 essay "The Forgotten Reaping-Hook: Sex in *My Ántonia*" set the tone for revisionist scholarship with its critique of what Gelfant terms Cather's "negations and evasions" of sexuality, race, and history (97). Attributing this evasiveness to pastoral nostalgia, Gelfant finds Cather's narrator, Jim Burden, to be "disingenuous and self-deluded" in his withdrawal from a disappointing present into memories of his Nebraska childhood (79). Yet another of Cather's characters with "an intuitive fear of sex," Jim "substitutes wish for reality in celebrating the past. His flight from sexuality parallels a flight from historical truth" (81). Subsequent readings of *My Ántonia* repeatedly refer to Gelfant, amplifying her thesis. In 1982, Deborah Lambert inferred that Cather was "a lesbian who could not, or did not, acknowledge her homosexuality, and who, in her fiction, transformed her emotional life and experiences into acceptable, heterosexual forms" (119–20). More recently, Mike Fischer has examined *My Ántonia* in the context of plains history, interpreting it as "a story of origins for whites only" that "ignores the most significant Other in Nebraskan history: the Native Americans" (31).

The title of his 1990 essay bespeaks the spirit of ideological deconstruction: "Pastoralism and Its Discontents: Willa Cather and the Burden of Imperialism."

However insightful, these studies have by no means sounded the thematic depths of *My Ántonia,* the most well loved of Cather's works. The very critique of pastoralism performed by Cather's recent critics is in fact underway in this novel, which, as biographer James Woodress notes, combines "character, setting, myth, and incident . . . into a narrative of great emotional power" (293). *My Ántonia,* like *O Pioneers!* before it, poses aesthetic ideals derived from Romanticism and from the pioneers' immigrant cultures as alternatives to utilitarian and provincial attitudes. While celebrating Nebraska's early homesteaders, Cather recognizes the psychological and social forces tending to undermine their attachment to place.

The central theme of *My Ántonia* is the nostalgic (and tragically futile) desire to recapture the innocence of childhood when material and social success has not fulfilled spiritual and emotional needs. The life of Jim Burden, the novel's narrator, serves as a synecdoche for midwestern society in its transition between the nineteenth and twentieth centuries: his childhood is spent in the country, his adolescence in a small town, and his adulthood in cities. Along the way, Jim has lost something, as has his developing civilization.

Jim (like Carl Linstrum of *O Pioneers!*) is a sensitive and restless man. Our first view of him is in motion, traveling through Iowa in a train "flash[ing] through never-ending miles of ripe wheat, by country towns and bright-flowered pastures and oak groves wilting in the sun." In the novel's brief introduction, the author meets Jim on the train; the two old friends grew up together in the same Nebraska town, and both now live in New York. Despite his worldly success, Jim has not found happiness as an adult. A man of a "romantic disposition" and "quiet tastes," Jim is unsuitably married to a sophisticated woman who strikes the author as "unimpressionable and temperamentally incapable of enthusiasm." Dissatisfied with the present, Jim dwells on his Nebraska childhood, particularly his friendship with a Bohemian girl named Ántonia who signifies "the country, the conditions, the whole adventure of [his] childhood" (711–12). Since reestablishing contact with Ántonia after many years, Jim has been writing a memoir of their friendship. When he gives the manuscript, written from his first-person point of view, to the author, the novel proper begins.

Jim's first impressions of Nebraska reflect Cather's own early experiences on the prairie. At the age of ten he comes to Nebraska from Virginia upon the death of his parents. In his train voyage west, Jim experiences the same dislocation Cather felt; he remembers nothing about crossing the great Missouri River, and "the only thing very noticeable about Nebraska was that it was still, all day long, Nebraska" (716). The prairie is for him a mere expanse of space, a place only in name and "not a country at all, but the material out of which countries are made." Though Jim claims not to have been homesick, he admits that he felt "erased, blotted out" by his initial impression of Nebraska (718). He surrenders himself to an apparent emptiness that he will fill with experience.

Cather devotes the second chapter to Jim's first explorations of his grandfather's farm, where he finds that the prairie landscape varies more than he had thought. Jim visits his grandmother's garden, which Cather envisions as a peaceable kingdom, a prairie Eden where the serpents are likely to be harmless bull-snakes. Jim's grandmother even protects a chicken-thieving badger, saying she "won't let the men harm him" because in "a new country a body feels friendly to the animals." Her forbearance contrasts with a historical reality of which Cather betrays awareness by describing "motion in the landscape . . . as if the shaggy grass were a sort of loose hide, and underneath it herds of wild buffalo were galloping, galloping" (723–24). Like the name Cather gives the nearby town—Black Hawk, after the Sauk chief—the metaphor reminds us of the violence of American expansionism. The slaughter of the bison herds by commercial hunters, a key strategy in the genocidal assault on the plains nations, underlies the text of one of Cather's most lyrical and evocative scenes.

The chapter builds up to another of Cather's memorable epiphanies of place, when Grandmother leaves Jim at his request to sit alone at the center of the garden. Once he is still and observant, the plant and animal world around him comes fully alive, and he discovers a "new feeling of lightness and content":

> I kept as still as I could. Nothing happened. I did not expect anything to happen. I was something that lay under the sun and felt

> it, like the pumpkins, and I did not want to be anything more. I
> was entirely happy. Perhaps we feel like that when we die and
> become a part of something entire, whether it is sun and air, or
> goodness and knowledge. At any rate, that is happiness; to be
> dissolved into something complete and great. When it comes to
> one, it comes as naturally as sleep. (724)

The passage is outstanding in Cather's work; it meant enough to her that
the definition of happiness contained within it was inscribed on her tombstone in Jaffrey, New Hampshire. A model of the midwestern epiphany
of place, it recounts a sublime experience in a nonsublime landscape.

From this point, Jim feels at home in Nebraska, which he knows as a
place with aesthetic variety and differentiation. Cather evokes the prairie's
topography and biota with great lyricism and descriptive detail. Among
the places Jim comes to love are the "sunflower-bordered roads," "damp
spots" at the edges of "pale-yellow cornfields" where "the smartweed soon
turned a rich copper color," a neighbor's catalpa grove, and "a big elm
tree that grew up out of a deep crack in the earth and had a hawk's nest
in its branches" (730). Jim learns to look closely to find the poetry in what
would seem a prosaic landscape to a casual and unengaged observer.

Since we know from the introduction that Jim will live in New York,
Cather establishes with his introduction to Ántonia the conventional
pastoral pairing of a city person with a rural counterpart. Like Ivar in *O
Pioneers!* Ántonia's family lives on a beautiful but unpromising piece of
land, a place of "broken, grassy clay cliffs," "cottonwoods and ash trees,"
and "rough red hillocks" (726). Also like Ivar, they live in an earth cave
dwelling, the best they can manage, from which they emerge as if the
earth is giving birth. Ántonia embodies pastoral values: "the goodness of
planting and tending and harvesting" and the love of place (926). "I'd always be miserable in a city," she will one day tell Jim. "I'd die of lone-
someness. I like to be where I know every stack and tree, and where all the
ground is friendly" (909–10). Ántonia brings Old World intuitions about
nature and beauty to this very American landscape. Jim teaches her to
speak and write English, but Ántonia inspires in Jim an enthusiasm for
life and the glory of nature.

While Ántonia comes to feel a deep sense of belonging in the New
World, other immigrants find the transition more difficult, and even im-

possible. Cather develops two stories on the tragedy of displacement. One involves the bachelors Pavel and Peter, who share a farm and a history of ill fortune. Working hard to get out of debt, Pavel fatally strains himself. On his deathbed, he reveals why he had emigrated from Russia with Peter: they had sacrificed two people to save their own lives. While driving a newly wedded couple through a forest at night, they were chased by a large pack of wolves that had already brought down six other sledges. To lighten their load and thereby save himself and Peter, Pavel threw the newlyweds to the wolves. They survived the night only to become exiles, shunned by neighbors and family alike for their horrible deed. Once in America, they hid their terrible secret but were plagued by bad luck. Pavel dies a painful death in a foreign land, and Peter leaves the Divide to work in a railway construction camp.

The fate of Pavel and Peter anticipates that of their friend Mr. Shimerda, who hears Pavel's deathbed confession. Mr. Shimerda, who never wanted to leave Europe, is terribly homesick for his native Bohemia. Unlike his conceited and rather ignorant wife, Mr. Shimerda is dignified, sensitive, and educated; Ántonia later tells Jim that her father "know a great deal; how to make the fine cloth like what you not got here. He play horn and violin, and he read so many books that the priests in Bohemie [sic] come to talk to him" (792). In Nebraska, Mr. Shimerda is displaced from the cultural life he so treasures. He cares for his family, showing particular solicitousness for Ántonia's education, but is melancholy and ultimately suicidal. He shoots himself during the worst snowstorm of the winter, during the bleak frozen season when the plains landscape is least consoling.

Cather develops two remarkable vignettes relating to the aftermath of Mr. Shimerda's suicide and the theme of immigrant homesickness. The first occurs while the adults in Jim's household are occupied with funeral arrangements and the official investigation. Left alone in his grandparents' house, Jim considers Mr. Shimerda's sad fate. "I knew it was homesickness that had killed Mr. Shimerda," he reports, "and I wondered whether his released spirit would not eventually find its way back to his own country" (779). This recalls Jim's arrival in Nebraska, when he felt that he had left his parents' spirits back in Virginia among the places familiar to them, "the sheep-fold down by the creek, or along the white road that led to the mountain pastures" (718). Alone at home that winter day, Jim senses Mr. Shimerda's spirit with him in the room, resting before its long journey back to Bohemia. Years later, when Ántonia herself wonders if "maybe my father's spirit can go back to those old places," Jim recalls that winter day and his intuition: "I said I felt sure then that he was on his way back to his own country, and that even now, when I passed his grave, I always thought of him as being among the woods and fields that were so dear to him" (860–61).

Mr. Shimerda's unusual grave occasions the second vignette resulting from his death. In accordance with Bohemian tradition, Mrs. Shimerda and her son Ambrosch decide that the old man should be buried on the southwest corner of their land, at the very point where section roads will converge once roads and fences follow Jefferson's rectangular survey. Something curious happens though: years later, when the wildness has been plowed out of the land and "the roads no longer ran about like wild things, but followed the surveyed section-lines," the location remains untouched. Someone sees to it that the converging roads curve slightly in order to avoid Mr. Shimerda's grave. Surrounded by native prairie grass, the grave becomes a sacred place in several senses: religious, psychological, and ecological. There is another image in the novel that most readers and critics think of as central to *My Ántonia:* the plow silhouetted against the flaming sunset that Jim and Ántonia see soon before Jim goes to college—a hieroglyph of the pastoral ideal. But in a novel so concerned with wilderness and pastoralism, place and the tragedy of displacement, the image of Mr. Shimerda's grave bears equal consideration:

> The grave, with its tall red grass that was never mowed, was like a little island; and at twilight, under a new moon or the clear evening star, the dusty roads used to look like soft grey rivers flowing past it. I never came upon the place without emotion, and in all that country it was the spot most dear to me. I loved the dim superstition, the propitiatory intent, that had put the grave there; and still more I loved the spirit that could not carry out the sentence—the error from the surveyed lines, the clemency of the soft earth roads along which the home-coming wagons rattled after sunset. (789)

The spirit that could not carry out the sentence is the spirit of place Cather hoped would emerge in the Midwest: circularity to temper linearity, wildness to survive development, and Old World aesthetic and spiritual sensibilities to complement American utilitarianism and "common sense." By such small gestures pastoral values might endure in the new materialistic age.

After the tragic winter, the seasonal cycle of Jim's first year is completed by spring—"the throb of it, the light restlessness, the vital essence of it everywhere" (790)—and summer, which brings "that breathless, brilliant heat which makes the plains of Kansas and Nebraska the best corn country in the world" (801). Jim lives on his grandfather's farm for three years but narrates only the events of the first, which for Jim constitutes the "best days" of his life, and of American society, in Cather's view. Ántonia, who faces a difficult future breaking the land, expresses the conventional pastoral desire to stop time so that "no winter [will] ever come again" (802). But neither life nor history can stop; Jim's move to town coincides with the beginning of his adolescence and the period of small-town dominance on the midwestern cultural landscape.

The town of Black Hawk, like Hanover in *O Pioneers!* and Sandtown in "The Enchanted Bluff," is a fictionalization of Cather's actual hometown of Red Cloud, Nebraska. Like her contemporaries Sherwood Anderson and Sinclair Lewis, Cather cast a critical eye on midwestern small-town life just before and after the turn of the century. Jim first describes Black Hawk, glowingly, as "a clean, well-planted little prairie town, with white fences and good green yards about the dwelling, wide, dusty streets, and shapely little trees growing along the wooden sidewalks" (805). As an adolescent with burgeoning social (and sexual) desires, Jim benefits from living where he can attend school, dances, and musical recitals. But Black Hawk is marked by conformity, boredom, snobbishness, and materialism; it is a town full of Babbitts like Alexandra Bergson's brothers Lou and Oscar. In yet another winter scene—the bleak season again reinforcing the theme of environmental and spiritual malaise—Jim explores the back streets of Black Hawk, where he deduces much about his townspeople from their architecture: "On starlight nights I used to pace up and down those long, cold streets, scowling at the little, sleeping houses on either side, with their storm-windows and covered back porches. They were flimsy shelters, most of them poorly built of light wood, with spindle porch-posts horribly mutilated by the turning-lathe. Yet for all their frailness, how much jealousy and envy and unhappiness some of them managed to contain!" (850). In striving to maintain the impression of propriety, the people of Black Hawk exercise extreme caution in speech and action. As in Lewis's *Main Street,* colorful immigrant traditions that might enliven the place are ignored and even reviled. The dominant attitude is that "foreigners were ignorant people who couldn't speak English," even though there is no one in town with "the intelligence or cultivation, much less the personal distinction, of Ántonia's father" (839). Jim's best experiences of the town are those that recall pastoral values and transplanted European culture: the home of the neighboring Harling family, which is like a little farm; frequent visits from farmers come to town; and, most importantly, the presence of Ántonia and other immigrant girls, like Lena Lingard, who have hired into local families as domestic help. In preferring the company of the hired girls to that of the "refined" but dull town girls, Jim breaks unwritten social codes based on distinctions of ethnicity and social class. Unlike most Black Hawk boys, who "looked forward to marrying Black Hawk girls, and living in a brand-new little house with best chairs that must not be sat upon, and hand-painted china that must not be used" (840), Jim is loath to conceal his affection and admiration for Ántonia, Lena, and the other girls "who helped to break up the wild sod, [and] learned so much from life, from poverty, from their mothers and grandmothers." Their beauty, vigor, and knowledge derive from European traditions and their direct experience of an American landscape; they "had been early awakened and made observant by coming at a tender age from an old country to a new" (838).

One might expect Jim to court one of the country girls, but he defers to the very prejudice he abjures in his townspeople. Despite his attraction to Ántonia, their relationship stays on the level of a childhood friendship; even his dreams about Ántonia innocently recall the places and play of their country childhood, "sliding down straw-stacks as we used to do; climbing the yellow mountains over and over, and slipping down the smooth sides into soft piles of chaff." His recurring dream about the Swedish beauty Lena Lingard is, however, strongly sexual: in a harvested field Lena "came across the stubble barefoot, in a short skirt, with a curved reaping-hook in her hand . . . flushed like the dawn, with a kind of luminous rosiness all about her." Lena sits by Jim and says, "Now they are all gone, and I can kiss you as much as I like" (854). Jim does in fact have something of an affair with Lena once he is in Lincoln attending the university, but the dalliance distracts him from his studies and he is soon off to Harvard, eventually settling in New York and resigning himself to a conventional and unhappy marriage.

Jim's aversion to sex has been the subject of much critical analysis. Referring to Jim's characterization, Woodress goes so far as to say that Cather's "greatest failing as an artist is her inability to depict heterosexual adult relationships affirmatively" (299). James E. Miller similarly argues that *My Ántonia* depicts not the fulfillment of the American dream, but its loss," finding in the name "Jim Burden" an allegory of "not only his acute sense of personal loss but also a deep sense of national unease, a *burden* of guilt for having missed a chance, for having passed up an opportunity" (102). Just as America traded agriculture for industry, so Jim passes up his chance with Ántonia for an unhappy marriage and a career as a railroad attorney. He tells her "I'd have liked to have you for a sweetheart, or a wife, or my mother or my sister—anything that a woman can be to a man" (910), but then leaves the Divide for twenty years. He embraces the aesthetic and not the physical aspects of Ántonia and the place, nostalgically preserving both in his memory as "a succession of . . . pictures, fixed there like the old woodcuts of one's first primer" (926). In dread of change, Jim sublimates life into art, because he feels that some "memories are realities, and are better than anything that can ever happen to one again" (912).

One such sublimation of life into art is occasioned by Jim's reading of Virgil's pastorals. One evening in Lincoln, while reviewing *Georgics,* Jim mulls over the melancholy thought that "the best days are the first to flee." He then turns to an earlier passage in which Virgil proclaims "*'Primus ego in patriam mecum . . . deducam Musas';* for I shall be the first, if I live, to bring the Muse into my country" (876). Before he can get far with his study, Lena Lingard knocks at the door, there to visit Jim for the first time. Though Lena is as beautiful as ever, she does not arouse Jim's sexual interest as much as his nostalgia for the people and places of his childhood. As soon as the actual flesh and blood Lena, sensuous Swedish farm girl turned successful fashion designer, has left him to his books, Jim reverts to his fantasy image of her, now transformed by his experience of literary art: "[M]y old dream about Lena coming across the harvest-field in her short skirt . . . floated before me on the page like a picture, and underneath it stood the mournful line: *'Optima dies . . . prima fugit'*" (The

best days are the first to flee). The lesson he has drawn from this conjoining of life and art is "the relation between girls like [Lena and Ántonia]
and the poetry of Virgil. If there were no girls like them in the world,
there would be no poetry" (880).

Cather's citation of Virgil certainly reinforces the novel's dominantly
nostalgic tone, but it also universalizes the Nebraska locality. Gaston
Cleric, Jim's mentor at the University of Nebraska, had explained to his
students that what Virgil meant by *patria* was "not a nation or even a
province, but the little rural neighborhood on the Mincio where the poet
was born." Virgil brought poetry not to Rome, but "to his own little
'country'; to his father's fields, 'sloping down to the river and to the old
beech trees with broken tops'" (876). Jim's relation of Virgil and the
"hired girls" of Black Hawk is an imaginative leap substantiated by his
memoir, which brings the muse to the Divide, his (and Cather's) *patria*.

But Jim is only half an artist, and, like Carl Linstrum in *O Pioneers!*
whose talent is confined to the engraving of others' work, he must content himself with secondhand pastoral—an aesthetic appreciation of the
very real art that Ántonia has created with the Nebraska landscape as
her medium. Jim's belated return to the Divide reenacts his boyhood arrival, with Ántonia to greet him instead of his grandmother, and another
beautiful garden landscape to explore. Cather again describes a place in
which trees and children are at home. In the orchards and grape arbors
where Ántonia's many sons and daughters play, Jim experiences the
same deep peace he felt as a child in his grandmother's garden, a feeling
that recurs when his discovery of a remnant of the old pioneer road
brings him "the sense of coming home to himself" (937).

This contentment, however, is only a respite from a disappointing life.
Because Ántonia has always been at home with herself and her place,
the lofty affirmation with which Jim concludes the novel is a half-truth:
"Whatever we had missed, we possessed together the precious, the in-
communicable past" (937). Ántonia also possesses the present; however
stereotyped by Jim as an earth mother, "a rich mine of life, like the
founder of early races" (926), she is an admirable figure. Susan Rosowski
aptly concludes of *My Ántonia* that the "male myths of adventure have
led to pointless wandering and lonely exile, and the women, originally
assigned roles of passivity, have become the vital sources of meaning"
(*Voyage Perilous,* 91). Jim's solitary fate speaks to the passing of an era, but

Ántonia's success as an agriculturist and matriarch confirms the persistence of pastoral ideals in the Midwest.

*My Ántonia* marked the end of Cather's first period as a novelist, a period characterized by celebration of America's past and optimism for its future. Cather wrote in 1936 that the "world broke in two in 1922 or thereabouts" (*Stories,* 811). There were a number of reasons for her new pessimism. Though she had reached the height of her popularity and critical acclaim, Cather felt let down by success. Her personal and professional lives were in transition: her best friend, Isabelle Hambourg, had permanently expatriated to Europe, and her novel of World War I, *One of Ours* (1922), won the Pulitzer Prize but received mixed reviews. Cather's disillusionment, however, was deeper than personal or professional. Like many other authors and artists of the period, Cather was affected in her attitude toward American life and culture by major events of the time. Woodress reiterates a familiar historical litany: "World War I, Prohibition, Communist witch hunts, the gaudy extravagances of the Jazz Age—all these extrinsic factors that sent other American writers to self-imposed exile in Europe contributed to Cather's sense of alienation" (336).

Cather never accepted the modern era, from the glorification of technology to the work of "young poets and painters of advanced ideas and mediocre ability" (*My Ántonia,* 712). Materialism, she felt, now dominated American society to the detriment of aesthetic ideals she associated with the pioneer era. "The generation now in the driver's seat," she wrote in the 1923 essay "Nebraska: The End of the First Cycle," "hates to make anything, wants to live and die in an automobile, scudding past those acres where the old men used to follow the long corn-rows up and down. They want to buy everything ready-made: clothes, food, education, music, pleasure." Changes in higher education particularly concerned Cather; she feared that the University of Nebraska, her alma mater, was becoming "a gigantic trade school" devoted to the study of "machines, mercantile processes, 'the principles of business'; everything that has to do with the game of getting on in the world—and nothing else." Exceeding its Jeffersonian mission as a land-grant institution to promote useful knowledge, the university emphasized "the most utilitarian subjects in the course of study" at the expense of the humanities, which as Cather knew from experience tend to "develop taste and enrich personality" (238).

Cather responded to social change, however, not as an advocate or activist, but as an artist. While the novels of her second or middle period all disparage materialism, Cather treated them as opportunities to perfect her narrative skills. She wrote *One of Ours* (1922), *A Lost Lady* (1923), *The Professor's House* (1925), and *My Mortal Enemy* (1926) using formal principles set forth in her 1922 essay "The Novel Démeublé." The "novel *démeublé*" or "unfurnished novel" dispenses with the descriptive cataloging of objects and physical sensations that Cather felt cluttered many works of realist fiction. By reducing exposition, description, and dialogue to an essential minimum, such a novel creates "the inexplicable presence of the thing not named . . . the verbal mood, the emotional aura of the fact or the thing or the deed" (*Stories,* 837).

These novels personify crass materialism in representative characters: Bayliss Wheeler in *One of Ours,* for example, and the grasping wife and daughters of Godfrey St. Peters in *The Professor's House.* Ivy Peters of *A Lost Lady,* Cather's third and final novel of pioneer Nebraska, is an unmitigated villain who tortures animals as a boy and grows up to be a dishonest lawyer. By draining a marsh beloved by many, Peters obliterates "a few acres of something he hated, though he could not name it," asserting "power over the people who had loved those unproductive meadows for their idleness and silvery beauty." Ivy is the prototype of the new capitalist speculator who will commodify the prairie, cheat the Indians, and "root out the great brooding spirit of freedom" by destroying "the space, the colour, the princely carelessness of the pioneer." Nebraska society has come to be dominated not by individuals like Alexandra and Ántonia but by a placeless commercial "generation of shrewd young men, trained to petty economies by hard times," who "do exactly what Ivy Peters had done when he drained the . . . marsh" (106–7).

The major works of Cather's third and final period—*Death Comes for the Archbishop* (1927), *Shadows on the Rock* (1931), and *Sapphira and the Slave Girl* (1940)—represent further withdrawal from modern realities. While some readers see these novels as masterworks culminating Cather's career, there is a long critical tradition that views them as regressive and escapist. As America sunk into the Great Depression, leftists lambasted Cather for writing historical romances instead of polemical novels of social realism. Notable among these critics was Granville Hicks, who accused Cather in his 1933 essay "The Case against Willa Cather" of falling "into supine romanticism because of a refusal to examine life as it is." Writers like Cather, Hicks charged, "cannot accept the cruelty and rapacity" of industrialism, but "are so much bound up in it that they cannot throw themselves, as the revolutionary writers have done, into the movement to destroy and rebuild it" (147). Hicks's Marxist analysis anticipated the work of recent feminist critics, who unfavorably compare Cather's later works with her earlier pastorals. Deborah Lambert, for example, argues that "Cather's movement toward the past in these novels— toward authority, permanence, and Rome—is also a movement into a world dominated by patriarchy. The writer who could envision an Alexandra [Bergson of O Pioneers!] . . . came to be a celebrant of male activity and institutions" (122–23). Similarly, Blanche Gelfant charges Cather with "historical blindness" for denying that the past she so admired "transmitted the crassness, disorder, and violence which 'ruined' the present for her and drove her to hermitic withdrawal. She blamed villainous men, such as Ivy Peters in A Lost Lady, for the decline of a heroic age" (82).

Cather responded to her critics by defending the artist as an expressive individualist. In an open letter (later titled "Escapism"), addressed to the editor of Commonweal in 1936, she argued that the poet's role in society was not "to devote himself to propaganda and fan the flames of indignation" but to inspire others by creating beauty (968). True poets are "useful" only in the sense that "they refresh and recharge the spirit of those who can read their language." Cather's critics struck her as utilitarians, however well-meaning, engaged in an unfortunate "revolt against individualism" (971). For Cather, always a Romantic and sometimes an aesthete, art dealt with intangible ideals more than material realities. "Religion and art," she asserted, "spring from the same root and are close kin. Economics and art are strangers" (972). This, she insisted, was as true of literature as it was of the Native American ceramics she had admired in the Southwest. She claimed aesthetic kinship with the ancient potters who "experimented with form and color to gratify something that had no concern with food and shelter" (968).

Cather was not an escapist, or a hermit or artistic anchorite. She *was,* however, an intensely private person who valued her wealth inasmuch as it bought her time and space to work on her art. She lived comfortably in New York City, where she relished the proximity of libraries, museums,

and especially her beloved Metropolitan Opera. She summered in New
Hampshire and at Grand Manan, New Brunswick, and traveled whenever possible to New Mexico and to Europe. But she did not forget Nebraska, or her friends and family there. Frequent trips back to Red Cloud
inspired her to create stories that are arguably her finest later works:
"Neighbor Rosicky," "Old Mrs. Harris," and "The Best Years," all elegies
to her elders and the first generation of European immigrants in Nebraska. During the Depression she also acted as a benefactor to several
farm families, saving them from foreclosure and destitution. Unlike many
modernist writers, she did not expatriate or withdraw into an amoral
cosmopolitanism. As Rosowski, one of Cather's more sympathetic critics,
writes, "Cather's belief in an essential relationship with place remained
firm, as did her linking to the land traits of character, attitudes, qualities
of feelings, and imagination" ("Willa Cather," 93).[2]

Cather's strength is as an artist, not as a historian or social advocate.
She was a Jeffersonian and a Romantic, and her only rebellion was the
one she recommends in "Nebraska: The End of the First Cycle." Urging
young people to "revolt against all the machine-made materialism
about them" and to "go back to the old sources of culture and wisdom,"
Cather calls on them not to "believe that to live easily is to live happily"
(238). Not surprisingly, she argues for the richness and diversity of the
state's European immigrants as a primary resource in this pursuit:

> I have always the hope that something went into the ground with
> those pioneers that will one day come out again. Something that
> will come out not only in sturdy traits of character, but in elastic-
> ity of mind, in an honest attitude toward the realities of life, in
> certain qualities of feeling and imagination. . . . It is in that great
> cosmopolitan country known as the Middle West that we may
> hope to see the hard molds of American provincialism broken
> up; that we may hope to find young talent which will challenge
> the pale proprieties, the insincere, conventional optimism of our
> art and thought. (237–38)

The passage stands not only as a gloss on Cather's midwestern fiction,
but as a prediction of pastoral writers yet to come. Leopold, Roethke,
Wright, Harrison, and others are prefigured there: writers who follow

Cather, sometimes consciously, in portraying midwestern places and the need for cultural expressions of commensurate beauty. Cather's aesthetic strengths derive, like her ethical weaknesses, from the same Romantic sources that her successors would question and revise to fit their new understandings of American history and landscape. If Cather erred in imagining America, after Whitman, as "not a country at all, but the material out of which countries are made" (*My Ántonia,* 718), she did identify cultural and natural diversity as ultimate values in a democratic society. In the unmatched beauty of her prose, she set the standard for midwestern pastoral. Like Whitman, who describes himself as a "teacher of athletes," she might have said of her admirers and critics, "He most honors my style who learns under it to destroy the teacher" (83).

three

# Aldo
# Leopold

We must regard the *land* as a commanding and increasing
power on the citizen, the sanative and Americanizing influence, which promises to disclose new virtues for ages to
come.

—Ralph Waldo Emerson, "Nature" (1844)

The pastoral impulse behind Willa Cather's Nebraska novels also manifested itself in the life and work of Aldo Leopold (1877–1948), ecologist
and essayist. Leopold is best remembered as the author of *A Sand County
Almanac* (1949), a classic of American nature writing primarily noted for
the thesis of its capstone essay, "The Land Ethic": that society needs to
expand its ethical boundaries to include "man's relation to land and to
the animals and plants which grow upon it" (203). Leopold's "land ethic"
and the book that expresses it have profoundly influenced the modern
environmental movement and new fields of study such as environmental
history, environmental ethics, restoration ecology, and bioregionalism.
As recent ecocritics have demonstrated, Leopold derived from and contributed to long-standing traditions in Romantic literature, moral philosophy, and biological science. He is most often considered in the context of
nature writing, a literary genre that tends to pose aesthetic, moral, and
ecological alternatives to the economic, pragmatic, and human-centered
view of nature dominant in American society at large. But Leopold's
ecophilosophy and literary manner also had a decidedly regional dimension. He was, by birth, outlook, and ultimate residence, of the American

Midwest, as influenced by his region's landscape, culture, and history as Emerson and Thoreau were by their native New England. In attempting to mediate the perennial American conflict between holistic and materialistic attitudes toward nature, Leopold drew on his midwestern experience as well as the unique version of pastoral idealism evident in the region's history and literature.

Leopold was born and raised in Burlington, Iowa, on the Mississippi River. Like Samuel Clemens before him, Leopold had many of his first significant experiences of nature near the greatest American river, the heartland stream praised by T. S. Eliot as "a strong brown god" (191). Enough wild country yet endured in the region for Leopold to know something of the pioneer experience—tramping through fields and woods, hunting, or just observing wildlife. Yet the older, wilder Midwest was passing into history. In this era before game laws, unregulated hunting for the commercial market was bringing wild bird populations to the verge of extinction, or beyond. By slaughtering the passenger pigeon and other species, the market hunter, as Leopold's biographer Curt Meine writes, played the role "in the wildlife drama that the lumber baron played in the northwoods and the sodbuster on the plains: the reaper of the primeval crop" (18).

A more benevolent pastoralism was modeled for Leopold by his father, a prominent Burlington businessman who instructed his sons during hunting trips to the Illinois side of the river. Carl Leopold, as Meine recounts, had "a well-developed personal code of sportsmanship" that included a personal bag limit and required a certain shot or none at all (18). He inculcated a basic conservationism in his son by allowing Aldo to shoot partridges only in flight, never from trees (reducing the likelihood of success by making the shot more difficult). Leopold would one day write that "to forego a sure shot in the tree in favor of a hopeless one at the fleeing bird was my first exercise in ethical codes." In his essay "Red Legs Kicking," Leopold remembers the shooting of his first partridge not as an exploit to boast about, but as a moment when he intensely appreciated the integrity and beauty of a wild place. In a characteristic understatement, Leopold there conveys Romantic esteem for the child's sense of wonder. "I could draw a map today," he writes, "of each clump of red bunchberry and each blue aster that adorned the mossy spot where he lay, my first partridge on the wing. I suspect my present affection for bunchberries and asters dates from that moment" (*Sand County*, 121–22).[1]

But, as Leopold observes, "One of the penalties of an ecological education is that one lives alone in a world of wounds" (*Round River*, 165). While he was at college, "progress" consumed his sacred place, that little remnant of wildness in the agrarian Midwest, prompting Leopold's "first doubt about man in the role of conqueror"—the role Tocqueville had described as typical of utilitarian Americans. "I came home one Christmas," he recalled, "to find that land promoters, with the help of the Corps of Engineers, had dyked and drained my boyhood hunting grounds on the Mississippi River bottoms. The job was so complete that I could not even trace the outlines of my beloved lakes and sloughs under their new blanket of cornstalks." The conversion of this marsh to cropland was for Leopold a formative experience; his shock and "sense of loss" were such that he did not write about his former hunting grounds until late in his life: "[M]y old lake had been under corn for forty years before I wrote 'Red Legs Kicking'" (Foreword, 282–83). Aldo Leopold turned his sorrow to commitment, continuing his ecological education so as to help heal this "world of wounds" as a "doctor who sees the marks of death in a community that believes itself well and does not want to be told otherwise" (*Round River*, 165). His special contribution to midwestern pastoral literature, and to American nature writing as a whole, would be the conjoining of modern ecological science with the Romantic spirit of place.

Like the Hemingways of Oak Park, Illinois, Leopold's well-to-do family traveled by boat and rail each summer to a resort community in northern Michigan; Leopold's first encounters with near-wilderness occurred at Marquette Island in the Les Cheneaux group in northern Lake Huron. Like Hemingway at Walloon Lake, Leopold was more interested in fishing, boating, and hunting than in social diversions available among the "summer people." He explored Marquette Island intensely, drawing detailed maps of the well-forested terrain and continuing his special interest in ornithology. According to Meine, Leopold's father maintained strict conservation rules while on vacation, seeing to it that "Aldo never kept a bass under a pound-and-a-half, nor a pike under three pounds." Northern Michigan was, as Meine describes it, "a land rich in the raw material of adventure, and wild enough to inspire the imagination" (23–24). Though Leopold never fulfilled his dream of canoeing northward into wild Ontario toward Hudson Bay, his early encounters with the woods and waters of Les Cheneaux and the Michigan mainland instilled in him a love for nature in untrammeled expanses, and an ardent desire to see it preserved.

Leopold earned bachelor's and master's degrees at Yale, in forestry programs founded by conservationist Gifford Pinchot in 1900. For Pinchot, the first U.S. Forest Service chief (under president Theodore Roosevelt), the "first principle of conservation [was] development, the use of the natural resources now existing on this continent for the benefit of the people who live here now" (43). Though Leopold did not at first significantly deviate from this reductively economic view of nature (it was many years, for example, before he decided that predatory animals deserve protection), he was from the beginning of his career interested in expanding the application of conservation principles beyond the Forest Service mandate for timber management. In fifteen years as a forester in Arizona and New Mexico, Leopold focused on issues relating to game protection, including the need for hunting laws and habitat preservation. His leadership among conservationists in the Southwest included playing a critical role in the establishment of the Gila Wilderness Area, the first tract to be so designated. Leopold learned during his Forest Service years to build community consensus for conservation measures. He wrote articles in popular *and* professional journals, and established rapport with ranchers and hunters as well as scientists and government officials. His final position with the Forest Service, as Associate Director of the Forest Products Laboratory in Madison, Wisconsin, removed Leopold from fieldwork for four years (1924–1928). But he had returned to the Midwest, his home and the regional focus of his work during the last twenty-four years of his life.

Leopold's first major project after leaving the Forest Service was a game survey of eight midwestern states, sponsored by the Sporting Arms and Ammunition Manufacturers' Institute. Between 1928 and 1931, Leopold gathered data relating to hunting laws and practices, habitat, and animal populations in Wisconsin, Minnesota, Iowa, Missouri, Illinois, Indiana, Ohio, and Michigan; this information went into his *Report on a Game Survey of the North Central States* (1931). "Affection born of nativity," Leopold writes in the *Report,* "is probably in part responsible for my conviction that no region in the world was originally more richly endowed with game than" the Midwest (15). But decades of intensive commercial farming had decimated game populations by destroying their habitat, necessitating a new understanding between government, landowners, and the public. Laws, certainly, were needed to regulate hunting and other uses of land, but the success of game management rested with private landowners, particularly farmers. Leopold wrote his second book with that insight in mind; *Game Management* (1933) provided landowners, professionals, and bureaucrats alike with sound techniques for correcting the adverse conditions he had observed during the midwestern survey. These two publications became essential to conservation research and public policy at midcentury, earning Leopold the title of "father of game management."

Leopold's appointment in 1933 as professor in a new Department of Game Management at the University of Wisconsin provided him with a base to conduct further research and disseminate his philosophy. While maintaining his prominent role in the national conservation movement (he was a founding member of the Wilderness Society in 1935), Leopold applied himself most vigorously to conservation at the local level. He instructed young farmers as well as graduate students in game management theory and technique; he gave radio talks on conservation, addressing his commentary to the Wisconsin agricultural community; he helped establish a University Arboretum at Madison for educational, recreational, and research purposes; he served on the new Wisconsin State Conservation Department's game and fisheries committees; he initiated cooperative ventures between farmers and sportsmen to improve habitat. Finally, and most significantly for Leopold's enduring influence, he bought eighty acres of land on the Wisconsin River in central Wisconsin, a place where he and his family—wife Estella and five children—would enjoy close contact with wild nature and put game management theory to work in the field. Through each of these endeavors Leopold sought to reconcile democratic individualism with the lessons of ecology, to take midwestern pastoralism beyond utilitarian considerations of the immediately useful and practical to encompass the long-term health of the land. Leopold was, as Meine describes him, "an Anglo-Saxon midwesterner, nonpolitical, nondoctrinaire," and more: he was a Jeffersonian ecologist (352).

The sand country of Wisconsin lies at the convergence of three biotic provinces: prairie, deciduous hardwoods, and northern coniferous forest. Interestingly, two other major figures in American environmental thought spent significant portions of their lives in the area: frontier historian Frederick Jackson Turner and preservationist John Muir spent their boyhoods not far from the abandoned farm Leopold bought in 1935.[2] Turner, who was briefly Leopold's neighbor and acquaintance in Madison, grew up in Portage and studied at the University of Wisconsin; his famous "frontier thesis" originated in research into land-tenure patterns around his home town. Muir, who is most famous for his writings about the Sierra Nevada of California and his fight for wilderness protection in the West, came to the sand country with his family from Scotland in 1849. Muir experienced the midwestern wilderness first hand, helping to turn a rugged forest into productive farmland. Whereas Turner celebrated the pioneer period for its supposed democratizing effect, Muir loved the Wisconsin landscape for its own sake, writing his memoir *The Story of My Boyhood and Youth* (1912) as a transcendentalist celebration of the wild nature he believed to be literally sacred, revelatory of God's splendor. The sand country, as Muir's account implies, was never cut out for intensive farming. Overproduction of wheat, excessive grazing, clear-cut lumbering, and marsh drainage caused erosion, peat fires, and the creation of inland sand dunes. As environmental historian Susan Flader relates, the land Aldo Leopold bought in 1935 was hardly a mid-American Arcadia. "Less than half the land in any of the sand counties was in farms," she writes, "and of that very little was actively cultivated. The rest was considered wasteland—weeds, brush, runty jack pine, scrub oak, and raw peat sprouting dense thickets of seemingly worthless aspen. Much of the land had reverted to the counties for nonpayment of real estate and drainage taxes. There it reposed, for few would think of buying it" (49). Leopold, in fact, selected his Wisconsin farm "for its lack of goodness and its lack of highway; indeed my whole neighborhood lies in a backwash of the River Progress" (*Sand County,* 46–47). Seeing the place as a living laboratory for applied ecology, Leopold set himself to healing wounds inflicted on the land by a long history of abuse. In the terminology of contemporary bioregionalism, he "reinhabited" the country of Turner and Muir, finding that country "may be rich despite a conspicuous poverty of physical endowment, and its quality may not be apparent at first glance, nor at all times" (*Sand County,* 164).

    For the rest of his life Leopold spent every weekend and spare moment at the farm, staying in a converted chicken coop affectionately known as "the shack." He and his family planted native trees and other vegetation, provided cover for wildlife, and kept a detailed record of their work and observations. By this time, Leopold was a convert from utilitarian, Pinchot-style conservation; he now embraced a holistic view of land management that considered the welfare not only of game animals, but of all creatures, including predators, within the context of the entire "land community." He was still an avid hunter, but the chase had become just one of many possible outdoor activities. His motivation in owning and improving the land would transcend diversion, research, or environmental restoration—the larger purpose was ultimately educational. Leopold meant to present his sand country experience as a model for others to follow, and to that end he wrote narratives about life at the shack for publications ranging from *Wisconsin Agriculturalist and Farmer* to *Audubon*. By 1941, Leopold was envisioning a book of collected essays combining narrative description of what *is* in nature and current land use with ecological exhortation—a prescription of what *ought* to be the norm in human-nature relations. Up until his death in 1948 Leopold worked on the manuscript that his family and friends would edit and posthumously publish as *A Sand County Almanac*.

*A Sand County Almanac* is arranged into three parts. Part I, the "Almanac" itself, reflects the influence of Thoreau's *Walden* in representing the passage of a full year's cycle, January to December, at Leopold's "week-end refuge from too much modernity: 'the shack'" (vii–viii). Part II is concerned with "The Quality of Landscape" not only in the Midwest, but across North America, as Leopold recounts episodes in his life that taught him vital lessons in conservation. Part III is titled "The Upshot" for its directly philosophical arguments concerning a "Conservation Esthetic," "Wilderness," and, most importantly, "The Land Ethic." This arrangement acquaints us with a man through his life and works before explicitly seeking to convert us to his way of thinking. By moving from the local to the universal, from natural history through autobiography to ecological theory, the structure of Leopold's book creates, as John Tallmadge comments, "a climate of belief that will make us receptive to Leopold's doctrine of land citizenship" (114). If Leopold changes his reader's outlook, he does so by first providing entertainment and instruction regarding ecological issues as they affect particular places and people. Like all good nature writing, *A Sand County Almanac* succeeds as both polemic and poetry, as science and literary pastoral.

Leopold's philosophy centers on the concept of a "land community," elaborated on in "The Land Ethic." There Leopold argues that western culture has gradually expanded its definition of "community" by extending its range of ethical consideration. Having evolved from tribal obligations to a general humanitarianism, society needs to include nature itself in its ethical constructs. "The land ethic," Leopold writes, "simply enlarges the boundaries of the community to include soils, waters, plants, and animals, or collectively: the land." It "changes the role of *Homo sapiens* from conqueror of the land-community to plain member and citizen of it" (*Sand County,* 204). Leopold's use of the term "community" is consistent with early twentieth-century science, particularly as formulated by his friend British ecologist Charles Elton, whose seminal *Animal Ecology* (1927) describes nature's "food chains," in which organisms occupy "niches" in a "community," much like humans in a socioeconomic order. (In avoidance of anthropomorphism, most scientists now prefer the term "ecosystem" to convey the concept of biological interdependence.) Leopold favored the cultural connotations of "community," a word sacred to Romantics like Thoreau (who often spoke of his place in a "society" of nature) and to American democrats since Jefferson. From ecological and ethical values Leopold proceeds to aesthetics, employing a pastoral metaphor in asserting that "land yields a cultural harvest" (ix). This harvest includes works of art and literature—such as *A Sand County Almanac*—that celebrate and defend "the integrity, stability, and beauty of the biotic community" (224–25).

Leopold writes in a relaxed and conversational style, using "simple rhetorical figures" and "turns of phrase" to achieve what Tallmadge calls the "memorable succinctness" of his prose (116). Figurative language is especially important in *A Sand County Almanac,* including the recurring metaphor of landscape as language and literature, as a book from which nature-literate people can read lessons in ecology, ethics, and aesthetics.[3] "Every farm woodland," Leopold declares, "in addition to yielding lumber, fuel, and posts, should provide its owner a liberal education" (73). Thus, "every farm is a textbook on animal ecology" (81), and "he who owns a veteran bur oak owns more than a tree. He owns a historical library" (30).

This is the premise of "Good Oak," the essay for February in which Leopold tells of sawing down an old oak tree that had been killed by lightning. Leopold introduces an environmental history of Wisconsin by imagining his saw "biting its way, stroke by stroke, decade by decade, into the chronology of a lifetime, written in concentric annual rings of good oak." After "a dozen pulls of the saw to transect the few years of our ownership, during which we have learned to love and cherish this farm," Leopold cuts into "the reign of the bootlegger" who wasted the soil and burned the farmhouse; he then continues to saw progressively back into history (9).

Some of the stories Leopold reads in the wood grain are encouraging, such as John Muir's attempt to establish a wildflower sanctuary just thirty miles from Leopold's farm; according to Leopold, 1865, the year of Muir's effort, "still stands in Wisconsin history as the birthyear of mercy for things natural, wild, and free" (16). Most of the history, however, is a continuum of environmental neglect and abuse, a chronology of years such as 1899, when "the last passenger pigeon collided with a charge of shot near Babcock, two counties to the north" (12). Leopold concludes the essay by comparing the saw with the wedge and the ax as a tool for splitting wood and as "an allegory for historians" (16). The metaphor is also likely to appeal to people, such as farmers, who may be more convinced by an ecological argument if it is phrased in colloquial, commonsensical language. By speaking the vernacular of rural Wisconsin, Leopold creates for himself a persona, described by James I. McClintock in *Nature's Kindred Spirits* (1994) as "a twentieth-century variant of the mythic American yeoman farmer, the traditional repository of Jeffersonian virtue and homespun wisdom" (28).

Comments made by environmental historian Donald Worster touch on the colloquialism of Leopold's metaphorical language. Worster argues that Leopold's description of land ecology as both "mechanism" and "organism" constitutes a "vacillation between root metaphors . . . consistently identified with fundamentally antithetical world views" (290). "Mechanism" invokes eighteenth-century physics and views associated with Newton, Descartes, and others who describe nature as a machine, understandable in its component parts. Mechanistic thinking has developed through the centuries toward more sophisticated expressions in science and social thought, which according to Worster explain "all nature as a system of matter in motion, entirely subject to the laws of physics and chemistry" (379). Such a vision of nature lends itself to utilitarian

confidence in the technological management of nature for human benefit. Like many intellectual historians, Worster notes an "Arcadian"
countertradition of resistance to mechanism as a reductive and insuffi-
cient explanation of nature's order. Influential proponents of organicism
include natural historians, Romantic poets, and, in Leopold's lifetime,
philosophers and scientists such as Alfred North Whitehead, William
Morton Wheeler, and several specialists in animal ecology at the University of Chicago. According to Worster, these figures agreed that nature
should be "viewed as a 'complex organism,' not unlike the human body"
(380). Nothing can be understood in isolation; everything in nature is
interdependent.

Worster's point about Leopold's equivocation is well taken. Although
he was well aware of the connotations of "mechanism," Leopold repeatedly used the term when it would have been more consistent to speak of
land ecology as an "organism." Even in "The Land Ethic," the ultimate
summation of his philosophy, references to the "community clock" and
the "biotic mechanism" abound. Yet in concluding that Leopold's land
ethic is "in many ways . . . merely a more enlightened, long-range pru-
dence: a surer means to an infinite expansion of material wealth," Worster
overstates his case, as when he claims that by Leopold's use of "agronomic terms . . . the entire earth became a crop to be harvested, though
not one wholly planted or cultivated by man" (289). Leopold applies the
word "harvest" to the cultural, rather than economic, rewards of prudent
land management; he strenuously objects to those in his own field,
forestry, who are "quite content to grow trees like cabbages, with cellu-
lose as the basic forest commodity." Such specialists feel "no inhibition
against violence; [their] ideology is agronomic" (*Sand County,* 221). Leopold's ideology is pastoral, not agronomic, as Worster has it; his land ethic
is practical rather than materialistic. While ceding to the human claim
on nature for resources, Leopold insists that economics must be modeled
after ecology, not vice versa.

This lesson, not surprisingly, arose from the rural landscape that was
Leopold's first concern. A major cause of environmental distress in the
Midwest (including erosion, water pollution, and habitat loss) was and still
is the kind of agriculture Leopold calls "clean farming . . . a food chain
aimed solely at economic profit and purged of all non-conforming links,"
including native flora and fauna. Leopold abjures this "*Pax Germanica* of

the agricultural world," a bleak monoculture that he would replace with a simultaneously ecological and democratic diversity: "a food chain aimed to harmonize the wild and the tame in the joint interest of stability, productivity, and beauty" (*Round River*, 164). Far from advocacy of economic hegemony over nature, Leopold's stated purpose was to encourage a "healthy contempt for a plethora of material blessings" (*Sand County*, ix). Rejecting Pinchot-style resource management as a "[hopelessly lopsided] system of conservation based solely on economic self-interest," Leopold sought a pastoral balance between human needs and imperatives of ecology and aesthetics (*Sand County*, 214).

In addition to inherent inconsistencies in Leopold's philosophy, we should look to the regional sources of his occasionally mechanistic language. To initiate social change Leopold needed to tailor his rhetoric to his audience, which includes farmers and other midwesterners steeped in the region's ethic of rural utilitarianism. Priding themselves on their practicality, such readers are familiar with machinery and even affectionate toward it. Farmers rely on tractors and other equipment; townspeople think of their cars as essential to their personal freedom. In addressing a readership for whom the machine is a fact of life, Leopold found mechanistic metaphor indispensable. A passage from the essay "The Farmer as a Conservationist," published in *American Forests* in 1939 and in posthumous volumes of Leopold's work, illustrates his usage well:

> This is the age of engineers. For proof of this I look not so much to Boulder Dams or China Clippers as to the farmer boy tending his tractor or building his own radio. In a surprising number of men there burns a curiosity about machines and loving care in their construction, maintenance, and use. This bent for mechanisms, even though clothed in greasy overalls, is often the pure fire of intellect. It is the earmark of our time.
>
> Everyone knows this, but what few realize is that an equal bent for the mechanisms of nature is a possible earmark of some future generation. (164–65)

Invoking the midwestern archetype of the tinkerer, Leopold projects that representative figure into an ecologically enlightened future. He praises the tinkerer, but subversively; by speaking in utilitarian terms, Leopold establishes a rapport that enables him to introduce nature's noninstrumental value into the conversation. In "The Farmer as a Conservationist," therefore, he offers several definitions of conservation, including the mechanistic assertion that conservation means "keeping the resource in working order" (164). In a later passage, however, Leopold suggests that "conservation implies self-expression in [the] landscape, rather than blind compliance with economic dogma" (172). Utilitarian individualism, in other words, can serve ecological ends only if midwesterners develop foresight in their working relationship with land. They must "try to see the *trend* of our tinkerings with fields and forests, water and soils" (167).[4]

Leopold accepted that the midwestern countryside, the most productive farmland in the world, would be cultivated and intensely managed. But, as he states in the essay "Conservation," "To keep every cog and wheel is the first precaution of intelligent tinkering" (*Round River,* 147). Intelligent tinkering entails a stewardship that works with rather than against ecology, that allows for enclaves of wild nature. Leopold notes that many such places survive, reminding observers of formerly intact ecosystems. Driving through Illinois, for example, he sees that in "the narrow thread of sod between the shaved banks and the toppling fences grow the relics of . . . the prairie" (*Sand County,* 117). As have many midwestern writers, Leopold notices that midwestern graveyards often harbor native species of plants that have been extirpated elsewhere. "Every July," Leopold writes in "Prairie Birthday," "I watch eagerly a certain country graveyard that I pass in driving to and from my farm":

> It is extraordinary only in being triangular instead of square, and in harboring, within the sharp angle of its fence, a pinpoint remnant of the native prairie on which the graveyard was established in the 1840s. Heretofore unreachable by scythe or mower, the yard-square relic of original Wisconsin gives birth, each July, to a man-high stalk of compass plant or cutleaf Silphium, spangled with saucer-sized yellow blooms resembling sunflowers. It is the sole remnant of this plant along this highway, and perhaps the sole remnant in the western half of our county. What a thousand acres of Silphiums looked like when they tickled the bellies of the buffalo is a question never again to be answered, and perhaps not even asked. (*Sand County,* 45)

The flowers, whose description as "man-high" emphasizes their citizenship in the land community, are beautiful to Leopold for their own sake and because they constitute an important page in the history book of nature, a page that informs us about the great herds of bison that once roamed freely across the plains, and about the region's troubled social history. Because Silphium is a long-lived plant, the specimen in the cemetery may have been a hundred years old; it may have "watched the fugitive Black Hawk retreat from the Madison lakes to the Wisconsin River. . . . Certainly it saw the successive funerals of the local pioneers as they retired, one by one, to their repose beneath the bluestem" (49). When Leopold returned in August to find that a road crew had removed the fence and cut the Silphium, he was angered and hurt by this desecration of a sacred place—a desecration more offensive for being part of a well-intended, though misguided, system of land management. Leopold emphasizes the spiritual as well as ecological dimensions of the loss by considering the nominal steward of the graveyard's consecrated ground: "If I were to tell a preacher of the adjoining church that the road crew has been burning history books in his cemetery, under the guise of mowing weeds, he would be amazed and uncomprehending. How could a weed be a book?" (46)

The commodification and abuse of midwestern landscape result, in part, from an inadequate sense of the beautiful in nature. In his essay on "The Land Aesthetic," J. Baird Callicott describes how the "prevailing natural aesthetic . . . is not autonomous but derivative from art," particularly from eighteenth-century notions of the "picturesque," perspectives on nature that suggest pictures or paintings. The way most people look at nature is "conventionalized, not well informed by the ecological and evolutionary revolutions in natural history; and it is sensational and self-referential, not genuinely oriented to nature on nature's terms. In a word, it is trivial" (160). We appreciate rugged forests and sublime mountain landscapes because our culture conditions us to value them; our national park system, for example, originated as a means to preserve such places—Yosemite, Yellowstone, and so forth. Few have loved the grand American wilderness as much as Aldo Leopold, or worked as diligently for its preservation. But Leopold saw that historical and ecological ignorance leads to the aesthetic undervaluation and subsequent abuse of less obviously "beautiful" places like the sand country of Wisconsin. To counteract this harmful tendency in American culture, Leopold proposes an evolutionary land aesthetic, parallel and complementary to his land ethic. Leopold's aesthetic, as Callicott notes, strives to extend human perception of nature beyond the visual to include the other four senses, and, most importantly, "the mind, the faculty of cognition" (160). To this effect Leopold suggests that the "ability to perceive quality in nature begins, as in art with the pretty. It expands through successive stages of the beautiful to values as yet uncaptured by language" (*Sand County*, 96). Valuing nature for the integrity of its ecological processes enables one to "see America as history, to conceive of destiny as a becoming, to smell a hickory tree through the still lapse of ages" (*Sand County*, 112).

Such an ability to see into nature is especially important in a region like the American Midwest, where landscapes are often apparently prosaic and lacking in Romantic sublimity. In his essay "Country," as in "Prairie Birthday," Leopold invokes the memory of the American bison in respect to prevailing perceptions of midwestern landscapes:

> The taste for country displays the same diversity in aesthetic
> competence among individuals as the taste for opera, or oils.     .
> There are those who are willing to be herded in droves through
> "scenic" places; who find mountains grand if they be proper
> mountains with waterfalls, cliffs, and lakes. To such the Kansas
> plains are tedious. They see the endless corn, but not the heave
> and the grunt of ox teams breaking the prairie. History, for
> them, grows on campuses. They look at the low horizon, but
> they cannot see it, as [Spanish explorer Cabeza] de Vaca did,
> under the bellies of the buffalo.

Leopold learned to see nature in this way, "under the bellies of the buffalo," through long study of his sand country farm, where he discovered that in "country, as in people, a plain exterior often conceals hidden riches, to perceive which requires much living in and with" (*Round River*, 32–33). The most lyrical passages of the "Almanac" are descriptions of particular places that Leopold came to know intimately, such as a "streambank where hillside briars adjoin dank beds of frozen ferns and jewelweeds on the boggy bottom" (*Sand County*, 63), and the fork of a river, "narrow, deep, and fed by cold springs that gurgled out under its close-hemmed walls of alder" (37). These typically midwestern places offer hidden riches of subtle beauty to the sensitive and discerning observer. A deeper-than-visual curiosity is required to apprehend their significance; the observer needs to enter the picture, figuratively and literally: "There are woods that are plain to look at, but not to look into. Nothing is plainer than a cornbelt woodlot; yet if it be August, a crushed pennyroyal, or an over-ripe mayapple, tells you here is a place" (*Round River,* 32). Pennyroyal and mayapple dwell in this woodlot as members of the land community; Leopold's recognition of them by name serves as his passport into their domain. He achieved full naturalization (to complete the metaphor) as a citizen of the place by protecting and propagating these and other native life forms.

Recognizing that most people in the Midwest and elsewhere in America lack such an informed sense of place, Leopold proposes environmental education as the best means of counteracting the materialistic view of nature. Such education must transcend ordinary injunctions to "obey the law, vote right, join some organizations, and practice what conservation is profitable on your land" (*Sand County,* 207); it must build "an ethical underpinning for land economics and a universal curiosity to understand the land mechanism" ("The Round River," 202). Leopold admits an important role for government in conservation, but he felt that too many people wrongly delegate their responsibility for nature to bureaus and agencies. In the Midwest, where relatively little land is in the public domain (compared to in the West), commitment on the part of private landowners and amateur naturalists ( Jefferson's favored land stewards) is essential to successful "revolt against the tedium of the merely economic attitude toward land." Among Leopold's heroes in this revolt were farmers he knew who reintroduced native tamarack trees on their land, "an industrial chemist who [spent] his spare time reconstructing the history of the passenger pigeon," and an Ohio woman whose study of the common sparrow was recognized by professional ornithologists as a major contribution to the field (*Round River,* 57–60). Such commitment to nature, in Leopold's view, needs to be included in science curricula, which too often emphasize laboratory work like dissection at the expense of fieldwork that will teach students to see their "native countryside with appreciation and intelligence." Like Leopold's students at the University of Wisconsin, a college student in a class so designed could expect an examination such as the following, presumably tailored to fit his or her own state of residence:

> We are driving down a country road in northern Missouri. Here is a farmstead. Look at the trees in the yard and the soil in the field and tell us whether the original settler carved his farm out of prairie or woods. Did he eat prairie chicken or wild turkey for his Thanksgiving? What plants grew here originally which do not grow here now? Why did they disappear? What did the prairie plants have to do with creating the corn-yielding capacity of this soil? Why does this soil erode now but not then? (*Round River,* 62)

Leopold asks, in effect, that we "read the land" for lessons in human history and the intrinsic order and beauty, or "poetry," of nature. This kind of learning will in Leopold's view help us overcome "the most serious obstacle impeding the evolution of a land ethic . . . the fact that our educational and economic system is headed away from, rather than toward, an intense consciousness of land" (*Sand County,* 223).

Leopold harbored no illusions about the enormity of this project, which required no less than a reform of American middle-class values associated in his time with the business culture of small towns. In "A Criticism of the Booster Spirit," a 1923 speech to a civic group in Albuquerque, New Mexico, he takes small-town utilitarianism to task for promoting quantity over quality. "The booster's yardstick" he writes, "is the dollar, and if he recognizes any other standard of value, or any other agency of accomplishment, he makes it a point of pride not to admit it" (102). Yet even as he excoriates the booster's materialism, provinciality, and lack of aesthetic sophistication, Leopold admits "the possibility that true vitality and greatness underlies the booster idea." He cites local developers promoting regional style in architecture as evidence that boosterism, "harnessed to a finer ideal, may . . . accomplish good as well as big things" (104–5).

While concerning himself in that speech with issues of planning in the Southwest, Leopold draws on midwestern literature in framing his argument, alluding to Samuel Clemens and Carl Sandburg. He also models his personification of the booster after the title character in Sinclair

Lewis's novel *Babbitt*—published just one year before in 1922—which introduced the name into the American lexicon and established the philistine businessman as a midwestern archetype. After moving to Wisconsin in 1924, Leopold preferred the term "Babbitt" to "booster" for its regional specificity, as frequent allusions in his essays attest. In 1932, for example, he speaks of his "love for what Mr. Babbitt is trampling underfoot"; a year later, he refers to the same Mr. Babbitt as a "conservation-booster, who of late has been rewriting the conservation ticket in terms of 'tourist-bait'" (*River of the Mother,* 168, 189). Before long Leopold had coined an adjectival form of the name. In *A Sand County Almanac* he refers to the 1920s as "the Babbittian decade when everything grew bigger and better in heedlessness and arrogance" (10). He also writes that the "wonder" of the passenger pigeon is not that the species was driven to extinction, "but that he ever survived through all the millennia of pre-Babbittian time" (111).

In valuing wealth and social prestige above all else, Babbitt represents one dimension of the midwestern mind; another is the Jeffersonian yeoman farmer, personified by Leopold as an ecologist, hunter, and weekend bird-watcher. These two archetypes represent the tension between materialism and idealism in midwestern pastoral ideology. Since Babbitt prioritizes wealth, Leopold would transform our conception of wealth to include the intrinsic value of nature. To this end he occasionally resorts to humorously economic language: "If you are thriftily inclined, you will find pines congenial company, for unlike the hand-to-mouth hardwoods, they never pay current bills out of current earnings; they live solely on their savings of the year before" (*Sand County,* 82). Since Babbitt values his good reputation almost as much as prosperity, we must also redefine civic virtue to include responsibility to the entire land community; there must be "social stigma in the possession of a gullied farm, a wrecked forest, or a polluted stream" ("The Round River," 202). Addressing the man directly, Leopold assumes the polemical tone of public debate: "I demand of Mr. Babbitt that game and wild life be one of the normal products of every farm" (*River of the Mother,* 167). At stake is the definition of democracy: whether freedom in the United States is merely personal and economic or dependent on (and responsible for) ecological stability and diversity. As Leopold writes, alluding to *Babbitt* in the concluding paragraph of *Game Management,* "Twenty centuries of 'progress' have brought the average citizen a vote, a national anthem, a Ford, a bank account, and a high opinion of himself, but not the capacity to live in high density without befouling and denuding his environment, nor a conviction that such capacity, rather than such density, is the true test of whether he is civilized" (422–23).

Leopold's argument for land stewardship has a special resonance in the American Midwest because of his long and profound association with the region. His land ethic and land aesthetic are evident in the work of subsequent midwestern naturalists such as Stephanie Mills (b. 1948) and Wes Jackson (b. 1936). Mills, an eloquent advocate of bioregionalism and restoration ecology, has reinhabited a plot of land in northern Michigan. A pilgrimage to Leopold's Wisconsin farm strengthened Mills's commitment to her own damaged midwestern acreage; she writes that "as a result of those days spent in the regenerating landscape at the Leopold Memorial Reserve, my own surroundings are beginning to tell more of a story, and its ending is no longer a foregone, or paltry, conclusion" (111–12). Jackson, founder of the Land Institute near Salina, Kansas, is the best recent exemplar of Leopold's midwestern topophilia in the service of science.[5] Jackson's lifework is to replace corn and wheat agriculture, which requires intensive plowing, irrigation, and application of petrochemicals, with the cultivation of native perennial grasses. The "domestic prairie" toward which Jackson and his fellow researchers have targeted their experiments in selective breeding would offer high crop yields without the erosion, pollution, and aquifer depletion characteristic of modern farming on the Great Plains. It would constitute a pastoral middle ground offering both agricultural productivity and biological diversity. Jackson's argument for ecological education and commitment to local communities is distinctly Leopoldian, as is his caution for ecocritics and environmental activists, whose treatment, according to Jackson, "of wilderness as a holy shrine and Kansas or East Saint Louis as terrain of an altogether different sort is a form of schizophrenia," a philosophical double standard. "Either all the earth is holy or none is. Either every square foot of it deserves our respect or none does. . . . It is possible to love a small acreage in Kansas as much as John Muir loved the entire Sierra Nevada. This is fortunate, for the wilderness of the Sierra will disappear unless little pieces of nonwilderness become intensely loved by lots of people" (67).

An ardent admirer of both Jackson and Leopold is Scott Russell Sanders (b. 1945), author of several books of essays drawing on his life in southern Indiana and the midwestern writer who has done the most to develop the implications of Leopold's land ethic and aesthetic for the nature essay. In his foreword to *For the Health of the Land* (1999), a collection of rare and previously unpublished writings by Leopold, Sanders suggests the degree to which Leopold has inspired him by taking an imaginary walk in the Indiana countryside with the late ecologist.

> It is land that my family has recently bought, and with Leopold's help I can see the damage done by previous owners: the eroded gullies, the stumps from careless logging, the straightened creek, the rusted carcasses of refrigerators and trucks dumped along the road. The gullies can be mended, he assures me. The trash can be carted away. The creek can be slowed down and encouraged to wander. . . . With each glimpse of a wilder future for this land, I enter more deeply into the life of the place.

Touching on sources of Leopold's wisdom, Sanders writes that Leopold "knows all the trees in our Indiana woods, all the flowers, all the birds, because he is a midwesterner, and that is another reason I am drawn to him. As much as he loved wilderness, Leopold also loved farm country" (xviii–xix). That special concern for rural landscape and the stewardship of private property, Sanders notes, directly links Leopold to Thomas Jefferson and to an American tradition of "curious and skillful people who chose to settle in one place for a spell or a lifetime and who studied their neighborhoods with a loving eye." The Jeffersonian tradition, Sanders concludes, is best exemplified today by "ecological restorationists who are now working to heal injured lands" and others "striving to live with a simplicity that honors and welcomes wildness" (xvii–xviii).

Notable for a consistent message about informed inhabitation of local landscapes, Sanders's essays have appeared in widely read literary reviews and in several collections, including *The Paradise of Bombs* (1987), *Staying Put* (1993), and *The Force of Spirit* (2000). These books form an ongoing autobiography and commentary on culture, literature, and the lessons of everyday life. Sanders's essays derive their power as well as their charm from personal testimony about relationships and responsibility. While he values solitary study and exploration of nature, he writes, "What I see when I look at the land is also informed by the company I have kept, beginning with that of my parents" (*Secrets,* 85). Writing about his father's passion for both trees and tools, Sanders draws on midwestern rhetoric in a way that Leopold would have appreciated. "He could make from scratch a house or a hat, could mend a stalled watch or a silent radio. He possessed the tinkerer's genius that has flourished in the stables and cellars and shops of our nation for three hundred years" (*Writing,* 169–70).

As did Aldo Leopold, Sanders advocates reinhabiting a location in North America, learning about its natural and human history for the sake of citizenship as well as spiritual growth. A quote from Roethke's journals, one of two epigraphs to *Staying Put,* introduces the dilemma of America history: "We have failed to live up to our geography" (n.p.). The essays that follow evoke, therefore, both the grandeur and ecological complexity of North America and the tragic consequences of the "nation's history," which, Sanders admits, "does not encourage me, or anyone, to belong somewhere with a full heart" (xv). What Leopold calls "living in a world of wounds" figures in Sanders's loss of three childhood homes, including a "farm in Ohio" that was "erased entirely, the house and barn bulldozed by the army, the woods and fields flooded by a boondoggle dam" (xiv). These memories, along with episodes from his life as a husband and father, illustrate the need for a shift from a culture of placelessness to one of place. In the essay "Settling Down," Sanders notes, "Those who care about nothing beyond the confines of their parish are in truth parochial, and are at least mildly dangerous to their parish; on the other hand, those who *have* no parish, those who navigate ceaselessly among postal zones and area codes, those for whom the world is only a smear of highways and bank accounts and stores, are a danger not just to their parish but to the planet" (*Staying Put,* 114). With Bloomington, Indiana, as his parish, and the Ohio River valley as his watershed, Sanders strives in his writing, as in his life, for a cosmopolitan regionalism that recognizes the intimate ties of region to world, as well as person to place.

Leopold's appeal for Sanders and like-minded naturalists lies in his way of uniting apparently irreconcilable perspectives: materialism and idealism, science and spirituality, domestication and wildness. Between these dualities lies the mythic pastoral middlescape for which midwestern writers have long yearned. By reconnecting midwestern metaphors and archetypes to their Jeffersonian origins, Leopold pointed the way to a new, ecologically enlightened version of pastoral idealism. That *A Sand County Almanac* is revered by state game officers, farmers, and high school biology teachers, as well as by writers and conservation professionals, testifies to his success. Central to Leopold's philosophy is the virtue of forbearance; he once defined a conservationist as "one who is humbly aware that with each stroke he is writing his signature on the land" (*Sand County*, 68). With ax and shovel, Leopold wrote a bright new chapter in the often-troubled history of a remote Wisconsin county; with his expressive pen he wrote a book that makes that place a microcosm for a planet in need of love, respect, and understanding. His example is instructive for people in all places who seek to be better citizens of the earth's diversely beautiful land communities.

four

# Theodore
# Roethke

The smallest sprout shows there is really no death.

—Walt Whitman, "Song of Myself"

In 1948, Aldo Leopold died of a heart attack while fighting a brush fire on his Wisconsin farm. The same year saw the publication of *The Lost Son* by Theodore Roethke, the volume that secured his reputation as a major American poet. Like Leopold's *A Sand County Almanac,* published the following year, Roethke's second book conveys the spirit of a midwestern place, in this case, the Saginaw River valley of Michigan and the greenhouses once operated there by Roethke's family. Most textual analyses of this and Roethke's other books have focused on the poet's private sensibility, his often elliptical and Freudian journey through memory and grief in search of transcendence. The few regionalist examinations of Roethke's work mostly reflect on his late residence in the Pacific Northwest. Some claim that he found his ultimate sense of place during his fifteen years in Seattle, Washington, as a northwestern poet. While acknowledging these readings, the present chapter argues for Roethke's midwestern cultural identity and contribution to the region's tradition of literary pastoral. Much of Roethke's work (the formal love poetry, for example) attenuates place in favor of metaphysical abstraction and symbolism. Some of his best writing, however, draws significantly from midwestern landscape and cultural archetypes; the greenhouse, his central symbol, reconciles utilitarian and Romantic values in midwestern pastoral ideology. However else he may be described, Roethke was a midwesterner and the seminal figure in a poetry of place that includes notable work by James Wright, Jim Harrison, and many other subsequent midwestern writers.[1]

In *The Glass House: The Life of Theodore Roethke* (1968), Allan Seager touches on the poet's regional context, beginning with Tocqueville's Romantic impressions of the wilderness that was Saginaw in 1831. The violent history of the valley's Indian inhabitants, early immigration by New Englanders, and the environmental devastation wreaked by the logging era all come under the biographer's purview. But, as Seager notes, these legacies do not directly appear in Roethke's poetry:

> [Roethke] ignores all the vivid tales of the lumber boom, tales that expressed courage, will, and cunning that might have engaged another man. . . . He must have been aware of the Indians, for he collected a shoebox full of flint arrowheads in his rambles along the riverbanks. . . . But, for the most part, he pays no attention to the history of the valley which expresses in modes of physical action an energy like his own. It is as if he had inherited the best part and did not need to acknowledge it. (8)

Roethke's vision of place and landscape was personal rather than public, leading Seager to claim, alluding to Whitman, "It was himself he had to sing, not the circumambient world. He only used that" (123).

Since Roethke wrote of his father's property and the surrounding countryside with affection and specificity, there is an element of overstatement in Seager's latter assertion. As the poet told his British audience in a 1953 radio address, "It was a wonderful place for a child to grow up in and around":

> There were not only twenty-five acres in the town, mostly under glass and intensely cultivated, but farther out in the country the last stand of virgin timber in the Saginaw Valley, and, elsewhere, a wild area of cut-over second-growth timber, which my father and uncle made into a small game preserve.

As a child . . . I had several worlds to live in, which I felt
were mine. (*On the Poet,* 8).

The statement points to the perennial midwestern tension between pastoral and wild landscapes; like Cather and Leopold, Roethke admired
both and sought to reconcile the demands of human use with the self-
willed processes of natural growth and evolution. From his earliest evocations of Michigan seasons to the late "North American Sequence,"
Roethke wrote equally well of wild and tame places and the plants and
animals that inhabit them. At times, his is the eye of the naturalist, literal
and observant. He then expresses "a genuine love of nature" inspired in
part, as he confessed in a college essay, by his reading of American nature writers such as "Muir and Thoreau and Burroughs[, who] speak the
truth" (*On the Poet,* 4). On other occasions, he directs his nature imagery
toward psychological or mythic themes. At his best, Roethke was at once
literal and symbolic in his references to plants, animals, and landscapes.

The development of parallel description and symbolism is well underway in Roethke's first book, *Open House* (1941). "It took me ten years to
complete one little book," he wrote of that volume several years later,
"and now some of the things in it seem to creak. Still, I like about ten
pieces it in" (*On the Poet,* 16). Those ten likely included poems from the
second section, which turn from the book's pervasive abstraction toward
concrete subjects and Michigan locales. Among these is "The Heron,"
which recalls what Roethke describes as a "favorite place . . . a swampy
corner of the game sanctuary where herons always nested" (*On the Poet,*
8). Consisting of three quatrains in rhyme and iambic tetrameter, the
poem calls less attention to its formal precision than to its careful representation of the heron's behavior. Roethke repeatedly notes the bird's
posture or activity in relation to subtle variations in habitat, such as "a
hump / Of marsh grass heaped above a musk-rat hole." The pattern culminates in the final stanza, when the heron seizes his prey and makes an
elegant departure:

He jerks a frog across his bony lip,
Then points his heavy bill above the wood.
The wide wings flap but once to lift him up.
A single ripple starts from where he stood.

The genius of the place, the heron possesses "antic grace," a strength in stasis as well as in movement (14). Roethke's verse emulates the heron's composure, ease in motion, and observance of local detail. "The Heron" is the first in a number of "animal poems" that Roethke always titled after their subjects, including "The Bat," "Night Crow," "Snake," "Slug," "The Lizard," "The Meadow Mouse," and "The Pike." These poems, worthy of comparison to similar works by John Clare, D. H. Lawrence, and Emily Dickinson, all feature vivid imagery, economy of expression, and a radical identification with creature consciousness. "With bats, weasels, worms," Roethke writes in "Slug," "I rejoice in the kinship" (145).

In their focus on the singular, delicate, and too often overlooked, the animal poems correlate to Roethke's special feeling for subtlety in landscape. A line from the poem "Unfold! Unfold!" in *Praise to the End!* (1951) embodies the upper-midwestern origins of this sensibility: "On the jackpine [*sic*] plains I hunted the bird no one knows" (85). Jack pines, characteristic of northern Michigan, are scrubby, nondescript trees that emerge from sandy, fire-scorched terrain. Hemingway set his famous fishing story "Big Two-Hearted River" (1925) in the jack pine plains of Michigan's Upper Peninsula. While Hemingway's Nick Adams wanders the plains in pursuit of trout and solace after his traumatic experience of the First World War, Roethke seeks a particular bird, one unique to Michigan. Though he does not refer to it by name, his quarry is the endangered Kirtland's warbler, a species limited to a few hundred pairs nesting only in jack pines of a certain height in isolated northern Michigan locations. Roethke's quest to observe this uncelebrated "bird no one knows" symbolizes his attentiveness to midwestern biota, the root of nature imagery in all of his poems, even those not explicitly set in the region. "The first definitions, the fruits of the primary glances, can never be supplanted," Seager writes of Roethke's early years; "for the trees of one's childhood are the touchstones of all later trees, the grass of the back yard the measure of all greenness, and other lights fail because they are not the true sun that brightens those trees, that grass" (7). By exploring the Saginaw country, fishing and hunting in northern Michigan, and consulting books on the state's flora and fauna, Roethke obtained an accurate knowledge of living beings and natural processes.

Roethke unequivocally asserts a midwestern aesthetic in another poem from section 2 of *Open House,* "In Praise of Prairie":

The elm tree is our highest mountain peak;
A five-foot drop a valley, so to speak.

A man's head is an eminence upon
A field of barley spread beneath the sun.

Horizons have no strangeness to the eye.
Our feet are sometimes level with the sky.

(12)

While not literally prairie, much of the Saginaw valley is level country, cleared for agriculture, where one can see a large portion of unobstructed horizon. Since Roethke does not specify Saginaw, his setting suggests a generalized Midwest, the prairie as "America's characteristic landscape," as Whitman calls it (864). Roethke's use of the first person plural lends a sense of community to the poem; for once, his speaker is not a Romantic solitary but a collective voice for the region. In a public tone of declamation, Roethke correlates human qualities—honesty, generosity, and fellowship—to the intimate immensity of the prairie. There, grandeur is relative to an observer's physical stance (the "eminence" of a man's head, our feet "level with the sky") and perspective. That sublime experience does not require a stereotypically sublime landscape is a lesson Roethke knew from Thoreau and Whitman, as well as from Emerson, whose epiphany in *Nature* (the "transparent eye-ball" passage) occurs on no more dramatic a site than a "bare common" (*Essays*, 10). Again, a single phrase (this from his poem "The Small") conveys Roethke's poetic mission, inspired by his own native landscape and informed by the transcendentalists: "I live / To woo the fearful small" (142).

To the degree that the poem treats the plains with sympathy and candor, "In Praise of Prairie" conveys something close to Leopold's "land aesthetic." It is, however, something of an apprentice piece, lacking in personal presence and historical sensibility. Roethke does not yet see the prairie "under the bellies of the buffalo," to cite Leopold's metaphor for the sense of time implied by a land aesthetic. Changes in the land wrought by natural processes and by human intervention do not yet appear in the poet's vision of midwestern landscape.

Roethke was well aware of how drastically his home region had been altered in the half century preceding his birth. "The Saginaw Valley," he said in the 1953 British radio broadcast, "where I was born, had been great lumbering country in the 1880s. It is very fertile flat country in Michigan, and the principal towns, Saginaw and Flint, lie at the northern edge of what is now the central industrial area of the United States" (*On the Poet*, 7). In a manuscript poem "Suburbia: Michigan," published in his *Selected Letters*, Roethke laments the common lack of appreciation for regional history, associating such ignorance with tolerance of environmental degradation:

> The immediate past as remote as Carthage;
> Bulldozers levelled the curving hillside
> . . . . . . . . . . . . . . . . . . . . . . . . . . .
> Tourists stare at an absolute marvel:
> A monarch pine, saved by quixotic fancy.

(Found in Hartwick State Park, about one hundred miles north of Saginaw, the Monarch was the most impressive white pine in a remnant first-growth forest that still attracts thousands of visitors yearly.) Prophesying the postwar culture of convenience that would spread garish strip development across the countryside, Roethke pictures the people of Michigan living in "a land of lubritoriums [and] super milk-shakes," landmarks in a "geography of despair." Those who resist the spiritual abyss of materialism, who hold nature in more than instrumental value and will not "live by objects," are "driven from the land" to

> . . . seek the comfort of water,
> Crawl back to the eternal womb, the beneficent mother.
> Like dazed turtles in spring, they creep to the river
> To dangle bent pins at the mouth of a roaring sewer.
>
> (90–91)

The passage anticipates James Wright's bleaker Ohio River poems, in which old men and children brave polluted waters and littered shores for the sake of contact, however diminished, with local nature. Roethke's Tittabawasee River, and the Saginaw into which it flows, are still degraded, though more by nonpoint pollution (road runoff and agricultural chemicals) than by contamination flowing out of pipes. "Suburbia: Michigan" remains, unfortunately, an accurate depiction of a powerful influence on midwestern cultural geography: the utilitarian drive to subordinate local landscape and biota to economic concerns.

A line from that poem, almost a casual aside, articulates Roethke's dissent from mainstream midwestern–American values: "Who said, 'Yes, but,' was never a hero" (90). The booster, the tinkerer, and other utilitarian archetypes may be celebrated in Saginaw and America at large, but the poet, Roethke implies, is an outcast. Among those who have questioned material progress—in effect, saying "Yes, but"—we must count Roethke, but in the company of his Romantic precursors. "*Early,* when it really matters," Roethke wrote in his letters, "I read, and really read, Emerson (mostly prose), Thoreau, Whitman, Blake and Wordsworth" (*Selected Letters,* 230). In *Theodore Roethke: An American Romantic* (1979), still one of the best critical studies, Jay Parini argues for Roethke as "the central American Romantic poet of [his] generation . . . a Romantic descended from Blake, Wordsworth, and Yeats, but one whose language is idiomatically American and whose meaning derives from the Emersonian tradition" (15). Like the transcendentalists, Roethke believed in the spiritual significance of nature, in the child's clarity of perception, and in experience over received wisdom. He also continued their critique of utilitarian progressivism: the dominant notion that industrial advancement equals human progress, that the subordination of nature and the individual to technology and the market economy is inevitable, and even to be desired.

As a poet, Roethke naturally turned to metaphor in this task. Emerson, appropriately for the horse-drawn 1800s, writes, "Things are in the saddle / And ride mankind" (*Collected Poems,* 63). Thoreau makes the same point, but specifically of advancing technology, when he writes, "We do not ride on the railroad; it rides upon us" (396). Roethke, as a twentieth-century disciple of Emerson and Thoreau, sought a modern image of the human journey, one resonant with regional implications. In Michigan, birthplace of utilitarian hero Henry Ford and the industry he personifies, that symbol is of course the automobile. Thus in "Highway: Michigan," one of his best early poems, Roethke treats the dominance of the automobile over the landscape and human life:

Here from the field's edge we survey
The progress of the jaded. Mile
On mile of traffic from the town
Rides by. . . .

(31)

From its first word, the preposition "here," this is a poem of place. Roethke favored the words "field" and "edge" for their psychological as well as spatial connotations; they frequently appear in his poems. While obviously suggestive of cultivation and other pastoral values, "field" in Roethke's vocabulary also signifies the embodiment of eternity in the physical world, as in the title poem of his last book, *The Far Field* (1964): "I learned not to fear infinity, / The far field, the windy cliffs of forever" (194).[2] "Edge," a word connoting risk and heightened awareness, implies the marginal realm between states of consciousness, and also what ecologists refer to as "ecotones." These transitional zones between environments—forest and field, for example, or field and stream—are distinguished by maximum biotic diversity and energy exchange. Places favored by many plants and animals, they are of special interest to ecologists and literary naturalists.

The edge in "Highway: Michigan," however, runs between an ever-diminishing pastoral world and the concrete and steel environment of "drivers from production lines." Contrary to the twentieth-century utilitarian myth of the automobile as an instrument of individual freedom and expression, Roethke describes the autoworkers and commuters of Michigan as subordinate to modern transportation technology. That the drivers are "jaded" implies a comparison to horses ridden to exhaustion. To adapt Emerson, "Things are in the driver's seat and ride mankind." Thus the synecdochic clause "Mile / on mile of traffic from the town / Rides by," which endows the cars, collectively "traffic," with agency and control. The passive drivers are mere "prisoners of speed," subordinate to the products of their labor. Far from Henry Ford's vision of the off-duty autoworker "enjoy[ing] with his family the blessing of hours of pleasure in God's great open spaces" (73), these laborers simply wish to escape the factories where they work. Destination is unimportant; they seek refuge not in nature's embrace but in motion, a "mania [that] keeps them on the move." In this vision of industrial America, the only possible escape from sovereign technology is death. The poem concludes with a fatal collision, described with nightmarish understatement as a "meet[ing]" of vehicles: "We shiver at the siren's blast. / One driver, pinned beneath the seat, / Escapes from the machine at last" (31). "Highway: Michigan" succeeds as poetry and as social commentary on the basis of its extended metaphor of the car riding the driver. Because "Suburbia: Michigan," apparently projected as a companion piece, lacks such a unifying conceit, it only at moments transcends its fundamentally prosaic quality. Both poems, however, confirm Roethke's early discernment of social and historical dimensions of the Midwest essential to his writing.

The first of the "Plans for Work" included in Roethke's 1945 application for a Guggenheim grant suggests the terms of that regional consciousness; he proposes "a dramatic-narrative piece in prose and verse about Michigan and Wisconsin, past and present, which would center around the return of Paul Bunyan as a kind of enlightened and worldly folk-hero" (qtd. in Seager, 148). This "first project is hardly to be taken seriously," Seager tells us. "He really did not intend to do anything about Paul Bunyan" (148). Roethke's interest in the topic, however, merits consideration. In his essay "The Round River," Aldo Leopold turns the folklore of Paul Bunyan, who symbolizes the aggressive spirit of resource extraction that razed the pine forests of the upper Midwest, toward a lesson in ecological interdependence. Likewise, Roethke's projected fable would return Bunyan to the Great Lakes not as a prolific exploiter of trees, but as an "enlightened and worldly folk-hero," perhaps chastened by the excesses of the logging era. Given his difficulty with "Suburbia: Michigan," which never made it beyond the drafting stage, Roethke likely would have fared no better with this even more ambitious project. The proposal, however, should be "taken seriously" in that it shows Roethke reimagining midwestern archetypes, considering how symbols of utilitarian individualism might be subverted for Romantic and ecological purposes.

Roethke's second Guggenheim proposal more closely resembles his work in progress: "a series of lyrics about the Michigan countryside which have symbolical values. I have already begun these. They are not mere description, but have at least two levels of reference" (qtd. in Seager, 148). These were the "greenhouse poems," which Roethke had begun soon after the publication of *Open House* in 1941, while teaching creative writing at Penn State. His work accelerated during his residency at Bennington College in Vermont (1943–47), where he met Kenneth Burke and William Carlos Williams, acquaintances crucial to his poetic development. These two men, a literary scholar and a modernist poet who had known each other since the 1920s, encouraged Roethke to abandon the often precious abstraction of his first book, take greater risks with language, and draw more on his own experience. Their influence was such that when Roethke sent a manuscript of his long sequence "The Lost Son" to Williams in 1946, he wrote, "In a sense it's your poem, yours and K. Burke's" (*Selected Letters,* 122).

In terms of Roethke's treatment of place, Williams's influence is the more pertinent. Among the major modernists, Williams alone offered Roethke and other young poets a philosophy and aesthetic of the local. While his most famous dictum, "No ideas but in things" (9), speaks to an insistence on literalism and imagery, Williams's frequent comments on locality in art ground his objectivism in cultural geography. "Place is the only reality," he wrote in 1952, "the true core of the universal. We live in only one place at a time but far from being bound to it, only through it do we realize our freedom. Place then ceases to be a restriction, we do not have to abandon our familiar and known to achieve distinction. . . . [Only if we] make ourselves sufficiently aware of it do we join with others in other places" (qtd. in Peterson, 5). This literary program entailed opposition to the abstraction, elitism, and Eurocentrism of many of Williams's contemporaries. Unlike T. S. Eliot and other famous expatriates, Williams stayed in the United States, practicing medicine in Rutherford, New Jersey, and writing poetry based on his observations of local life. When Roethke first met him in 1944, Williams was working on *Paterson,* the epic poem that he would publish in five books between 1946 and 1963. Like Thoreau's *Walden,* also named for its location, *Paterson* is a book of discovery and inhabitation, its central metaphor being "that a man in himself is a city, beginning, seeking, achieving and concluding his life in ways which the various aspects of a city may embody" (7). Thus Paterson is simultaneously a character in the poem (Dr. Paterson, Williams's alter ego) and the city in New Jersey, personified as a mythical giant lying "in the valley under the Passaic Falls / its spent water forming the outline of his back" (14). In the tradition of Whitman, Williams wrote about an American place using a personal and idiosyncratic American language.

So too would Roethke, who shared with Williams a sense of himself as outsider to the literary establishment. In their correspondence, Williams urged the younger poet to defy the editors of the day, with their predilection for carefully constructed formal verse. Roethke needed to proceed boldly with the greenhouse poems, which represented his true subject matter and style. "These are the best things of yours that I've seen," Williams wrote, beginning a letter that mixed high praise with considered criticism of Roethke's work: "Your great contribution to modern poetry may well be that you have found or are finding a way to express that generosity of spirit in a polished steel mesh or frame that can and must hold it against injury. If you can continue to make poems along that line, as you have shown you can do in this batch of poems, there is no reason why you should not become one of the most distinguished poets of the day. I think here and there you have already done the trick" (qtd. in Kusch, 32–33). Roethke took great encouragement from Williams's response, even confessing to Williams that he had "carried the letter around for a time: something to hold against the world." He needed such affirmation in 1944, after his first greenhouse poems had been rejected by major poetry journals. "I do think the conceptual boys are too much in the saddle: anything observed or simple or sensuous or personal is suspect right now" (*Selected Letters*, 111). Noting Roethke's allusion to Emerson's "things are in the saddle," Robert Kusch argues that "Roethke is distinguishing between a poetry that is spiritless, limited and fully resolved, and one that renews itself by those ranges of associations grouped around the surprises of the earth" (37). In other words, Roethke is after a modern pastoral, one that engages life in the technological era without making a fetish of technique. Williams's statement suggests the unusual symbolic power of Roethke's greenhouse, which contains and protects a Romantic, organically conceived "generosity of spirit" within a modernist-inspired formal structure. By focusing on Michigan landscape and the details of greenhouse operations, Roethke fulfills Williams's belief in "the poet who lives locally, and whose senses are applied no way else than locally to particulars, who is the agent and the maker of all culture" (*Selected Letters*, 225).

Two poems that Williams thought particularly promising were "Cuttings" and "Cuttings *(later)*," which Roethke placed first in *The Lost Son*. These announce botanical life and horticultural processes as the book's central topics, and establish the "two levels of reference," literal and psychological, that Roethke noted in his Guggenheim proposal. By "cuttings" Roethke means small sections removed from a parent plant for propagation. Also known as "starts," they are placed into a nitrogen-rich medium that accelerates root growth, creating new life where death would otherwise set in. The first poem closely observes the process, accelerating movement so that the cuttings seem as active and conscious as Roethke's herons, snakes, and other animals:

> Sticks-in-a-drowse droop over sugary loam,
> Their intricate stem-fur dries;
> But still the delicate slips keep coaxing up water;
> The small cells bulge. . . .

> (35)

The musicality of Roethke's language, persistent throughout the book, suits his subject here. Alliteration, first of "drowse," "droops," and "dries," emphasizes the effects of gravity and cellular death, then suggests a resistant life force, as a sprouting "nub . . . nudges" aside a particle of soil. The same expression of physicality in sound occurs in "Cuttings *(later),*" in which Roethke makes explicit the comparison between plant and human life: "In my veins, in my bones I feel it,— / The small waters seeping upward" (35).

Whitman is a presence here, the poet of "Song of Myself" for whom "a spear of summer grass" infers the transcendental realm (27). "The smallest sprout shows there is really no death," Whitman writes, a declaration central to his life's work, the lush and ever-growing *Leaves of Grass* (32). Like Whitman and Emerson before him, Roethke recognized in the natural world what he would later call a "steady storm of correspondences" (231). The doctrine of correspondence, taken from the Romantics as well as from Plato and mystics like Swedenborg and Boehme, informs Roethke's every natural image, as well as the careful choice of words in "Cuttings *(later)*." Propagation is a "resurrection of dry sticks" that requires no ecclesiastical tradition to give it significance (35). Roethke's mysticism reminds us of Whitman, who taught that "to glance with an eye or show a bean in its pod confounds the learning of all time" (85). Roethke asks of the cuttings, "What saint strained so much, / Rose on such lopped limbs to a new life?" The answer to this rhetorical question is "None"; sacredness has nothing to do with theology, and everything to do with biology, evolution, and the primeval life force that the poet recognizes in his own body and spirit, and that he describes in distinctly botanical terms: "I quail, lean to beginnings, sheath-wet" (35).

The poems immediately following in *The Lost Son* continue the motif of sprouting, of plant life breaking out, at times frighteningly, in the environs of the greenhouse. "Root Cellar" features "[s]hoots [that] dangled and drooped, / Lolling obscenely from mildewed crates" (36); "Weed Puller" evokes the young Theodore working as assigned "[u]nder the concrete benches / Hacking at black hairy roots,— / Those lewd monkey-tails hanging from drainholes." The mythical and psychosexual connotations are obvious; these phallic images and rich smells ("a congress of stinks!") embody a general descent into a subterranean world of unconscious fears and desires. This "perverse life" would seem incoherent and aimless but for the fact that without "lime and dung and ground bones" there would be no "[l]ilies, pale-pink cyclamen, roses, / Whole fields lovely and inviolate" (37). Without regression there is no advancement; without dreams and memories, no poetry, at least not the kind Roethke wished to write. Parini asserts that the greenhouse poems resulted from "one crucial lesson . . . that life *includes* death and is magnified by it." Noting Roethke's intellectual sources as they appear in his 1940s notebooks, he describes them as companions in a mythological journey: "Like Dante venturing into the underworld with Virgil as a guide, Roethke enters the unconscious with Burke leading him and with the spirits of Freud, Jung, and the Romantic poets in attendance. The goal of this quest finds perfect expression in [Roethke's journal] entry: 'All the present has fallen: I am only what I remember'" (68).

At the center of Roethke's memories stood his father, Otto Roethke, an implied presence in the first greenhouse poems and an explicit one in subsequent verses. Otto went to Saginaw as a child, when his family immigrated from Germany in 1872. His father, Wilhelm Roethke, started with twenty-two acres where he grew vegetables and where he later built a greenhouse for the cultivation of flowers. Wilhelm willed the business to his sons, two of whom, Otto and Charles, bought out their brother Emil's share before expanding operations. According to Roethke, the greenhouses were a marvel of Germanic perfectionism, his father "the youngest son of a strange brood, / A Prussian who learned early to be rude / To fools and frauds" (216). In the poem "Otto," collected in *The Far Field,* Roethke characterizes the man's fierce independence and proprietorship, recalling how he fired warning shots at poachers in his game preserve, then "walked toward [them], / Without his rifle, and slapped each one hard." Yet Otto's "hand could fit into a woman's glove," and it was said that "[t]he Indians loved him, and the Polish poor." At once graceful, nurturing, and tough, the greenhouse keeper illustrates Roethke's thesis that "who loves the small can be both saint and boor." This contradictory character appears in the poet's description of his father at work:

> A florist does not woo the beautiful:
> He potted plants as if he hated them.
> What root of his ever denied its stem?
> When flowers grew, their bloom extended him.
>
> (216)

This sternness and deliberation derived, according to Roethke, from his father's ethnicity. The greenhouses, he wrote, were "both heaven and hell, a kind of tropics created in the savage climate of Michigan, where austere German-Americans turned their love of order and their terrifying efficiency into something truly beautiful" (*On the Poet,* 8–9). *Tüchtigkeit,* meaning correctness, doing things right, was a family byword, applied to chores in and around the greenhouses. "If [Otto] loved flowers, the love did not show up in his daily work," Seager writes. "The love was revealed rather in little touches like the harmony of color between the sweet peas and the carnations. No customer would have seen this. He did it for himself because it seemed right, *tüchtig*" (15).

That orderliness and efficiency are consistent with midwestern utilitarianism, to which German immigrants made notable contributions. Papa Otto is a yeoman farmer, a Jeffersonian freeholder whose crop of flowers feeds the human spirit rather than body. His heroic ability to summon forth beauty at times approaches the godlike, as in "Old Florist," the first poem in *The Lost Son* to characterize the man at work. Structuring the poem around present participles and active verbs, Roethke emphasizes his father's competence and life-giving powers:

That hump of a man bunching chrysanthemums
Or pinching-back asters, or planting azaleas,
Tamping and stamping dirt into pots,—
How he could flick and pick
Rotten leaves or yellowy petals. . . .

The whole poem takes place in a mythic realm, beginning with the suggestion of Pan or any number of earth gods in the image of a "hump of a man" hovering over the plants. "Old Florist" resembles a creation story, with the florist as trickster figure. Assonance (as in h*u*mp / b*u*nching / chrysanthem*u*ms) and internal rhyme (tamping and stamping; flick and pick) lend an incantatory music to the proceedings. Wielding powers of life and death as he nurtures the plants and kills weeds and pests, the florist is a figure of gravity, his activity centered and purposeful. The poem's final image confirms this impression of constancy and dominion, as the florist stands "all night watering roses" (40). He is a dutiful yeoman, his individuality inseparable from his work and from the place he has created.

In addition to embodying certain characteristics of the midwestern yeoman farmer, the greenhouse keeper may be considered a version of the region's tinkerer archetype. The greenhouse, after all, is a technological creation maintained by empirical observation and mechanical ingenuity. "In spite of the fact that it was a working commercial greenhouse," Roethke recalls, "a good deal of space, time and money was spent in experiment" (qtd. in Seager, 13). Any number of variables had to be accounted for: temperature, humidity, soil composition, weeds, pests, as well as the environment *outside* the greenhouses. Horticulture entailed a continual struggle with "the savage climate of Michigan," as Roethke calls it, seasonal extremes of heat and cold that cracked glass, dried putty, and generally threatened the greenhouse project. This effort was motivated not only by profit, but also, as Roethke implied, by an inventive, curious, and therefore heroic sensibility.

Such contention between artisan and weather occurs in "Big Wind," a poem based on a particularly violent storm in the Saginaw valley. Roethke sets the scene and mood in the rhetorical question of the poem's first lines:

Where were the greenhouses going,
Lunging into the lashing

> Wind driving water
> So far down the river
> All the faucets stopped?—
>
> (39)

Seager confirmed the story by consulting a cousin of Roethke's and the files of the *Saginaw News,* which featured "a photograph taken the morning after the storm. The water was indeed gone from the river; boats were careened on their sides; and only a few puddles were left in the riverbed. This has happened two or three times in Saginaw's history when the wind was right" (150). With intake from the river temporarily suspended, water pressure dropped to nothing in the city, endangering the greenhouses. This was in November, when the roses were kept alive with steam heat. The situation called for quick thinking:

> So we drained the manure-machine
> For the steam plant,
> Pumping the stale mixture
> Into the rusty boilers. . . .
>
> (39)

The manure machine, as Roethke describes it in a prose account, "was not just a contraption but a veritable Roman bath: about forty by twenty-five feet, with an assembly of pipes, faucets, steam-gauges, [and] a cat-walk for the attending mixer of the brew" (qtd. in Seager, 13). The transfer of malodorous liquid from this machine to the steam plant is an inspired act, reminiscent of the experimentalism of Edison, the Wright brothers, and the young Henry Ford. The plural pronoun "we," however, implies collective effort, the work of a community rather than one resourceful individual. Deliberation and worry are likely shared not only by Otto and his son, but also by other members of the family and their workers, named elsewhere as Max Laurisch, George the watchman, and Fraus Bauman, Schmidt, and Schwartze. Eschewing the solitude associated with the tinkerer archetype, Roethke turns to an extended metaphor of the greenhouse as a ship, with the workers as a loyal crew guiding her through turbulent seas:

But she rode it out,
That old rose-house,
She hove into the teeth of it,
The core and pith of that ugly storm,
Ploughing with her stiff prow,
Bucking into the wind-waves. . . .

. . . . . . . . . . . . . . . .

She sailed until the calm morning,
Carrying her full cargo of roses.

(39)

"Big Wind" is a richly suggestive poem. A rewarding study can be made of its lyrical structure, including the assonance, consonance, and litany of verbs that create such rhythm and drama. Roethke seems to have ancient sagas in mind, *Beowulf* perhaps, not only in the motif of adventure at sea but also in his insistently Anglo-Saxon diction and poetics. (The phrase "wind-waves," for example, is a kenning, a type of metaphorical compound favored by Old English bards.) In this miniature epic, heroism entails human ascendancy over technology, which is wielded not for its own sake but to protect organic beauty: a "cargo of roses." In "Highway: Michigan," Roethke depicts lonely individuals alienated from their work, their place, and one another. Driven by technology, the autoworkers in that poem "flee in what their hands have made" (31). The greenhouse crew of "Big Wind," by contrast, "stayed all night, / Stuffing the holes with burlap" (39). They work together as a community, taking technology by the helm—throwing, as it were, the saddle back on things.

Roethke thereby reconciles, if temporarily, technology and agriculture, utility and aesthetic values in midwestern pastoral ideology. The greenhouse reverses Leo Marx's metaphor for American pastoralism— the "machine in the garden." A "garden in the machine," it symbolizes the possibility of appropriate technology that would sustain rather than destroy nature and human lives. Utilitarian "love of order and terrifying efficiency," which might otherwise create wage slavery and a blighted, monocultural landscape, has been turned "into something truly beautiful": not only roses, but also love and a responsible sense of place in the Saginaw valley of Michigan.

Not that the florist has achieved a perfect harmony of self and nature. In the poem "Moss-Gathering," Roethke remembers a task by which the economy of the greenhouses impinged on "the natural order of things": his job was to hike into the woods in search of moss for use in "lining cemetery baskets." For people who have lost a loved one, such a form of natural beauty can provide solace. But taking the moss from its rightful place, where it is most beautiful, seemed terribly wrong:

> . . . something always went out of me when I dug loose those
>    carpets
> Of green, or plunged to my elbows in the spongy yellowish
>    moss of the marshes:
> And afterwards I always felt mean, jogging back over the
>    logging road. . . .
> . . . . . . . . . . . . . . . . . . . . . . . . . .
> As if I had committed, against the whole scheme of life, a
>    desecration.
>
>                             (38)

That the boy walks home on a logging road connects his experience to the larger context of environmental history. Between the Civil War and First World War, the old-growth white pine forests of Michigan were indiscriminately cut. For a time, Saginaw produced more board feet than any other American city, a dubious distinction it passed to other cities when the local timber gave out. Tremendous fires, fed on slashings left over from the cut, further devastated what forest remained. The ecological toll was heavy: the loss of ancient woods, the destruction of rivers, the extinction of animals such as the grayling (a beautiful native fish) and the passenger pigeon. In a region of second-growth forests and intense use of land for agriculture and industry, locations evocative of former natural grandeur assume a greater beauty and solemnity. Such are the marshes in "Moss-Gathering," a poem about sacred places and their violation. Roethke's narrative reminds us of the need for wildness in populated country, a truth that midwestern agrarians have too often disregarded.

Roethke's personal history, as well as that of his region, troubles his quest for a restored unity with nature. The greenhouse poems are more poignant if read in regard to two biographical facts: the death of his father when Roethke was fifteen, and the poet's manic depression, which resulted in serious mental episodes and institutionalization. The poetic search for reconciliation with his powerful and sometimes harsh father, and for consolation of his grief and psychological distress, inspired the title poem of Roethke's second book: "The Lost Son," not only the longest but also "the central poem in Roethke's canon" (Parini, 96).

"The Lost Son" has occasioned more close reading than any of Roethke's other poems. Parini interprets it according to Freudian ideas about regression and patterns of myth and ritual described by Carl Jung, Mircea Eliade, and Joseph Campbell. Such approaches have a long history in Roethke scholarship, beginning with Kenneth Burke's seminal 1950 essay "The Vegetal Radicalism of Theodore Roethke." Burke sees nature imagery in "The Lost Son" as "a kind of psychology, an empathetic vocabulary for expressing rudimentary motives felt, rightly or wrongly, to transcend particular periods of time." Flowers, for example, "are children in general, or girls specifically" (85). Following Burke's precedent, critics have read the poem as "an appeal for order . . . a request for spiritual survival in the primal sucking waters patterned on the immemorial night journey" (Sullivan, 41–42) and as a "profoundly cathartic work" concerned with "the poet's private conflict of devotion and rivalry that formed the basis of his filial anxiety" (Kalaidjian, 51).

Another close explication of the poem is not called for here, but rather a discussion of its setting in Saginaw and modification of pastoral convention. "The Lost Son" depicts an emotional and spiritual crisis occurring in two landscapes: the literal one around the greenhouses and the psychic one of Roethke's fears, memories, and grief. If one keeps the geographical dimension in mind, Roethke's psychic symbolism becomes clearer. In other words, the mental episode recounted in "The Lost Son" *takes place*.

The first fact of the poem is that Otto is dead and that his son is "lost" in grief. Titled "The Flight," the first section shows the poet moving through the local landscape, seeking consolation in nature. He begins in the graveyard, mourning at his father's tomb:

> At Woodlawn I heard the dead cry:
> I was lulled by the slamming of iron,
> A slow drip over stones,
> Toads brooding wells.

"Woodlawn" refers to Oakwood Cemetery in Saginaw, where Roethke's father was buried and where the poet's ashes would one day be interred. By renaming the place, Roethke establishes a pastoral setting, a "lawn" or "pasture of flat stones" as he subsequently calls it. In this ironic pastoral, however, there is no ease or sense of nature's benevolence. He summons familiar animal spirits—snails, birds, and worms. But nature seems to mock him in his distress: "All the leaves stuck out their tongues," and when he "[f]ished in an old wound . . . / Nothing nibbled [his] line, / Not even the minnows came" (50).

The speaker then moves through the cemetery, "[r]unning lightly over spongy grounds, / Past the pasture of flat stones." This ironically pastoral scene includes not only headstones and "three elms," but also "sheep strewn on a field" above the Tittabawasee River, toward which the mourner turns (51). In "The Premonition," a poem in *Open House* that anticipates the autobiographical emphasis of Roethke's subsequent writing, he contrasts the permanence of the river with the transience of human life. He remembers how Otto "dipped his hand in the shallow" so that "[w]ater ran over and under / Hair on a narrow wrist bone" (6). In "The Lost Son" he searches along the river that his father taught him to love for some sign that will help him rise from despair:

> Hunting along the river,
> Down among the rubbish, the bug-riddled foliage,
> By the muddy pond-edge, by the bog-holes,
> By the shrunken lake, hunting, in the heat of summer.

From that literal setting the poet turns to metaphor. The object of his search becomes a symbolic animal, a ratlike creature that feels like "the skin of a cat / And the back of an eel." Subsequent sections of the poem take us into "The Pit" and "The Gibber," landscapes of pain in the poet's mind. Roethke takes his language as close as possible to the experience of mania—chaotic, panicked, and regressive:

> The weeds whined,
> The snakes cried,
> The cows and briars
> Said to me: Die.

$$(51–52)$$

After passing through this psychic underworld we surface in Roethke's childhood, walking through the greenhouses at night. The memory evokes feelings of security ("a single light / Swinging by the fire-pit") and self-transcendence. While the crisis has played out in "the heat of summer," the final two sections occur in winter. The season represents calm and clarity after emotional heat and confusion:

> The light in the morning came slowly over the white
> Snow.
> There were many kinds of cool
> Air.
> Then came steam.
>
> Pipe-knock.
>
> (54)

From darkness we emerge into light, from "the kingdom of bang and blab" into the domain of Otto, the greenhouse keeper who kept the boiler running and therefore the plants alive (51). His arrival, which signifies life, hope, and the ordering of chaos, is announced by "Pipe-knock." In his essay "Open Letter," Roethke explains the dual meaning of this phrase. "With the coming of steam," he writes, "the pipes begin knocking violently in a greenhouse. But 'Papa,' or the florist, as he approached, often would knock the pipe he was smoking on the sides of the benches, or on the pipes. Then, with the coming of steam and 'papa'—the papa on earth and heaven are blended—there is the sense of motion in the greenhouse, my symbol for the whole of life, a womb, a heaven-on-earth" (*On the Poet,* 39).

Human labor, with technology well in hand, has sustained life and beauty in what might otherwise be a dead time. Winter's stillness and quiet provide the solace that the lost son vainly sought in exuberant summer. Having inverted pastoral convention by celebrating winter instead of spring or summer, the poem concludes with a tentative resolution:

> A lively understandable spirit
> Once entertained you.
> It will come again.
> Be still.
> Wait.
>
> (55)

That spirit is one of place, identified with Otto, the greenhouses, and the Michigan countryside of Roethke's childhood. The epiphany here deferred occurs, joyfully and deeply, in the book's final poems, in which happiness is more affecting after the struggle recounted in "The Lost Son." Roethke writes of the darker poems in *The Lost Son* beginning "in the mire; as if man is no more than a shape writhing from the old rock." The regional sources of this emergence strike him as essential:

> This may be due, in part, to the Michigan from which I come. Sometimes one gets the feeling that not even the animals have been there before; but the marsh, the mire, the Void, is always there, immediate and terrifying. It is a splendid place for schooling the spirit. It is America.
>
> None the less, in spite of all the muck and welter, the dark, the *dreck* of these poems, I count myself among the happy poets. (*On the Poet,* 40)

Plants and animals, therefore, again reassure in the verses following the title poem of *The Lost Son.* One of these, "A Field of Light," conveys Roethke's association of happiness with space and sight even in its title. There, Emerson's "naked eyeball" looks out at nature with Roethkean attentiveness to its "lovely diminutives":

> I saw the separateness of all things!
> My heart lifted up with the great grasses;
> The weeds believed me, and the nesting birds.
>
> (60)

This vision occurs in morning, which Roethke associated with the child's clarity of perception. After the mythical night of despair, after a journey through bogs of obsession and fear, the poet returns to vision and praise. In "The Shape of the Fire," which concludes *The Lost Son,* he weaves memories of morning in the greenhouse and sundown on a Michigan lake. Happiness, an emotion Roethke leaves unnamed but not undefined, is synonymous with vision: "To see cyclamen veins become clearer in early sunlight, / And mist lifting out of the brown cat-tails." It is also synonymous with patience, something he learned from his father's art, and science, of horticulture:

To know that light falls and fills, often without our knowing,
As an opaque vase fills to the brim from a quick pouring,
Fills and trembles at the edge yet does not flow over,
Still holding and feeding the stem of the contained flower.

(64)

The work of Roethke's middle period at first reinforces the experimentalism of *The Lost Son*. *Praise to the End!* (1951) continues his exploration of the child's dream world, with further excursions into Joycean and Mother Goose–inspired wordplay. The book's title, taken from Wordsworth's long autobiographical poem *The Prelude,* reminds us of Roethke's Romantic heritage while suggesting the direction his writing would take: toward a dialogue with his poetic masters and toward traditional forms. In several poems he assumes something of the style, and even personality, of Dante, Ralegh, Davies, Blake, and Yeats. "Imitation," Roethke writes in the essay "How to Write like Someone Else," "is one of the great methods, perhaps *the* method, of learning to write. The ancients, the Elizabethans, knew this, profited by it, and were not disturbed" (*On the Poet,* 69). So Roethke could confess, in "Four for Sir John Davies":

I take this cadence from a man named Yeats;
I take it, and I give it back again:
For other tunes and other wanton beats
Have tossed my heart and fiddled through my brain.

(101)

As a result, Roethke's poems became more philosophical, less place centered and literal. The symbols remain the same: the tree, the worm or snail, the river and field, all originating in the Michigan countryside of his youth. But setting is indefinite, for the most part, in *The Waking* (1953) and *Words for the Wind* (1958), books less "American" in subject matter and language than *The Lost Son*. It is as if Roethke, having broken new ground with his second book, wished to consolidate his progress and to master certain technical aspects of his craft. Again, to quote his prose: "In a time when the romantic notion of the inspired writer still has considerable credence, true 'imitation' takes a certain courage. One dares to stand up to a great style, to compete with papa" (*On the Poet,* 69–70).

The choice of the word "papa" to signify the great poets reveals that Roethke saw himself as competing not only with Blake and Yeats, but also with his actual father, Otto. Lines from "The Lost Son" come to mind: "Scurry of warm over small plants. / Ordnung! Ordnung! / Papa is coming!" (54). Roethke relates mastery of poetic craft to his father's expertise with plants and horticultural techniques. Both poet and florist work with forms—greenhouses, fields, villanelles, stanzas—that give shape or order (*ordnung*) to nature. Using rhyme, meter, and allusion with the same *tüchtigkeit* that Otto applied to his arrangement of flowers, Roethke is a literary pastoralist even when writing in modes other than pastoral. He admits as much in "The Swan," one of many traditional love poems written to his young wife, Beatrice: "I am my father's son, I am John Donne / Whenever I see her with nothing on" (135).

The craftsmanship and competitiveness of Roethke's middle period can also be understood in relation to his desire for national and international esteem. To achieve a reputation as a major poet he felt it necessary to demonstrate ability with diverse poetic forms and subjects, and to place himself, by association, among immortals like Donne, Blake, and Yeats. But good work was not its own reward; Roethke craved awards, good reviews, promotions, and pay raises as public acknowledgment of his success. According to Seager, Roethke "played poetry the way he played tennis, competitively. . . . He was like Hemingway. To view literature as a contest to be won is a Saginaw Valley, Middle-Western, American set of mind" (192). This attitude appeared in Roethke's jealousy of fellow poets—the reputation of Robert Lowell being of particular concern—and in the pathology of his manic episodes. Seager describes the fantasies about a lost family fortune, the get-rich schemes, and plans for political power that typically accompanied Roethke's hospitalization for delusion and erratic behavior. There were "dark hints of treachery, skulduggery by trusted relatives . . . something criminal to do with the sale of the greenhouse after his father's death" (175). All of these fears might be assuaged by public recognition and better pay as a professor of creative writing.

Roethke always felt that poetry was unappreciated in America. At times, in his notebooks and at parties and poetry readings, he reacted to this state of affairs by adopting the persona of a social outcast or criminal. He delighted in relating apocryphal tales about his college years in

Ann Arbor during Prohibition, when he had supposedly been on close terms with the gangsters of Detroit and Chicago. Eventually his fantasies ran to the opposite extreme, toward social acceptance and influence. "Hell," he told Seager, "a poet ought to be as big a guy in a town as a banker" (45). If American society is artless and utilitarian, artists should demand the respect accorded professionals whose work is more obviously "productive" or "useful."

Many of Seager's stories follow that pattern: Roethke meeting a governor, demanding that he be introduced as a *poet,* not a professor; Roethke in the back of a patron's Rolls Royce, scribbling to his wife a note that read, "Don't act impressed"; Roethke at a job interview, telling the president of Bennington College, "I may look like a beer salesman, but I'm a poet."[3] There was a Romantic bravado to all of this, something like Beethoven's arrogance toward the nobility. But Roethke was also acting on democratic impulse. This was an immigrant's son, a proud man who had pulled weeds, shoveled manure, and worked in a Saginaw pickle factory. Roethke longed for the kind of recognition that Pablo Neruda enjoyed in Chile, and Dylan Thomas in Wales. "I mean almost nothing to the people of my own state," he wrote in 1955, "to the man in the street—and desire that regard most passionately" (*On the Poet,* 15). Seager elaborates: "He wanted all his life to be widely read, and since he grew up in it, he was aware of the almost corrosive apathy of the public at large, aware and oppressed by it and he wanted to explode it if he could. Poetry, he believed, should have an acknowledged civic place in the life of his time and a large part of his work as a teacher was an unremitting labor to create an audience for it" (126).

The difficulty of this project lay not only in the reluctance of Americans to embrace poetry and poets, but also in the nature of Roethke's writing. He wrote in a high literary style about private concerns: his memories, fears, and mystical yearnings. Reading his poetry, particularly that of the middle period, one would hardly guess that Roethke had lived through two world wars, the Great Depression, and the postwar expansion of American economic and military power. These topics do appear in his notebooks, as edited by David Wagoner in *Straw for the Fire* (1974). In the 1950s, for example, he brooded over the cold war, cultural mediocrity, and his frustrated search for a public voice. He writes, "Democracy: where the semi-literate make laws and the illiterate enforce them" (240). And elsewhere: "Was it my time for writing poems about McCarthy . . . my time for dictating memoranda about what's wrong with America . . . or my time for crying?" (88).

Missing from these musings is an essential context, one that made *The Lost Son* so successful: place. When Roethke found a public voice, it would not be a political one addressed to current events. What broadened his vision was a late meditation on American landscape, apparently originating in a cross-country trip he made in 1950, the first time he had seen the nation by automobile. The poetic result of Roethke's excursion was the "North American Sequence," six long poems that open his last book, the posthumously published *The Far Field*. These poems—"The Longing," "Meditation at Oyster River," "Journey to the Interior," "The Long Waters," "The Far Field," and "The Rose"—take a sweeping view of the continent, from the Pacific Northwest to the Great Plains and the poet's beloved Michigan. Borrowing Whitman's long lines and insistent cataloging of physical nature, Roethke strives in these poems for equanimity in the face of death and for mystical union with the forms of nature— plants, animals, rock, and water—that he has encountered in particular places in North America. By means of a recurring metaphor of automobile travel, Roethke symbolizes transcendence as "a long journey out of the self," which is also a "journey to the interior" of North America (187).

Roethke's American vision begins as a response to the despair and alienation of modern industrial society, which he characterizes in "The Longing" as a "kingdom of stinks and sighs." The problem is one of ecopsychology, to use a recent term for the relation of environmental conditions to emotional well-being:

> How to transcend this sensual emptiness?
> (Dreams drain the spirit if we dream too long.)
> In a bleak time, when a week of rain is a year,
> The slag-heaps fume at the edge of the raw cities:
> The gulls wheel over their singular garbage,
> The great trees no longer shimmer;
> Not even the soot dances.
>
> (181)

The geography here is generalized, the "raw cities" as suggestive of New York or Detroit as of Roethke's adopted home of Seattle, Washington. This

picture of urban anomie is typically modernist, recalling major works of
Crane, Pound, and Eliot. Roethke, however, does not share Crane's confidence in technology, Pound's economic determinism, or Eliot's aristo-
cratic Anglicanism. The third section of "The Longing" is specifically an-
timodernist, first in its response to the problem of "sensual emptiness":

> I would with the fish, the blackening salmon, and the mad
>     lemmings,
> The children dancing, the flowers widening.
> Who sighs from far away?
> I would unlearn the lingo of exasperation, all the distortions of
>     malice and hatred;
> I would believe my pain: and the eye quiet on the growing rose;
> I would delight in my hands, the branch singing, altering the
>     excessive bird;
>
>                              (182)

The catalog recalls Whitman's injunction to "Love the earth and sun and
the animals," to "re-examine all you have been told at school or church
or in any book, [and] dismiss whatever insults your own soul" so that
"your very flesh shall be a great poem" (11). Despite his admiration of
European culture and dismay at American provincialism (he refers in his
notes to a "sense [in which] American means eccentric, warped, and confined"), Roethke rejects modernist pessimism and cosmopolitanism; he
reasserts Whitman's faith in an integrated self and a democratic cultural
geography (*Straw*, 244). The symbol for self remains Whitman's blade of
grass, at once ephemeral and eternal, particular and universal: "A leaf, I
would love the leaves, delighting in the redolent disorder of this mortal
life" (182).

Elsewhere in *The Far Field*, Roethke invokes Whitman as his American muse: "Be with me, Whitman, maker of catalogues: For the world
invades me again" (212). The conclusion of "The Longing," however,
surpasses the ethical and ecological limits of Whitman's pastoralism:

> On the Bullhead, in the Dakotas, where the eagles eat well,
> In the country of few lakes, in the tall buffalo grass at the base
>     of the clay buttes,
> In the summer heat, I can smell the dead buffalo,

> The stench of their damp fur drying in the sun,
> The buffalo chips drying.
>
> (182–83)

This moment in Roethke's collected poetry represents his arrival at a mature land aesthetic. He now sees the prairie in relation to ecological history, as does Aldo Leopold, "under the bellies of the buffalo" (*Round River,* 33). Whitman had imagined the prairie becoming the heart of American agriculture, industry, and therefore of population and national identity. Exploration, conquest, and development, however, resulted in the diminishment of natural diversity regretted by Leopold and Roethke and symbolized by both in the tragic near extinction of the American bison. Rejecting abstract notions of American nationhood, Roethke uses prepositions and geographical names to insist on place as the true source of culture. America to him is rivers, lakes, and landforms; it is the Bullhead and the Dakotas, not flags, anthems, and myths of American exceptionalism.

Roethke, however, goes a step further than Leopold in his ethical and aesthetic perspective on American cultural history and geography. The Native American, excluded from Whitman's America and Willa Cather's Nebraska, and only mentioned by Leopold in respect to Wisconsin, appears in the final stanza of "The Longing," the introductory poem of Roethke's "North American Sequence":

> Old men should be explorers?
> I'll be an Indian.
> Oglala?
> Iroquois.
>
> (183)

The passage invites a number of interpretations. Roethke's initial question responds to T. S. Eliot, who asserts in *Four Quartets,* "Home is where one starts from. . . . Old men should be explorers / Here and there do not matter" (189). Eliot's notion of "exploration" is in keeping with orthodox Christianity, which distinguishes God from the Creation and eternity from worldly experience. Time, not place, is the sacred dimension in this cosmology, by which Eliot's expatriation might be justified as a courageous identification with universal rather than regional currents of thought. The *Four Quartets* do contend for Eliot's American connections, specifically the Mississippi River and Massachusetts coastal scenes of his childhood. "We will not cease from exploration," he writes in this regard, "[a]nd the end of all our exploring / Will be to arrive where we started / And know the place for the first time" (208). But this knowledge is metaphysical, not phenomenological; Eliot abstracts place, observing North America at a distance rather than involving himself intimately with the continent's history and landscape. For Roethke, however, home is not merely a point of departure, and "here and there" are of the utmost importance. By refusing to adopt Eliot's explorer archetype he rejects the expatriate poet's Anglo-Catholicism; by assuming that of the Indian, he professes an autochthonous spirituality of place.

Roethke's declaration also bespeaks familiarity with critic Philip Rahv's "Paleface and Redskin." First published in 1939 and included in the book *Image and Idea* (1949; revised 1957), Rahv's essay famously divides Anglo-American literature into two camps representing "a dichotomy between experience and consciousness . . . between energy and sensibility, between conduct and theories of conduct, between life conceived as an opportunity and life conceived as a discipline" (1). Whitman is Rahv's prototypical "redskin," one who "accepts his environment, at times to the degree of fusion with it"; Henry James exemplifies the "paleface," a highbrow who "continually hankers after religious norms, tending toward a refined estrangement from reality" (2). Rahv argues that these figures personify a divided consciousness in American literature, a lack of "balance of impulse with sensitiveness, of natural power with philosophical depth" (3). Writers in the mid-twentieth century, Rahv implies, needed to reconcile this dichotomy by drawing on both traditions. Yet while he acknowledges the strengths and deficiencies of both camps, Rahv privileges James and the genteel tradition, which he believes is more likely to overcome the dissociation of sense from sensibility.[4] The "paleface," he writes, "was frequently able to transcend or to deviate sharply from the norms of his group, and he is to be credited with most of the rigors and charms of the classic American books" (6).

By studying poets from Donne to Yeats and Eliot, Roethke advanced technically and intellectually. Many of his notable late poems, such as "In a Dark Time," continue in the metaphysical and formalist vein of his work midcareer. By stating "I'll be an Indian," however, Roethke dissents from Rahv's elitism, declaring himself instead for a cultural stance closer to that of Whitman and Williams. The project of *The Far Field* is in fact the reconciliation of experience and consciousness, but in terms of place, landscape, and memory, both personal and cultural. In this regard Roethke's declaration echoes D. H. Lawrence's insistence in *Studies in Classic American Literature* (1923) on "blood consciousness," by which Lawrence means a spirituality that embraces sensuous bodily experience. While not uncritical of Whitman (whom he described as monomaniacal and lacking in moral differentiation), Lawrence saw Whitman as the first American writer to free the body from puritanical shame and restraint. By developing "blood consciousness," as did Whitman, the Anglo-American can overcome alienation from nature and the impulse to dominate nature. The white man's spirit, Lawrence writes, "can cease to be the opposite and negative of the red man's spirit. It can open into a new great area of consciousness, in which there is room for the red spirit too" (61).

Whereas Rahv and Lawrence merely appropriate the Indian as a convenient symbol, Roethke's reference to Indians is also geographical and historical. His identification with the Iroquois rather than the Oglala Sioux turns him eastward from the Great Plains to his origin in the Great Lakes watershed (the Iroquois homeland includes Lake Ontario and the St. Lawrence valley). Both tribes, however, figure prominently in American history for their determined resistance to conquest by white invaders. Roethke, Seager tells us, planned to follow up on the "North American Sequence" by writing "an epic dealing with the injustices done to the Indians and based on an automobile journey across the continent where he would pass the site of each tribe's final defeat or betrayal" (279). Roethke's successful 1959 application for a Ford Foundation grant refers to this project as "beginning with a long dirge which will express through suggestive and highly charged symbolical language the guilts we Americans feel as a people for our mistakes and misdeeds in history and in time. I believe, in other words, that it behooves us to be humble before the eye of history." Roethke meant to address the central failing of American pastoral after Whitman: its elision of Native American experience and denial of the nation's violent past. By exposing "some of the lies of history; our triumphs of rage and cunning; our mania, our despairs; our furtive joys," he would "attempt to expiate some of our collective mistakes" (qtd. in Seager, 257–58).

One interpretation of this final, uncompleted project casts Roethke as "the regional writer impressively widening his range to become the national epic poet, and even more, an American conscience in the world's history." So argues Kermit Vanderbilt, a colleague of Roethke's at the University of Washington who describes *The Far Field* as "the logical culmination of Roethke's poetic and American sojourn out of the Midwest and through his native land to maturity and reconciliation in the Northwest" (203). Speaking of "Michigan beginnings and Northwest consummations,"Vanderbilt makes a case, as the title of his essay has it, for "Theodore Roethke as a Northwest Poet" (207).

There is justice to Vanderbilt's claim. Roethke wrote sensuously and specifically of Washington State in "North American Sequence," evoking a place "[w]here the fresh and salt waters meet, / And the sea-winds move through the pine trees, / A country of bays and inlets, and small streams flowing seaward" (190). The ocean figures in these poems much as in Whitman's "Out of the Cradle Endlessly Rocking"; before its depth and immensity, the poet reconciles himself to death (that of his beloved father, as well as his own, which was not long in coming) and loss (of his childhood, of innocence and grace). In the final lines of "The Long Waters," for example, he perceives "in the advancing and retreating waters" of the Pacific the trinity of his life restored: father, son, and the holy spirit of the greenhouse:

> The shape that came from my sleep, weeping:
> The eternal one, the child, the swaying vine branch,
> The numinous ring around the opening flower,
> The friend that runs before me on the windy headlands,
> Neither voice nor vision.

The lost son here propitiates Otto, the godlike father who proved too soon mortal. Roethke's mythic quest has led him from light to dark and to light again, from primal unity through disintegration and finally to a restored oneness of self and nature: "I lose and find myself in the long water; / I am gathered together once more; / I embrace the world" (192).

Roethke's ties to the Pacific Coast, however, have been overstated, his midwestern character too readily slighted. In light of the poet's long reflection on the region's landscape and cultural archetypes, Vanderbilt's more extravagant claims ring falsely; it is patently untrue that "Roethke felt no spirit of place in the environs of Saginaw" or that he "was never a midwestern regionalist" (189–90). Even in the "North American Sequence," his most "northwestern" work, Roethke returns to Michigan in every poem. Engaged in "Meditation at Oyster River," for example, he contemplates "the first trembling of a Michigan brook in April" and "the Tittebawasee [*sic*], in the time between winter and spring" (185). In "Journey to the Interior" he similarly recalls driving on a "highway ribboning out in a straight line to the North, / To the sand dunes and fish flies," past "wooden stores of silvery pine and weather-beaten red courthouses (187–88). "The Far Field" evokes his father's Saginaw property, "[a]t the field's end, in the corner missed by the mower, / Where the turf drops off into a grass-hidden culvert," littered with the remains of animals, flowers, and "broken machinery" (193).

Roethke finally unites his northwestern present and midwestern past in "The Rose," which dismisses "those to whom place is unimportant," an oblique reference to T. S. Eliot, who uses an abstracted rose in several poems to symbolize a distinctly Christian version of transcendence. Observing the Pacific Ocean and a "rose in the sea-wind" that "[s]tays in its true place," Roethke reconciles with his father and with the Midwest. He expresses preference for actual rather than merely symbolic flowers, for the reality of sacred place instead of a promised hereafter:

> . . . I think of roses, roses,
> White and red, in the wide six-hundred-foot greenhouses,
> And my father standing astride the cement benches,
> Lifting me high over the four-foot stems, the Mrs. Russells,
>     and his own elaborate hybrids,
> And how those flowerheads seemed to flow toward me, to
>     beckon me, only a child, out of myself.
>
> What need for heaven, then,
> With that man, and those roses?
>                                                     (196–97)

In stressing Roethke's midwestern dimension, there is no need to diminish the significance of the Pacific Coast to his ultimate vision of North American cultural geography. He was indeed a northwestern poet, not only in the imagery of his late verse, but also in the legacy he left in Seattle. By many accounts, Roethke virtually created the poetry scene in his adopted city, through his pioneering work in the teaching of creative writing and by the climate created by his presence. Internationally known poets came to read in Seattle "or detoured there en route down or up the coast because Roethke had made the Northwest a vital corner of American poetry" (Vanderbilt, 200–201). If a tradition of northwestern poetry exists, Roethke stands at the head; major writers of the region indebted to his example include David Wagoner, Carolyn Kizer (both students of Roethke's at the University of Washington), Richard Hugo, and William Stafford (Vanderbilt, 213). Critic Lars Nordström extends this list to include Gary Snyder, poet of northern California and preeminent spokesperson for the bioregional movement. That Roethke even affected the subsequent renaissance of Native American writing in the Northwest and elsewhere is suggested in "Lines for Roethke Twenty Years after His Death" by Duane Niatum. A poet and editor who belongs to Washington's Klallam tribe, Niatum eulogizes the late poet as one who "asked us to hear the softest vocable of wind, / whether slow or swift, rising or falling to earth; / its fragments will drop into place in the end" (103). Roethke's writing and a fortunate visit to his poetry class, Niatum reveals in the preface to his collected poems, "directed me to the right lyrical road" (*Drawings*, 9).

The fact remains, however, that Roethke named his last book *The Far Field,* not *The Windy Cliffs of Forever;* his title evokes midwestern rather than northwestern landscape. That the "field" is "far" suggests not only nostalgia for the beloved places and people of his childhood, but also that the reformation of pastoral ideology, in Roethke's poetry and in midwestern culture as a whole, had only begun. Reading the "North American Sequence" and the Ford Foundation project in light of the poet's psychobiography, Allan Seager argues for Saginaw as Roethke's spiritual and cultural *axis mundi:* "If we think in terms of the growth of Ted's mind, it seems to have taken nearly his whole lifetime to come to terms emotionally and spiritually with the presences of the Saginaw Valley, his father, his mother, the greenhouse, the field and its creatures.

. . . The epic he had planned may have started from the memories of what he had heard there of the debasement of the Chippewas and the extinction of the Sauks" (279).

Roethke's migration resembles the departure of earlier midwestern writers who believed they could best depict the region from a distance. Lamenting in his notebook "the Siberian pitilessness, the essential ruthlessness of the Middle West as I knew it," Roethke echoes Sherwood Anderson, Willa Cather, and Sinclair Lewis on midwestern utilitarianism and cultural isolation (*Straw,* 98). Unlike those authors, however, Roethke wished to maintain residence in the Midwest. He sought professorships at Michigan colleges on several occasions and taught briefly at Michigan State College (now University) before succumbing to his first major mental episode. He repeatedly returned to Saginaw, especially during the writing of *The Lost Son,* to absorb place details and atmosphere necessary for his poetry. Ultimately, the University of Washington worked around Roethke's health problems, and it was there that he completed *The Lost Son* and subsequent books. Washington's retention, therefore, of Roethke's manuscripts is quite deserved, as is every benefit of their association with his life and work. That key individuals in Michigan failed to recognize Roethke's greatness (and even, as Seager reveals, conspired against his employment in the state) demonstrates the underdeveloped regional consciousness and persistent provinciality of many in the Midwest.[5] Roethke, like many midwestern writers before him, had to find his own path back to place, even if his place was not ready to embrace itself in him. His path led, necessarily perhaps, through the Pacific Northwest.

Roethke's midwestern legacy is evident, as we will see, in the poetry of James Wright and Jim Harrison, both of whom delved further into the nation's history of environmental destruction and genocidal assault on native peoples. Both work in "the Roethkean mode" that Harry Williams, author of *"The Edge Is What I Have": Theodore Roethke and After* (1977), attributes to Wright and Robert Bly, poets sharing "Roethke's repugnance for a high-speed, technocratic society in their poetry, a poetry that strives for an insistence on a personal but archetypal autonomy as a prelude to their animistic themes" (155). The Roethkean mode of pastoral is also evident in the poetry of writers associated with landscapes of Roethke's home state of Michigan. Besides Harrison, poets with a transcendental sense of Michigan include Dan Gerber and Judith Minty.[6] While Gerber's Michigan poems often evoke Roethkean "minimals" in the landscape, Minty's often suggest what Roethke might have written had he stayed in his home state and meditated on the Great Lakes rather than on the Pacific Ocean. Thomas Lynch, whose poem "Learning Gravity" refers to Roethke's 1935 stay at Mercywood Sanitarium near Ann Arbor, has written memorably of his work as an undertaker in Milford, Michigan. Having learned the profession from his father, Lynch derives truths from his work much as Roethke learned about life and death in his father's greenhouse. Finally, Philip Levine and Jim Daniels have traveled further than any other poets down Roethke's "Highway: Michigan"; Levine's book *They Feed They Lion* (1972) and Daniels's *Places/Everyone* (1985) offer indelible portraits of factory work and the industrial landscape of Detroit, automobile capital of Michigan, the United States, and the world.[7] While diverse in style, these poets all portray midwestern life and landscape, after Roethke, in tension between the machine and the garden, between industrialism and the pastoral ideal.

Roethke was not the first writer to explore that conflict, but he was the first to articulate it in poetry of undisputed greatness. Many of his best poems came out of his middle period, when he tended to traditional forms and metaphysical symbolism. His late period is distinguished by the "North American Sequence," with its varied settings and long, Whitmanesque lines. Yet *The Lost Son* remains at the center of Roethke's oeuvre, the most unified of his books and that by which all of his poetry must be read. Poems as much of place as of mind, the greenhouse verses reflect a landscape simultaneously symbolic and literal, in which universal themes of love, loss, suffering, and redemption play out in a specific geographical and historical context: the upper Midwest as experienced by German immigrants at the beginning of the twentieth century. Roethke sought and sometimes achieved harmony between local, American sounds and European lyricism, between nature's elusive minimals and a transcendental vision of integrity and joy. The note is clearly struck in "Once More, the Round," the last poem in Roethke's last book and, appropriately, the last word in this chapter:

Now I adore my life
With the Bird, the abiding Leaf,
With the Fish, the questing Snail
And the Eye altering all . . .

. . . . . . . . . . . . . . . .

And everything comes to One,
As we dance on, dance on, dance on.

(243)

# five

# James
# Wright

One day the demons of America must be placated, the
ghosts must be appeased, the Spirit of Place atoned for.
Then the true passionate love for American soil will appear. As yet, there is too much menace in the landscape.

—D. H. Lawrence, *Studies in Classic American Literature*

Among Roethke's students at the University of Washington during the
1950s was James Wright, who remembered his teacher as "a genuine
poet . . . one of the chosen ones" (*Collected Prose,* 155). Later writers have
come to think of Wright in similar terms. Born and raised in the industrial city of Martins Ferry, Ohio, across the Ohio River from West Virginia, Wright was a self-described "jaded pastoralist" who saw the earth
from the perspective of his native Ohio valley as "rifted paradise": a
beautiful place significantly degraded by human inhabitation and industry (328, 3).[1] In his pastoral poetry Wright struggles between contrary
views of the humanized landscape, the human body, and the efficacy of
poetry in making sense of a seemingly fallen world. Some of Wright's
poems are set in a pastoral paradise, like the "field of sunlight" in the
poem "Lying in a Hammock at William Duffy's Farm in Pine Island,
Minnesota," where even the "droppings of last year's horses / Blaze up
into golden stones" (122). At such moments Wright tends to a Whitmanian physicality, as in the final lines of "Northern Pike": "There must be
something very beautiful in my body, / I am so happy" (217). More

often, however, Wright speaks of a "loneliness of body," of "the rotting slit of my body," analogous to the corruption of Ohio and its much-abused river (205–6). He despairs then of himself, of nature, and of the significance of his work as a poet. Lines from the poem "Many of Our Waters: Variations on a Poem by a Black Child" encapsulate Wright's connection of landscape, body, and poetry. They are spoken to the polluted Ohio River, one of Wright's major images and settings:

> Oh my back-broken beloved Ohio.
> I, too, was beautiful, once,
> Just like you.
> We were both still a little
> Young, then.
> Now, all I am is a poet,
> Just like you.
>
> (212)

Wright is of a divided mind about Ohio, the Midwest, and America as a whole; his native country is by turns a garden and a graveyard. Torn between celebration and bereavement, Wright wishes alternately to embrace and escape place, person, and poetry, the sources of his joy and grief.

This duality stemmed from both experience and temperament. Wright's childhood coincided with the Great Depression, which hit hard in Martins Ferry and neighboring areas, depending as they did on coal mines, steel mills, and factories for employment. Dudley Wright, the poet's father, was often laid off from his job at a glass company, and the family changed residences several times. "By the time I was ten years old," Wright recalls in his "Childhood Sketch," "we had lived in at least half a dozen houses, which were scattered apart from one another as widely as possible in a small town of 16,000 inhabitants" (*Collected Prose,* 330). James C. Dougherty suggests that the "compassion and economic insecurity that characterize so many of Wright's poems probably have their roots in the financial catastrophe" of the Depression (4). Vagrants, criminals, and lonely poverty-stricken girls populate his work; anger at cruelty and sympathy for the abused and misunderstood characterize poems from every stage of his career.

From an early age, Wright wished to escape the landscape and society of his youth. "Our problem," Wright told interviewer Dave Smith, "when we were boys in Martins Ferry, Ohio . . . was to get out" (*Collected Prose,* 195). Wright's ticket out was the army, which sent him straight from high school to occupied Japan in 1946. In 1948, he entered Kenyon College, from which he graduated in 1952, the same year in which he published his first poem and married for the first time. In 1953, Wright began graduate studies at the University of Washington, celebrated the birth of his first son, and won a major prize, the Yale Series of Younger Poets, for his first book, *The Green Wall.* By the time that book appeared in 1957, Wright had accepted a teaching position at the University of Minnesota and had written many of the poems that would appear in his second book, *Saint Judas* (1959). By all appearances he had achieved success: a doctorate in English, an assistant professorship at a major university, and a reputation as an important younger poet. He seemed to have "gotten out" of Martins Ferry and left his past behind him.

The late 1950s and early 1960s were, however, years of emotional struggle for Wright. Depression and nervous exhaustion, worsened by alcohol dependency, required hospitalization; his first marriage failed, and his life in Minneapolis became almost unbearably lonely. These sufferings were connected to childhood memories and, as many of Wright's friends remember, were expressed in his physical carriage. Robert Bly, who recalls "an immense loneliness surrounding [Wright]" (*Remembering James Wright,* 7), writes that his friend's "body and his psyche, and the relations between them, were complicated. . . . He carried a great deal of anger in his neck and shoulders." That anger began in Ohio; Wright's "landscape was industrial . . . [and] his longing was not for his childhood heart—on the contrary, his hatred of childhood tormentors was close to the surface" (*American Poetry,* 76).

In his introduction to Wright's *Above the River: The Collected Poems,* Donald Hall illustrates Bly's point by recounting a visit of Wright's during this period to Ann Arbor, Michigan, during which a "good-natured and affable—if unstoppable—tirade suddenly turned black":

> Late at night he decided that *they* wanted him to go back to the mills. He made a speech about how he would never go back to the mills, no matter how much *they* tried to push him there; he

had fought *them* all his life. And he stormed upstairs to bed. In the morning, he walked outside in the frost of early morning without eating or speaking. . . .

A few days later, letters began arriving from Minneapolis. . . . "I knew musicians and possible poets and even ordinary lovable human beings, and I saw them with brutal regularity going into Wheeling Steel, turning into stupid and resigned slobs with beer bellies and glassy eyes." Every now and then, he said, this madness came over him. (xxxi)

Speculating on Wright's psychological distress, Hall compares him to Roethke. "Both men were provincial, literary, and shy; both relied on comic routines to get them through social situations. . . . And both men drank too much." Roethke's condition was the more serious, "a thought disorder, not merely a mood disorder," though alcohol abuse was also symptomatic in Wright's case (xxviii).

Wright's depression, like Roethke's, was complicated by unresolved conflicts related to place. He suffered from nostalgia, which as Paul Gruchow points out "came into currency as a medical word in nineteenth-century Germany to describe the failure to thrive of . . . displaced people. . . . Nostalgia is the clinical term for homesickness, for the desire to be rooted in a place—to know clearly, that is, what time it is" (*Grass Roots,* 7). Wright characterized his nostalgia as "an abrupt pang that rises not only from the shape of my parents' lives but also from the very disruption of the earth in southeastern Ohio" (*Collected Prose,* 330–34). Recognizing that his health, as well as his development as a poet, required that he confront his sense of displacement, Wright became impatient with his mannered writing style; he began to strive for greater clarity and geographical specificity in his poems.

Wright, fortunately, found literary precedent for his quest. D. H. Lawrence's *Studies in Classic American Literature* (1923) proved useful, particularly the chapter "The Spirit of Place," which Wright considered "a very beautiful essay" worthy of close study by poets. "There is such a genius of place," he wrote, "a presence, and because there is, people's feelings accumulate about it. You can share in that feeling when you become aware of particular historical events and the significance of monuments and so on" (*Collected Prose,* 194). Monuments, in fact, do figure significantly in

Wright's poetry, especially graves of notable (or notorious) people. A signature piece in Wright's collected poems is "At the Executed Murderer's Grave," which deals with George Doty, executed by the State of Ohio for the rape and murder of a girl. Critics, including Jane Robinett, generally regard the poem "as a turning point in the development of this poet's career, the point at which he breaks away from his apprenticeship and begins his real work" (49). Forsaking the abstraction and complicated syntax of his early poems, Wright specifically identifies himself in relation to place:

> My name is James A. Wright, and I was born
> Twenty-five miles from this infected grave
> In Martins Ferry, Ohio, where one slave
> To Hazel-Atlas Glass became my father.
> He tried to teach me kindness. I return
> Only in memory now, aloof, unhurried,
> To dead Ohio, where I might lie buried,
> Had I not run away before my time.
> Ohio caught George Doty. Clean as lime,
> His skull rots empty here.

The setting of this poem in a midwestern graveyard recalls not only Edgar Lee Masters's *Spoon River Anthology,* but also Roethke's own breakthrough in "The Lost Son," which enacts a spiritual crisis in a Michigan cemetery. Where Roethke's sustained emotion was grief, however, Wright is concerned with guilt: the obvious criminal guilt of Doty, an "idiot" who "demanded love from girls, / And murdered one," as well as the guilt Wright purports to share with Doty by virtue of their common humanity in a fallen and corrupt world. Admitting to his own "sneaking crimes," Wright insists on the universality of evil; in his view, Doty constituted an extreme manifestation of the malice and destructiveness latent in all people: "Staring politely, they will not mark my face / From any murderer's, buried in this place. / Why should they? We are nothing but a man" (82–84). Wright's sense of guilt in this poem is mythic rather than historical; Doty's grave is to be found in the "rifted paradise" of Eden after the fall. Wright's comments about Edenic imagery in his first book, *The Green Wall,* also apply to "At the Executed Murderer's Grave":

"I tried to begin with the fall of man, and acknowledge that the fall of man was a good thing, the felix culpa, the happy guilt. And then I tried to weave my way in and out through nature poems and people suffering in nature because they were conscious" (qtd. in Stitt, *World's,* 205–6).

Noting the contradiction in this statement, Peter Stitt wonders "just how 'happy' was the fall of man in Wright's view if he also was convinced that it caused such a wealth of conscious 'suffering'" (*World's,* 165). Since the poet feels himself tainted by sin and guilt, there is little hope for redemption. Wright associates poetry with grasping materialism, characterizing it as mercenary and therefore psychically and socially ineffectual:

> I croon my tears at fifty cents per line.
> . . . . . . . . . . . . . . . . . . . . .
> Alive and dead, those giggling muckers who
> Saddled my nightmares thirty years ago
> Can do without my widely printed sighing
> Over their pains with paid sincerity.

Wright vows in this poem to change his approaches to life and to poetry. If his writing was once a "loud display, / Leaning for language on a dead man's voice" (that of E. A. Robinson, perhaps, or Robert Frost, whom Wright had once considered his poetic models), he is now "sick of lies" and ready "to face the past" with honesty and clear language. His subject—the broken people and abused landscape of Ohio—requires direct, not oblique, treatment. Conventional pastoral will not suffice:

> It does no good to woo the grass, to veil
> The quicklime hole of a man's defeat and shame.
> Nature-lovers are dead. To hell with them.
> I kick the clods away, and speak my name.

It is by speaking his name, and the name of his place, that Wright begins the poem. Nature here offers no refuge from guilt or fear, but by confronting these emotions the poet makes possible other responses to his environment. "At the Executed Murderer's Grave" serves as a bridge between Wright's early and later work: it rhymes and is metrical, but irregularly so; it occasionally lapses into archly literary language ("Open, dungeon! Open, roof of the ground!"), but hews closely to specifics of place and person (82–84).

Had he dwelled entirely on the country of his origin, Wright's collected work would be extremely bleak. Ohio is to Wright a place of death, with the Ohio River standing for the River Styx. For him to see beauty in that place, he needed to experience (and write about) other landscapes. The first and most memorable of these locations was the tall-grass prairie of western Minnesota, which Wright explored at the invitation of poet Robert Bly (b. 1926). The two met in 1958, when Wright was teaching at the University of Minnesota. During this crucial stage of his career, Wright was rejecting his previous poetic models and struggling toward a new style to match his thematic concern with character and landscape. Wright's new style was showcased in *The Branch Will Not Break* (1963), a book deeply influenced by Bly, who had published his own first book, *Silence in the Snowy Fields,* the previous year. The two books are often discussed in tandem, and rightly so, for Wright's stylistic and thematic growth as a poet owed much to Bly's friendship and example. The subsequent course of Wright's poetry needs to be understood in light of Bly's ideas about poetry and landscape.

Robert Bly, who was born and still lives in Minnesota, has profoundly influenced contemporary poetry, both as poet and critic. For the last half century he has been a tastemaker, a champion of the new and experimental, and, through his translations of European and South American poets like Rilke, Neruda, and Vallejo, an advocate of literary internationalism. Long before the best-selling book *Iron John* (1990) brought him fame as a leader of the men's consciousness movement, Bly edited a magazine called *The Fifties* (later, *The Sixties* and *The Seventies*) that promoted what he considered the best in contemporary poetry and poetics. This publication, which featured writing by Bly, Wright, and other like-minded individuals, established Bly as a major critical voice in American literature.

In his influential essay "A Wrong Turning in American Poetry" (1963), Bly argues against the "trust" placed by T. S. Eliot and other modernists "in the objective, outer world [rather] than in the inner world. As poets they want to concern themselves with objects." Bly inveighs against modernist objectivism and poetic formulas, including Eliot's "objective correlative," William Carlos Williams's dictum "No ideas but in things," and Ezra Pound's belief that "the proper and perfect symbol is the natural object." These prescriptions for poetry, according to Bly, derive from the American "puritan fear of the unconscious and the business drive toward dealing with outward things," which "meet in our poetry to push out the unconscious." Writers of the 1940s and 1950s who followed modernist and "New Critical" precepts created in Bly's view "a poetry without spiritual life . . . in which the poem is considered to be a construction independent of the poet," a dryly formalist verse either cluttered by objects or lost in flights of abstraction. Bly prefers the inwardness of non-English-language poets such as García Lorca, Neruda, and Rilke, for whom a "poem is something that penetrates for an instant into the unconscious." By means of vivid and associative imagery, these poets aim (as in transcendentalism and Zen Buddhism) "to make men more and more inward until they stop admiring objects, at which point they will be able to see them clearly, if they wish to." Bly suggests that connections between poetry, puritanical psychology, and utilitarianism can be broken if poets embrace Rilke and other great international figures in place of Eliot, Pound, and Williams as primary models (*American Poetry*, 7–35).

Bly's innovation was not confined to his absorption of international influences. The colloquial diction and simple declarative sentences of Bly's *Silence* poems came as something of a shock in 1962, when formalist verse was just beginning to lose its dominance in American poetry. Typical readings of these poems focus on their use of both mundane and "deep," surreal images to explore the unconscious mind and its relationship to the physical world. Thus, in "Laziness and Silence," Bly relates a "dream of moles with golden wings" which he experiences one fall day ("a Saturday afternoon in the football season") while sleeping near a lake. True to the dominant motion of the book, which is downward, into darknesses of mind and earth, the poet awakens to perceive the symbolic significance of the lake:

> I know that far out in the Minnesota lake
> Fish are nosing the mouths of cold springs,
> Whose water causes ripples in the sleeping sand,
> Like a spirit moving in a body.
>
> (53)

Whatever its private significance, the dream of moles has reminded the speaker of nature's hidden life and consciousness. The epigraph for Bly's book is a passage from German mystic Jacob Boehme: "We are all asleep in the outward man." It is by dreaming that the speaker of "Laziness and Silence" has awakened to his inner man, and to the natural landscape around him.

G. A. M. Janssens describes the cumulative effect of Bly's *Silence* poems as emerging from "a sense of space, of wide, bleak landscapes dotted with small midwestern towns, of the seasons, and of the time of the day" (204). The speaker of these poems embodies the Romantic archetype of a solitary figure in nature, a seeker of transcendental truth. Although he occasionally expresses a sense of bleak foreboding, Bly's characteristic emotion is a delight in nature reminiscent of Wordsworth, accompanied by an ease with his body recalling Whitman's celebration of the "body electric." The following lines are representative of the book's dominant tone: "Oh, on an early morning I think I shall live forever! / I am wrapped in my joyful flesh, / As the grass is wrapped in its clouds of green" (21). The directness and sincerity of such sentiments bothered some critics when *Silence in the Snowy Fields* first appeared. William Heyden, who later changed his mind about the book, initially felt (on the basis of his New Critical bias) that Bly's "risks . . . were all bad ones" leading to poetic errors: "Where was his 'heightened speech'? How, if to suggest something is to destroy it, could he write lines such as 'I have awakened at Missoula, Montana, utterly happy' ('In a Train') and 'There is a privacy I love in this snowy night' ('Driving to Town Late to Mail a Letter')? Didn't he know such bare statements were against the rules?" (13). James Wright endured similar criticisms of his own more tranquil poems, many of which he wrote while visiting Bly's farm in Minnesota. Bly attributed such reactions to the insularity of many in the literary and academic communities, "where the very process of studying poetry often increases one's store of irony, ambiguity, wariness, and anger." Like Whitman before them, Bly and Wright engaged in a Romantic rebellion against poetic formalism, which in the early 1960s meant fighting against "a kind of low level conspiracy to keep out of view the poems of tenderness and quiet" (*American Poetry*, 73).

For many poets of the period, including Bly and Wright, as well as Gary Snyder, Denise Levertov, and William Stafford, a revaluation of the contemplative in poetry necessitated a strong sense of place, a return to nature in order to explore human nature. As Bly once told an interviewer, "unless American poetry can grow naturally out of American ground, we may as well give up now and quit" (*Talking All Morning,* 56). Noting this statement by Bly, Howard Nelson writes that Bly's early work "belongs among the best regional writing this country has produced, [although] not regionalism of the superficial or strictly external variety. His scenes of farms, woods, and lakes are deepened; they have spiritual resonance. The inward world is entered in *Silence in the Snowy Fields* through the outward world: the soul is known through the body and the places it moves through" (7). From Bly's influence and example, Wright's poetry acquired this kind of regionalism, moving away from modernist abstraction and irony toward geographical specificity and directness of manner. As Wright told Stitt, Bly "made it clear to me that the tradition of poetry which I had tried to master, and in which I'd come to a dead end, was not the only one" (qtd. in Stitt, *World's,* 203). Wright undertook his own translations of modern European and South American poets, and began experimenting with imagery and free verse styles in his own poetry. The poems that resulted would firmly place Wright in the American neo-Romantic tradition of place poetry.

Wright's new aesthetic made its debut in *The Branch Will Not Break,* in which his happiest poems appear. According to Wright, his experiences walking around Bly's Minnesota farm, observing animals and the landscape, provided him with the "center of that book": "my rediscovery of the abounding delight of the body that I had forgotten about" (qtd. in Stitt, *World's,* 203). That rediscovery, however, came as a struggle, as Wright emphasizes through his arrangement of poems in the book. Bleak Ohio poems predominate at first, followed by increasingly peaceful visions of nature, mainly in Minnesota. The first poem, "As I Step over a Puddle at the End of Winter, I Think of an Ancient Chinese Governor," sets the tone, as Wright asks, "Where is the sea, that once solved the whole loneliness / Of the Midwest? Where is Minneapolis? I can see nothing / But the great terrible oak tree darkening with winter" (119). In keeping with those lines, most of the poems in the beginning of *The Branch Will Not Break* present the natural world as frightening, and people as alienated from their own places and bodies. Ohio is still associated with pollution, despair, and death, and Wright's frequent use of place names, like Martins Ferry, Tiltonsville, Benwood, and Marion, lends a poignant specificity to these poems. The frequently anthologized "Autumn Begins in Martins Ferry, Ohio," for example, pictures a football stadium full of lonely people projecting their shattered dreams onto youthful athletes who "grow suicidally beautiful / At the beginning of October, / And gallop terribly against each other's bodies" (121). In "A Message Hidden in an Empty Wine Bottle That I Threw into a Gully of Maple Trees One Night at an Indecent Hour," Wright observes the ghosts of women "dancing around a fire / By a pond of creosote and waste water from the river / In the dank fog of Ohio" (123). Corruption of body, spirit, and place is pervasive in Wright's imagery: the violence of bodies colliding in a football game, the acrid smell of creosote, and the dampness and chill in the Ohio air.

Given the almost charnel tone of these poems, the frequent appearance of grave and cemetery imagery is not surprising. From the poem "Miners":

> Somewhere in a vein of Bridgeport, Ohio;
> Deep in a coal hill behind Hanna's name;
> Below the tipples, and dark as a drowsy woodchuck;
> A man, alone,
> Stumbles upon the outside locks of a grave, whispering
> *Oh let me in.*
>
> (126)

And from "Two Poems about President Harding":

> A hundred slag piles north of us,
> At the mercy of the moon and rain,
> He lies in his ridiculous
> Tomb, our fellow citizen.

Wright's perspective on place has become less mythic and more historical, as in the poem about Warren G. Harding of Marion, Ohio, whose scandal-ridden administration ended when he died, according to rumor, "of crab meat on the way back from Alaska" (127–28). Ohio, which has produced more U.S. presidents than any other state except for Virginia, is emblematic of the entire nation's failure to come to terms with the native ground. Despite its pastoral ideal, the Midwest has produced a graveyard as much as a garden; Wright is looking for a way out of the first into the second, offering his pastoral poems (as the titles of two poems have it) as "A Prayer to Escape from the Market Place" and as a contribution to "The Undermining of the Defense Economy." He rejects the prevailing economic and political worldview of America, a rationalistic mindset that abhors weakness and seeks to control nature, human or otherwise. Thus Wright begins his poem on "Eisenhower's Visit to Franco, 1959" by lamenting how the "American hero," another president from the Midwest (Kansas, in Eisenhower's case), "must triumph over / The forces of darkness" (129). Given the social crises about to unfold in the United States in the 1960s, including the Vietnam War and the beginning of the contemporary environmental movement, Wright's vision of American society was both timely and prescient. As he concludes "Stages on a Journey Westward":

> America is over and done with.
> America,
> Plunged into the dark furrows
> Of the sea again.
>
> (125)

Typically, Wright turns to an agrarian metaphor ("furrows") to represent the psychic life of a nation in crisis.

After a group of political poems, Wright shifts from the wasteland of industrial Ohio to the pastoral plains of western Minnesota. The turning point of *The Branch Will Not Break* occurs in the poem "Two Hangovers," in which the book's title appears as a line. Wright first describes a morning in Ohio, where he has awoken from a dream

> Of green butterflies searching for diamonds
> In coal seams;
> And children chasing each other for a game
> Through hills of fresh graves.

The dream represents his search for redemption in a place where "[a]ll groves are bare" and "a sparrow outside / Sings of the Hanna Coal Co.

and the dead moon." He briefly achieves the longed for state of grace during hangover "Number Two: / I Try to Waken and Greet the World Once Again." The complete change of tone in this section, as well as the detail of a pine tree, suggests a Minnesota setting. "A brilliant blue jay . . . springing up and down, up and down, / On a branch" (132) brings the poet an intimation of immortality recalling Whitman's observation of the placidity and self-containment of animals, who "do not sweat and whine about their condition" (218). Wright's tone finally relaxes: "I laugh, as I see him abandon himself / To utter delight, for he knows as well as I do / That the branch will not break" (133).

Wright's discovery of a sustaining joy in nature comes as a respite not only from ego but also from the mediation of experience by literature. The title of the book's second poem wishes "Goodbye to the Poetry of Calcium"; the poem following the transition of "Two Hangovers" expresses both escape and arrival in its long title: "Depressed by a Book of Bad Poetry, I Walk toward an Unused Pasture and Invite the Insects to Join Me." Wright has taken transcendentalism to heart, following Emerson's pronouncement in "The American Scholar" that "[b]ooks are for the scholar's idle times. When he can read God directly, the hour is too precious to be wasted in other men's transcripts of their readings" (58). In a moment resonating with the graveyard imagery of so many of his poems, Wright drops the book of bad poetry "behind a stone," that he may unencumbered "climb a slight rise of grass" to observe ants and listen to grasshoppers and crickets. For once, Wright senses the possibility of being at home in nature, in his own body, and in the words of his poetry. His sense of wholeness wavers between the tentative and the consummate: the "old grasshoppers" have not yet begun to sing, though the poet is certain that "they have clear sounds to make." Nature strikes but one note, which is heard at the poem's conclusion: "lovely, far off, a dark cricket begins / In the maple trees." The sound is distant, but the poet has at least located its source. His motion toward the animal world and its un-self-conscious musicality is slow but persistent, like "the ants / Who are walking single file up the fence post," or the "tired" grasshoppers who "leap heavily" because "their thighs are burdened" (133). Wright still feels the "depressing" burden of the bad poetry book, and the confinement of the tradition it represents, but has begun to move with grace and attentiveness in the natural environment.

Most of the remaining poems in *The Branch Will Not Break* share this motif of a potential oneness with nature as experienced in particular locations, often in the company of animals. Several poems express yearning for transcendence even in their titles, as in "Trying to Pray," "Arriving in the Country Again," and "Beginning," in which "[t]he wheat leans back toward its own darkness, / And I lean toward mine" (135). In "A Prayer to Escape from the Market Place," Wright again rejects the primacy of the written word: "I renounce the blindness of the magazines. / I want to lie down under a tree." But the speaker captures only a fleeting glimpse of "everlasting happiness," as a "pheasant flutters, and I turn / Only to see him vanishing at the damp edge / Of the road" (140). Even Wright's most famous poem, "A Blessing," in which Wright and a friend (Bly in real life) visit two Indian ponies in a pasture "[j]ust off the highway to Rochester, Minnesota," is an incipient, rather than realized, epiphany of place.[2] Wright's contact with one of the horses awakens him to his own potential for freedom and belonging: "Suddenly I realize / That if I stepped out of my body I would break / Into blossom" (143). The enjambment of the last two lines stresses both the pain of growth ("breaking") and the beauty that results from a widening of consciousness ("blossoming"). The poet assumes a disjunction between physical and transcendental experience, feeling he must "step out of his body" to achieve grace. Still rather ill at ease with his body, he concludes the poem much as he does "Two Horses Playing in the Orchard," which appears earlier in the book: "I feel / Like half a horse myself, although / Too soon, too soon, already. Now" (134).

Three poems at the end of *The Branch Will Not Break,* however, are consummate epiphanies of place: "Today I Was Happy, So I Made This Poem," in which "The moon suddenly stands up in the darkness, / And I see that it is impossible to die" (141); "To the Evening Star: Central Minnesota," in which the poet exclaims, "Beautiful daylight of the body, your hands carry seashells" (142); and "Milkweed." Vividly evocative of place, the last merits quotation in full:

> While I stood here, in the open, lost in myself,
> I must have looked a long time
> Down the corn rows, beyond grass,
> The small house,

White walls, animals lumbering toward the barn.
I look down now. It is all changed.
Whatever it was I lost, whatever I wept for
Was a wild, gentle thing, the small dark eyes
Loving me in secret.
It is here. At a touch of my hand,
The air fills with delicate creatures
From the other world.[3]

(143–44)

In seeking spiritual significance in his surroundings, the poet has not until now truly perceived what is before him. Constrained by his ego, he has impatiently looked *down* the corn rows and *beyond* the grass. By releasing the milkweed seeds to float away in the wind, Wright also frees his own original nature from the confinement of rational thought and obsessive guilt and grief. It is not the world that has changed, but the poet's perception of it. The pastoral quest of *The Branch Will Not Break* has brought Wright, as Stitt describes, "from solipsistic self-absorption to identification with the animals, from an end-stopped despair at death to an inherent faith in natural immortality, from man to nature and beyond" (introduction, 15). He sees miraculousness in the ordinary, the beauty within himself as well as in nature: "I can be happy sometimes," Wright told Stitt in an interview. "And I'd forgotten that. And with those animals I remembered then. And that is what that book is about, the rediscovery. I didn't hate my body at all. I like myself very much" (*World's*, 204).

But as Wright also told Stitt, "I am not a happy man by talent. Sometimes I have been very happy, but characteristically I'm a miserable son of a bitch" (*World's*, 202). The contentment of *The Branch Will Not Break* proved to be short lived, as Wright continued his struggle with private and public griefs. In his next two books, *Shall We Gather at the River* (1968) and *Two Citizens* (1973), Wright "speak[s] of flat defeat / In a flat voice," once again "lonely / And sick for home" (158). Three themes dominate this period of Wright's career: loneliness and dislocation, American history as benighted and guilt ridden, and the blighted lives and landscapes of Ohio. This renewed ambivalence about place, poetry, and his body leads Wright to examine pastoralism both as a literary mode and as a social ideal.

The pastoral imagery of Wright's *Branch* poems—animals, trees, and grass—carries over into this period, but is treated quite differently. As did Willa Cather in her Nebraska novels, Wright symbolizes spiritual malaise with the bleakness of the prairie during the cold months. In "Late November in a Field," for example, Wright finds himself "walking alone in a bare place" observing a pair of squirrels whose "[f]rail paws rifle the troughs between cornstalks when the moon / Is looking away." In alluding to his poem "A Blessing," Wright seems to have given up all hope of transcendence in nature or in language:

> The earth is hard now,
> The soles of my shoes need repairs.
> I have nothing to ask a blessing for,
> Except these words.
> I wish they were
> Grass.
>
>                                    (160)

Wright is back in the graveyard, "Listening to the Mourners," as he titles another poem that finds him crouched "down by a roadside wind-break / At the edge of the prairie." But unlike the vague and mythical guilt of "At the Executed Murderer's Grave," Wright's grief is specific and historical. He mourns not only for himself, but for the dislocation of his nation from place and history:

> So: it is not me, it is not my love
> Alone lost.
> The grief that I hear is my life somewhere.
> . . . . . . . . . . . . . . . . . . . . .
> This field is the beginning of my native land,
> This place of skull where I hear myself weeping.
>
>                                    (161)

Wright's skull is more than a pastoral memento mori of individual mortality, given the increasingly historical emphasis of his poetry in this period. Appearing in a book that was published at the height of the Vietnam War in 1968, "Listening to the Mourners" alludes to the legacy of conquest in American attitudes about race, nationalism, and the natural environment. This linking of past and present violence in the name of national destiny was an insight Wright shared with his contemporaries in American poetry, who may well be the "mourners" referred to in the poem's title. In his book of essays *Earth House Hold* (1969), Gary Snyder recapitulates Lawrence's comment about the "menace" in the American landscape in a manner useful to our understanding of James Wright: "The American Indian is the vengeful ghost lurking in the back of the troubled American mind. Which is why we lash out with such ferocity and passion, so muddied a heart, at the black-haired young peasants and soldiers who are the 'Viet Cong.' That ghost will claim the next generation as its own. When this has happened, citizens of the USA will at last begin to be Americans, truly at home on the continent, in love with their land" (112). Robert Bly attacked the cultural roots of the Vietnam War in terms identical to Snyder's. At a poetry reading in 1969, Bly expressed the opinion that "what we're doing [in Vietnam] is repeating the crime with Indians. The Vietnamese are our Indians. We don't want to end this war! We didn't want to quit killing the Indians but we ran out of Indians, and they were all on reservations" (qtd. in Mersmann, 65). The comparison also appears in Bly's poetry. In his National Book Award–winning *The Light around the Body* (1968), Bly illustrates the frontier-Vietnam connection with statements such as "underneath all the cement of the Pentagon / There is a drop of Indian blood preserved in snow" (36).

According to James F. Mersmann, Bly's Vietnam poems attempt an "expiation of the burden of guilt accumulated from the rape of the frontier and the ecology, from puritanical morality and discipline, from killing Indians, from a history of violence and socio-economic inequities" (72). Mersmann's commentary also applies to James Wright. Whereas Bly borrowed from surrealism and Jungian psychology to explore the national psyche, Wright chose to continue writing extensively about his personal relationship to American places. It is natural that American Indians, the original inhabitants of the place, would arise as a theme in Wright's poetry, as in Roethke's and Snyder's. To discover a true love for America, Wright needed to follow Lawrence's directive in appeasing the nation's ghosts in atonement for the American spirit of place, the national "soul history" that Jim Harrison describes as stained "with the blood of over two hundred Native American civilizations we destroyed" (*Just before Dark,* 300).

Wright's first expression of national guilt over the Indians comes early in *The Branch Will Not Break,* in "Stages on a Journey Westward." The four parts of this poem retrace the westward movement of conquest, creating place images for Ohio during the Great Depression, western Minnesota, Nevada, and Washington State. Landscapes in each location bear the marks of callous economic exploitation. Wright's memory of Ohio is of his father standing in Depression-era bread lines before returning home "grimy with machinery" to sing his young son a lullaby, while "[o]utside the house, the slag heaps waited." In Minnesota, the winter wind howling

> out of the abandoned prairies
> . . . sounds like the voices of bums and gamblers,
> Rattling through the bare nineteenth-century whorehouses
> In Nevada.

Standing in a graveyard with "the half-educated sheriff of Mukilteo, Washington," Wright imagines the miners who "paused on the way up to Alaska . . . / [spading] their broken women's bodies / Into ditches of crab grass." Americans, here represented by bums, gamblers, prostitutes, and prospectors, have always been on their way to somewhere else, abandoning one place for another and leaving slag heaps and graves in their wake. These people and places haunt the American national conscience, which speaks to Wright one night in a dream:

> In western Minnesota, just now,
> I slept again.
> In my dream, I crouched over a fire.
> The only human beings between me and the Pacific Ocean
> Were old Indians, who wanted to kill me.
> They squat and stare for hours into small fires
> Far off in the mountains.
> The blades of their hatchets are dirty with the grease
> Of huge, silent buffaloes.
>
> (124–25)

Western Minnesota, according to Wright, is where you "start to get a hint of what the western United States is like" (*Collected Prose,* 195). The prairie begins there; before the arrival of settlers, the whole state was contested ground, home to woodland Ojibwa and their ancient adversaries, the Sioux. The American war of conquest against the Plains Indians began in Minnesota in reaction to the Sioux revolt of 1862, when Indians' resentment over being swindled out of their land led to the killing of hundreds of white settlers and the subsequent exile of the Minnesota Sioux. Wright's meditation on that historical event resulted in a poem essential to his oeuvre: "A Centenary Ode: Inscribed to Little Crow, Leader of the Sioux Rebellion in Minnesota, 1862."[4]

In that poem, Wright addresses Little Crow, identifying him as the "true father / Of my dark America." He first assumes a defensive tone: "I had nothing to do with it [Little Crow's death]. I was not here. / I was not born." Wright's Ohio ancestors, "a lot of singing drunks and good carpenters," also had an alibi: they were busy fighting on both sides of the Civil War. But they, and Wright, share a measure of guilt: "[I]t was not my fathers / Who murdered you. / Not much." Wright here implies that atonement for the genocide of America's native people must begin with a recognition of guilt, followed by appropriate mourning. But the exact location of Little Crow's grave is unknown, a fact that symbolizes the difficulty of national (and individual) redemption. "I don't know," Wright tells the chief,

> Where the fathers of Minneapolis finalized
> Your flayed carcass. . . .
>
> If only I knew where to mourn you,
> I would surely mourn.
>
> But I don't know.

Lacking a specific location or monument on which to meditate, Wright's thoughts shift from the conquered Sioux to Wright's own people; his confession to Little Crow that "[w]hen I close my eyes I lose you among / Old lonelinesses" suggests the psychic cost that all whites have paid for America's crime against the Indians. Despite the preservation of the

Union and the conquest of the West, white Americans are in another sense a defeated people who have never been more than superficially at home on the land. Wright feels himself fated to homelessness, like "Old Paddy Beck, [his] great-uncle . . . dead / At the old soldiers' home near Tiffin, Ohio." The concluding stanza projects this dislocation even beyond death:

> Oh all around us,
> The hobo jungles of America grow wild again.
> The pick handles bloom like your skinned spine.
> I don't even know where
> My own grave is.
>
> (186–87)

In *Reading the Fire* (1983), a study of Native American oral literature, Jarold Ramsey contrasts the Indian approach to geography and nature with "the vaguely guilty and nostalgic sense of place and feeling for landscape that we inherit from Romanticism; it is altogether sterner, more pragmatic as to ecological necessities, and more caught up in the narrative" (188). Ramsey's observation holds true of a number of Native American poets and novelists who emerged during the 1960s and 1970s, including Leslie Marmon Silko. Wright's correspondence with Silko, author of *Ceremony* (1977) and *Almanac of the Dead* (1991), represents a remarkable cultural convergence: the meeting, on equal terms, of Euro-American Romanticism and a Native American worldview. Their letters, published in *The Strength and Delicacy of Lace* (1986), do not dwell on the tragic aspects of American history or on literary aesthetics. Instead, Wright and Silko wrote of their admiration for each other's work, of their travels, of their daily struggles as individuals and artists. Each recognized in the other a kindred spirit, another author giving voice to previously voiceless people. Silko's narrative in *Ceremony* of Pueblo Indians facing threats to their traditional way of life is not far removed from Wright's elegies to Ohio people worn down by the industrial age. Both write from a tremendous sympathy for human suffering, particularly as caused by abrupt social change and geographical dislocation. Silko particularly appreciated Wright's mastery of colloquial English, which she contrasted with "that hideous, empty, artificial language television speaks": "the result of the past 50 years of working to eradicate regional usages, regional pronunciations, ie., regional and community expression from American English, always with the melting pot theory in mind. . . . That is what I love most in your writing, Jim, the gully and railroad track, the sumac and coal smoke—all could only be from the place you give us or that gives you to us, that Ohio country" (Anne Wright, 82). Silko admired Wright as a rare Anglo-American author who recognized the limitations of Romanticism, in particular the Whitmanian tendency to imaginative expansion at the expense of local truths. To invoke Ramsay's analysis, "pragmatism as to ecological necessities" required that Wright become "caught up in the narrative" of his own place and people. While retaining the vivid imagery and terse colloquialism of his middle period, Wright's later poems increasingly employ storytelling to convey his memories of the Ohio valley. Because he refused to idealize his place of origin or the people he knew there, the landscapes and portraits in Wright's later books are colored by both admiration and revulsion.

The poem "On a Phrase from Southern Ohio," for example, centers on Wright's memory of a patch of native wildflowers atop a strip-mined hill across the Ohio River in West Virginia, "the only / Beauty we found, outraged in that naked hell." The trip he shared with some "lazy and thieving" friends reenacts the conquest of North America as a myth of violation: white people cross a body of water, discover a sacred garden, and commit an act of racial violence:

> Well, we found two black boys up there
> In the wild cliff garden.
> Well, we beat the hell out of one
> And chased out the other.
>
> (300–301)

By finding an analogue for American history in his own experience, Wright sharpened the irony of his pastoralism: this narrative achieves the authenticity Wright wished for in "At the Executed Murderer's Grave" but could not achieve, because, as Robert Bly points out in his essay "The Work of James Wright," "a convicted rapist-murderer is a different piece of goods from James Wright" (100). The sense of guilt in the earlier poem seems contrived in comparison to the confession of "On a Phrase from Southern Ohio," which occurs in a fully realized context of environmental and social debasement. This is honest sorrow, rather than literary posturing. If nostalgia is the generic emotion of pastoral art, then Wright has revised the pastoral convention of yearning for a primal innocence and verdure. The Ohio River valley was always degraded in Wright's lifetime, and the discovery of a lovely remnant of wildness, "a garden of bloodroot, tangled there, a vicious secret / Of trilliums," only emphasizes the horrors of industrialism:

> It is summer chilblain, it is blowtorch, it is not
> Maiden and morning on the way up that cliff.
> Not where I come from.
>
> It is a slab of concrete that for all I know
> Is beginning to crumble.
>
> (300)

At times Wright is so strident in his condemnation of American society as to resemble Robinson Jeffers, whose poems denounce human solipsism and corruption as much as they celebrate the northern California coast that Jeffers made his home. Wright's poem "Ohioan Pastoral" is a catalog of ugliness quite similar to that in Jeffers's famous poem "November Surf," right down to the imagery of discarded condoms. Wright takes us to "the other side / Of Salt Creek," a place polluted by "orange rinds, / Oil cans, cold balloons of lovers," where a barn "[s]ags, sags and oozes / Down one side of the copperous gully." The poem's final image is bleaker yet: the sound of a "buried gas main" hissing "among the green rings / On fingers in coffins" (348). Again, corruption of body and nature persists even after death, because places that should have been treated with reverence have been ruthlessly defiled. The most concise expression of Wright's divided vision of the Midwest, "Ohioan Pastoral" implies an ironic optimism: salvation may lie in entropy—in the crumbling of the slab, in the erosion by natural forces of excessive human interference. Such was Jeffers's hope in imagining a storm that would cleanse North America beyond the sea lines, in a future with the "cities gone down, the people fewer and the hawks more numerous, / The rivers mouth to source pure." Even "inhumanist" Jeffers had to admit that "the two-footed / mammal" is "someways one of the nobler animals" (159), and Wright at his bleakest is reminded by nature of a persistent beauty in himself and other people that will not allow the bond between person and place to be severed—that will keep the branch from breaking. Since that branch appeared as the title of one book, the decision of Anne Wright, the poet's widow and literary executor, to derive the title for his complete poems from the last stanza of "On a Phrase from Southern Ohio" is consistent with the essential humanism of his work: "And still in my dreams I sway like one fainting strand / Of spiderweb, glittering and vanishing and frail / Above the river" (301).

Far more than Jeffers, Wright was guided by a profound sympathy for human suffering. Despite his anger at modern placelessness, Wright admired certain resilient individuals who confronted the harshness of life in industrial Ohio. The poem "A Flower Passage," for example, memorializes Joe Shank (elsewhere, John Shunk), a man who made a living recovering the bodies of drowned children from the Ohio River. In Wright's ironic pastoralism, Shank was a "[s]hepherd of the dead" who "dragged ... hooks / All over the rubble sludge and lifted / The twelve year old bones." As an adult Wright lived elsewhere, and could not bring flowers to Shank's funeral service. Instead he offers the memory of the same native plants discovered in "On a Phrase from Southern Ohio":

> The true sumac, and the foul trillium
> Whose varicose bloom swells the soil with its bruise;
> And a little later, I bring
> The still totally unbelievable spring beauty
> That for some hidden reason nobody raped
> To death in Ohio.
>
> (355)

In his "Childhood Sketch," Wright remembers feeling that Shank had "a kind of solitary holiness about him. . . . [H]e carried the visible terror of good and frightened people in his arms, and he was brave as even the river never knew how to be brave." Shank and the wildflowers represent an indestructible spirit, a genius of place as beautiful as the river "in its rawness and wildness," even though, as Wright recalled, "something was forever drifting past to remind us of the factories that lined the banks to the north" (*Collected Prose,* 332–33). In "The Old WPA Swimming Pool in Martins Ferry, Ohio," Wright attributes that spirit to his father and uncles, "good men who lived along that shore" who dug a hole ("No grave for once") so children would have a safe place to swim. Though redemption eludes them, these people have made the best of their situation: when

> the river,
> That is supposed to be some holiness
> Starts dying,
> They swim in the earth.
>
>                              (236)

In his poems and prose Wright testifies to a "goodness" and "holiness" that persists in places and people, however abused. As he wrote to Silko, "When you love a place, really and almost hopelessly love it, I think you love it even for its signs of disaster, just as you come to realize how you love the particular irregularities and even the scars on some person's face" (Anne Wright, 32).

Wright's love for his place of origin was deepened and clarified by his travels in Europe, where he experienced landscapes and cultures that had survived centuries of change, peaceful and violent. His last two books of poetry, *To a Blossoming Pear Tree* (1977) and the posthumous *This Journey* (1982), are dominated by poems set in France, Austria, Yugoslavia, and especially Italy, where he fell in love with the cities of Mantua (birthplace of Virgil, the greatest of all pastoral poets) and Verona, where Romeo and Juliet loved and died. Wright's visits to Italy with his wife, Anne, provided the happiest, most peaceful moments of his last years. Wright maintained his cynicism about pastoral poetry while in Europe; in "Notes of a Pastoralist," for example, he observes that the sheep in a field outside of Pisa "did not flock together / As they do in Spenser and Theocritus" (328). Yet these late poems pay homage to the ancient pastoral poets, whom Wright loved for writing about their homelands in language appropriate to their time and place. Horace and Virgil com-

municate across distances of geography and time by means of a visionary localism; as Emerson writes in "Self-Reliance," the ancients made
their places "venerable in the imagination . . . by sticking fast where they
were, like an axis in the earth." Since he traveled not to escape, but to
gain perspective on his experience (and use of language), Wright fairly
fits Emerson's description of a wise traveler: "When his necessities, his du-
ties, on any occasion call him from his house, or into foreign lands, he is
at home still . . . he goes the missionary of wisdom and virtue, and visits
cities and men like a sovereign, and not like an interloper or a valet"
(277).

Wright struggled throughout his career to balance his love of poetic
traditions ancient and modern with the necessity of writing in a natural
and regional idiom. As a young poet, he mastered the formal style of the
period, but soon resisted it as an unnecessary constraint on his imagination. "All this time," he confesses in "Many of Our Waters,"

> I've been slicking into my own words
> The beautiful language of my friends.
> I have to use my own, now.
> That's why this scattering poem sounds the way it does.
>
> (216)

By abandoning the iconoclasm and self-doubt of *Saint Judas* and *The
Branch Will Not Break,* Wright came to accept not only his Ohio experience, but also his own regional language, what he called "[t]he one
tongue I can write in / . . . my Ohioan" (261). When in *Two Citizens* he
addresses the Roman poet Horace, he is able to do so in a spirit of geographical and idiomatic mutuality:

> Easy, easy, I ask you, easy, easy
> Early, evening, by Tiber, by Ohio,
> Give the gift to each lovely other.
> I would be happy.
> . . . . . . . . . . . . . . . . .
> Quintus Horatius Flaccus, my good father,
> You were just the beginning, you quick and lonely

Metrical crystals of February.
It is just snow.

(228)

This conciliatory tone resounds throughout Wright's last two books, though some of his darkest visions of the United States, such as "Flower Passage" and "Ohioan Pastoral," appear in this period. The gift that Wright speaks of sharing with Horace is love of *patria,* of native language and landscape. Wright's last poems brim with confidence in the power of poetry to ease psychic pain, particularly homesickness and nostalgia. Wright longed for an Ohio of pastures and forests rather than strip mines and graveyards, its river pure from mouth to source. By contemplating the pastures, towns, and rivers beloved of the classical poets, and by trusting the redemptive power of his own writing, Wright came home to his ideal Ohio. The city of Mantua, for example, inspired him to meditate (as did Willa Cather in *My Ántonia*) on the famous lament of Virgil's *Georgics,* "Optima dies prima fugit":

The best days are the first
To flee, sang the lovely
Musician born in this town
So like my own.

(312)

Likewise, in the poem "One Last Look at the Adige: Verona in the Rain," Wright observes that the Ohio River

must have looked
Something like this
To the people who loved it
Long before I was born.

Wright has taken a broader view of history; though "Steubenville [Ohio] is a black crust," and America a "shallow hell where evil / Is an easy joke, forgotten / In a week," rivers yet flow to remind him of the earth (or paradise) just beneath the crust:

Now, Adige, flow on.
Adige, river on earth,
Only you can hear
A half-witted angel drawling Ohioan
In the warm Italian rain.

In the middle of my own life
I woke up and found myself
Dying, fair enough, still
Alive in the friendly city
Of my body, my secret Verona,
Milky and green,
My moving jewel, the last
Pure vein left to me.

(284–85)

Wright did not arrive at an easy resolution of his ambivalence toward poetry, place, and body. America, represented by the city of Martins Ferry, Ohio, is still in ruins, its pastoral dream alive but as tenuous as a branch, a spider web, a garden of trilliums atop a strip-mined hill. Wright's search for home did not bring him literally back to Ohio, but to a way of being, a gracefulness of word and deed. "The secret / Of this journey," Wright decided,

                  is to let the wind
        Blow its dust all over your body,
        To let it go on blowing, to step lightly, lightly
        All the way through your ruins, and not to lose
        Any sleep over the dead.

("The Journey," 338)

Wright finally placed his faith in poetry as his own best means to bridge the rift in paradise, to reestablish the vital link between person and place. He was a pastoralist, however jaded, who affirmed the basic message of American Romanticism since Emerson, what Bly calls "the truth of the soul's interior abundance": the belief "that nature is not below the divine, but is itself divine, 'perpetual youth.' Most important of all . . . that despite the Industrial Revolution certain things are as they have always been, and that in human growth the road of development goes through nature, not around it" (*The Winged Life,* 5). The best of James Wright's poetry, much of it about the reality and promise of the American Midwest, endures as testimony to that essential insight into our human residence on earth.

six

# Jim
# Harrison

Nature must be viewed humanly to be viewed at all; that
is, her scenes must be associated with humane affections,
such as are associated with one's native place.

—Henry David Thoreau, *Journals*

One important heir to the pastoral tradition of Cather, Leopold, Roethke,
and Wright is Jim Harrison, poet, novelist, and essayist. Born in 1937, Harrison spent his childhood on a farm in northern Michigan, a region
where he has lived most of his life and where much of his writing is set.
As a boy, Harrison spent hours, often at night, exploring wild areas such
as "a particular spot favored for a big moon—a grove of white birches
where deer wandered" and where he could observe blue herons and visit
an Indian burial mound ( *Just before Dark,* 280). Such walks helped him
cope with the vicissitudes of life: "a severe eye injury causing blindness
[in one eye] at age seven . . . the deaths of my father and nineteen-year-
old sister in an [auto] accident when I was twenty-one," and "a cycle of
predictably severe depressions, beginning at age fourteen" ( *Just before
Dark,* 310). These circumstances shaped his development as a writer. Pre-
dominantly rural in focus, Harrison's writing is strongly personal and
idiosyncratic. His poems and essays amount to an ongoing autobiography, and his pastoral fiction depicts protagonists whose midwestern origins and spiritual quest resemble his own. Harrison has synthesized the

concerns of his regional predecessors; themes of grief and the consoling beauty of nature, resistance to the dominant utilitarianism of American society, and historical understandings of place all lend coherence and continuity to the extensive body of this author's work.

Although best known as a novelist, Harrison established his reputation with two books of poetry, *Plain Song* (1965) and *Locations* (1968). These volumes appeared during a period of innovation in American verse. Poets such as Gary Snyder, Denise Levertov, and Robert Duncan had only recently published their first major work, and the Beat writers, particularly Allen Ginsberg, were still "news." While varying widely in subject matter and style, these poets all rejected academic formalism in favor of clear imagery and mythic resonances. They looked to Walt Whitman, William Carlos Williams, and Ezra Pound for inspiration more than to T. S. Eliot, who had been considered the exemplary modern poet by many poets of the 1940s and 1950s. They also embraced poetic traditions from nations other than the United States and England, and in languages other than English. In sum, American poetry of the 1960s tended to free verse and was at once more local and international in its influences and aims.

Harrison's relation as a young writer to these trends can be gauged by his two degrees in comparative literature at Michigan State University (BA 1960, MA 1966) and by comments he makes in the introduction to *The Shape of the Journey: New and Collected Poems* (1998). Here he contrasts the literary snobbery he encountered while working as "a road man for a book wholesaler" in the 1950s with the camaraderie of poets he met during his single year as a college instructor in 1966:

> I recall how startled I was in my early twenties in Boston when I discovered I was not allowed to like Roethke, the [Robert] Lowell of *Life Studies,* and also Duncan, Snyder, and [Charles] Olson, the latter three whom I came to know. I remember that in my brief time in academia, in our rather shabby rental in Stony Brook [New York], we had gatherings of poets as diverse as Denise Levertov, Louis Simpson, James Wright, and Robert Duncan who all effortlessly got along. But then, the poem is the thing and most of the rest are variations on the theme of gossip. (2–3)

The reference to Wright is particularly apt, given the harmony he and Robert Bly were striving to achieve between midwestern vernacular and influences from Latin America, Europe, and Asia. Multicultural reading had the same effect on Harrison as on Bly and Wright: it enabled him to turn from "the wretchedness of xenophobia and the repetitive vagaries of literary history" and to treat American experience without undue self-consciousness or nationalism. Harrison's *Plain Song,* which appeared just three years after Bly's *Silence in the Snowy Fields* and two years after Wright's *The Branch Will Not Break,* resembles the earlier books in its expansiveness and embrace of the local, personal, and quotidian. "I had been eating the contents of world poetry since I was fifteen," Harrison recalls, "and without any idea of what to spit out. I collected *Botteghe Oscure* [an international review from Italy that published Roethke and Wright], but also Bly's magazines *The Fifties* and *The Sixties.* I was obsessed with Lorca, W.C. Williams, Apollinaire, Rimbaud, and Walt Whitman but none of it much shows in the book, which is mostly poems out of my rural past" (3). In style as well as theme, Harrison's first book is notably midwestern. Even its title, *Plain Song,* suggests the region's landscape and unaffected vernacular speech. His own milieu, ultimately, interested Harrison more than modernist aestheticism. "My background was essentially populist," Harrison wrote in his master's thesis, "and it was impossible for me to become comfortably absorbed in [the modernists'] concerns" ( *Just before Dark,* 199).[1]

Memories of his family and the northern Michigan countryside, however, do absorb his interest. In "Sketch for a Job-Application Blank," for example, Harrison describes his own appearance ("My left eye is blind and jogs / Like a milky sparrow in its socket"), early fears ("electric fences, / my uncle's hounds, / the pump arm of an oil well, / the chop and whir of a combine in the sun"), and brief flirtation with evangelical Christianity. He also expresses ambivalence about his ethnic heritage:

> From my ancestors, the Swedes,
> I suppose I inherit the love of rainy woods,
> kegs of herring and neat whiskey. . . .
>> (But on the other side, from the German Mennonites,
>> their rag smoke prayers and porky daughters
>> I got intolerance, and aimless diligence.)[2]
>
>> (10–11)

The passage brings to mind Roethke's description of his own family as "austere German-Americans" whose "love of order" and "terrifying efficiency" resulted in the astonishing beauty of the greenhouses (*On the Poet*, 8). Something of their orderliness appears in Roethke's poetry, which is formally complex even when experimental. Harrison similarly attributes to his ancestry his feelings about nature ("the love of rainy woods") and work ("the aimless diligence" that led to the publication of twenty books by 1998). This "job application" is Harrison's *ars poetica;* the employment sought is that of Romantic poet. Harrison here announces the theme which continues to occupy him after nearly four decades: the Romantic quest for organic wholeness in which "self is the first sacrament" and he "who loves not the misery and taint / of the present tense is lost." This quest takes him from childhood fears to "a lunar arrogance," from his baptism "by immersion in the tank at Williamston [Michigan]" to a yearning for earthly pleasures such as the "night beside a pond / she dried my feet with her yellow hair" (10–11).

Harrison's poetry exhibits an intertextual relation to that of Roethke not only by chance of geography. In her review of *Locations,* Lisel Mueller writes that Harrison "shares with that other Michigan poet, Theodore Roethke, not only the longing to be part of the instinctual world, but also the remarkable knowledge of plant and animal life that comes only with long familiarity and close observation" (322). Harrison first encountered Roethke's poetry when he was a college sophomore, a discovery that encouraged his own early poetic efforts. Since his father worked in a field not dissimilar to that of Roethke's father (Winfield Sprague Harrison was a farmer and soil conservation agent), Harrison perceived "the direct sense that our backgrounds were similar enough that there was some hope for me as a poet, so I absorbed him rather than read him."[3] Like Roethke's, Harrison's Michigan is a landscape bruised by years of environmentally unsound economic activity, the natural beauty of which nonetheless offers relief from the stresses of modern industrial society. His poem "Northern Michigan" (from *Plain Song*) belongs with Roethke's "Highway: Michigan" in any anthology of writing about the state:

> On this back road the land
> has the juice taken out of it:

    stump fences surround nothing
    worth their tearing down
    by a deserted filling station
    a Veedol sign, the rusted hulk
    of a Frazer, "live bait"
    on battered tin.

Like Roethke, Harrison describes "the progress of the jaded," though
the "back road" lacks even the sheen of economic activity. The only
automobile in view is junked, and the gas station is closed. Similar to
Roethke "at the field's end, in the corner missed by the mower,"[4] Harrison juxtaposes a scene of human failure (his catalog of static human artifacts) with nature's exuberance, expressed by the active verbs of the
poem's second half. There he shows nature surviving even in a land with
"the juice taken out of it":

    In the far corner of the pasture,
    in the shadow of the wood lot
    a herd of twenty deer:
    three bucks
    are showing off—                        ·
    they jump in turn across the fence,
    flanks arch and twist to get higher
    in the twilight
    as the last light filters through the woods.

                        (16–17)

Harrison provides historical context for "Northern Michigan" in his first
novel, *Wolf* (1971), in which his semiautobiographical narrator describes
the same country as "lumbered off for a hundred years with few traces
of the grand white pine which once covered it, an occasional charred almost petrified stump four feet in diameter, evidence of trees which rose
nearly two hundred feet and covered the northern half of the state and
the Upper Peninsula, razed with truly insolent completeness by the lumber barons after the Civil War with all the money going to the cities of the
south—Saginaw, Lansing, Detroit—and east to Boston and New York"
(18). All of Harrison's writing involving Michigan scenes is informed by

this knowledge of how the land was stripped of its ancient grandeur. His historical allusions result in what Gary Snyder calls "instantly-apprehended because so-well-digested larger loopings of lore" (*Real Work*, 62). This kind of "lore digestion" operates in Harrison's novel *Sundog* (1984), the main character of which is named Corvus Strang: Corvus after the genus appellation of crows and ravens, birds common to northern Michigan, and Strang after James Strang, the nineteenth-century Mormon leader who declared himself king of Beaver Island in Lake Michigan. Harrison's Strang parallels his namesake in the religious fundamentalism of his youth and in his love for nature; his work on large construction projects around the world resembles a modern day version of King Strang's attempt to found a new Eden in the then wilderness of northern Michigan.

With regional history in mind, Harrison explores in his poetry special places in his familiar terrain, which like Roethke's Tittabawassee locales relieve confusion and psychic distress. Alluding to *The Poetics of Space* (1969) by French philosopher Gaston Bachelard, Harrison lists such natural features of northern Michigan as "gullies, hummocks in swamps, swales in the middle of large fields, the small alluvial fan created by feeder creeks, undercut river banks, miniature springs, dense thickets of the tops of hills: like Bachelard's attics, seashells, drawers, cellars, these places are a balm to me" ( *Just before Dark*, 262–63). The poem "Walking" explores many such places:

> Walking back on a chill morning past Kilmer's Lake
> into the first broad gully down its trough
> and over a ridge of poplar, scrub oak, and into
> a large gully, walking into the slow fresh warmth
> of midmorning to Spider Lake where I drank
> at a small spring remembered from ten years back;
> walking northwest two miles where another gully
> opened, seeing a stump on a knoll where my father
> stood one deer season, and tiring of sleet and cold
> burned a pine stump, the snow gathering fire-orange
> on a dull day; walking past charred stumps blackened
> by the '81 fire to a great hollow stump near a basswood
> swale. . . .

These lines are characteristic of Harrison's work in their wealth of prepositions—"into," "down," and "over," for example, which trace the speaker's movement—and the many topographical nouns, such as "lake," "gully," "ridge," "spring," "knoll," and "swale." These words are particular to the subtle gradations of Harrison's Michigan landscape, gradations that require a fine eye to observe and a specific vocabulary to describe. Harrison states in "Passacaglia on Getting Lost" the pleasure he takes in finding (and writing about) the kind of natural beauty many people overlook: "I prefer places valued by no one else. The Upper Peninsula has many of these places that lack the drama and differentiation favored by the garden variety nature buff. I have a personal stump back in a forest clearing. Someone, probably a deer hunter, has left a beer bottle beside the stump. I leave the beer bottle there to conceal the value of the stump" ( *Just before Dark,* 263). Harrison owns Leopold's land aesthetic, the ability to admire landscapes "under the bellies of the buffalo," that is, with natural history in mind rather than the facile, picturesque aesthetic of "the garden variety nature buff." The pine stump is Harrison's buffalo, a reminder of the logging era in the Upper Great Lakes, a period of ecological destruction that coincided with the near extinction of the buffalo on the Great Plains. In the sequence titled "Geo-Bestiary" (1998), the stump offers Harrison shelter from the thunderstorms of northern Michigan, and an opportunity for amateur phenology. Waiting for the rain to cease, he notices that animal droppings tell a story: "The coyote has been eating mice, / the bear berries, the bobcat a rabbit." Harrison's observations resemble a response to an exam question in one of Aldo Leopold's game conservation classes. They also reflect Harrison's practice of Zen meditation, by which one achieves a heightened consciousness by emptying the mind of thoughts, desires, and fears. "Here is a place to think about nothing," he writes, "which is what I do" (234).

In "Walking," Harrison mentions the 1881 fire as an important factor in local ecology. A more immediate context is personal association with certain locations. As if noting significant sites on a pilgrimage, Harrison drinks at the familiar spring and recognizes the knoll where his father burned the stump. In the poem's many subsequent lines, Harrison resumes his walk through cedar swamps, lakes, and finally to an island out in "the larger water" where he immerses himself in a hidden spring. While the moment lacks the explicit connotation of death and acceptance of mortality expressed by Roethke's watery "North American Sequence," it shares Roethke's relief and expanded sense of self. As he describes the many locations of "Walking," Harrison himself is not much more than the one who is doing the walking into, through, and over. The poem's final image, of the speaker "sliding far down into a deep cool / dark endless weight of water," transforms him from mere observer into an integral part of the landscape (54). Harrison's "larger water" recalls the conclusion of Roethke's "The Long Waters," as Roethke stares out into the Pacific: "I lose and find myself in the long water; / I am gathered together once more; / I embrace the world" (192). The flow of water shapes these poets' lives, as well as their landscapes; as Harrison has it in his long poem "The Theory and Practice of Rivers," which begins with a description of floating on "the rivers of [his] life":

> . . . the current
> lifts me up and out
> into the dark, gathering motion,
> drifting into an eddy
> with a sideways swirl,
> the sandbar cooler than the air:
> to speak it clearly,
> how the water goes
> is how the earth is shaped.
>
> (303)

Like Roethke and Wright, however, Harrison modifies his Romantic attraction to the natural world by insisting on the difficulties posed by such an embrace. A recurring motif in Harrison's writing is the experience of "getting lost," which literally means to lose one's bearings in the backcountry. In "Passacaglia on Getting Lost," Harrison states that "getting lost is to sense the 'animus' of nature," thereby recognizing the landscape as a living force, a natural context outside the ordinary, indoor, social world. "Perhaps getting lost temporarily destroys the acquisitive sense," he suggests (*Just before Dark*, 262–63). In "The Theory and Practice of Rivers," written in the isolation of his Upper Peninsula cabin, Harrison considers the locations of his life, including Key West, Los Angeles, and Grove Street in New York, where at age nineteen he discovered "red wine, garlic, Rimbaud, / and a red haired girl." At the river, which Harrison says "is as far as I move / from the world of numbers," he seeks a sense of himself independent of his memories and ambitions:

> What is it to actually go outside the nest
> we have built for ourselves, and earlier
> our father's nest: to go into a forest
> alone with our eyes open? It's different
> when you don't know what's over the hill—
> keep the river on your left, then you see
> the river on your right. I have simply
> forgotten left and right, even up and down,
> whirl then sleep on a cloudy day to forget
> direction. It is hard to learn how
> to be lost after so much training.
>
> (314)

Getting lost, according to Harrison, is less dangerous for the body than for the soul; as Swanson, the narrator of *Wolf* observes, "[T]he rare deaths that occur are simply a matter of the lost waiting too long to turn around" (18). Such was the fate of two snowmobilers near Harrison's cabin one winter. "They could have piled deadfall wood around their machines," Harrison writes in "Passacaglia," "and dropped matches into the remnants of the gas in the tanks, creating an enormous pyre for the search planes" (*Just before Dark,* 264). These men were doomed by their utilitarian attachment to machines: their "acquisitive sense" prevented consideration of the one act that could have saved their lives.

For a person whose resourcefulness would prevent such a tragedy, the more immediate danger in becoming lost is psychic: the possibility of projecting one's psychological crises onto the surroundings: "When we are lost we lose our peripheries. Our thoughts zoom outward and infect the landscape. Years later you can revisit an area and find these thoughts still diseasing the same landscape. It requires a particular kind of behavior to heal the location" (*Just before Dark,* 262). By behavior Harrison implies ritual. In poems such as "Walking" and "The Theory and Practice of Rivers," Harrison associates observation with *observance,* that is, with rite, ceremony, and sacrament. Arriving at a spring, knoll, or swale with a reverent attitude, one learns not only to see but also to cope with life, with the burdens of personal and social history. These matters come into focus in the back country because, as Harrison notes in koan-like fashion, "When you're lost you know who you are. You're the only one out there" ( *Just before Dark,* 264).

This is the case with Swanson, the narrator of *Wolf* whose life history is almost identical to the author's: the loss of sight in one eye, the deaths of his beloved sister and father in a car crash, a bohemian period in New York and Boston. Alone in the woods of northern Michigan, Swanson fishes and camps out, all the while brooding over his private sorrows and alienation from a society that seems bent on destroying all sacred places in the name of profit:

> From the vantage point of 1970 it appeared that all my move-
> ments since 1958 had been lateral rather than forward. I had
> printed three extremely slender books of poetry which took up
> approximately an inch of shelf space. A succession of not very
> interesting nervous breakdowns. The reading of perhaps a few
> thousand books and the absorption of no wisdom from them. . . .
> My real griefs were over the dead and the prospects of a disas-
> trous future; my affection for the presentness of the woods was
> easily accounted for. Trees offer no problems and even if all
> wilderness is despoiled I'll settle for a hundred acres and hide
> within it and defend it. (138–39)

There is little sentimentality about nature in *Wolf;* Swanson knows that he can neither escape his past nor discover a pristine sanctuary from in-dustrial society. Depressed, lonely, and beset by alcoholic cravings, Swan-son does not seek places of postcard beauty, but "swamps divided invisi-bly from the air by interlocking creeks and small rivers, made unbearable in spring and summer by mosquitoes and black flies, swamps dank with brackish water and pools of green slime, small knolls of fern, bog marshes of sphagnum, spongelike and tortuous to the human foot and bordered by impenetrable tamarack thickets" (18). This difficult terrain corre-sponds to Swanson's memory and feelings of dread, a psychic landscape that he is determined to explore at any emotional cost.

The premise of Harrison's first novel is not particularly original; *Wolf* follows Cooper's Leatherstocking tales and Hemingway's Nick Adams stories in an American tradition of wilderness romance. Such narratives center on male protagonists who flee from society into primitive country that restores their masculine vigor and instinct. Harrison's similarities to Hemingway are particularly obvious. Both authors depict semiautobiographical characters fishing and hunting in northern Michigan, describing the region's woods and waters with affectionate and sometimes luminous detail. Both struggled with alcoholism and suicidal thoughts; Swanson in *Wolf* briefly turns his rifle to his own forehead, contemplating "how Hemingway in unthinkable pain, mental and physical, picked the shotgun from the cabinet that morning" in 1961 (141).

Harrison's differences from Hemingway, however, overwhelm the largely superficial similarities. First, he did not kill himself. The fear that he might led him to confront the topic in his writing, as in *Letters to Yesenin* (1973), poems addressed to the Russian poet who hung himself in 1925. Love for his family, as Harrison writes in that book, sustained him: "My year-old daughter's red / robe hangs from the doorknob shouting *Stop*" (199). Ultimately, what saved Harrison from Hemingway's fate, besides effective psychiatric treatment, was the tonic of wild nature. Writing of fly fishing and the mayflies that cause trout to rise, Harrison observes that "few of us shoot ourselves during an evening hatch" ("Jim Harrison," 145). Swanson in *Wolf* comes to a similar conclusion after flirting with Hemingway's method of self-destruction: "I smiled to myself. How far again I was from taking my life with the woods covered with the skin of moonlight" (141).

That Harrison also differs from Hemingway as a literary naturalist is evident if we compare *Wolf* with the most famous Nick Adams story, "Big Two-Hearted River." While both are set in Michigan's Upper Peninsula, they express distinct attitudes about nature in distinct styles of prose. Writing in short declarative sentences, Hemingway dwells on details of setting and physical action. Nick pitches his tent, cooks dinner, and catches trout with a competence and deliberation recalling Cooper's Natty Bumppo and Clemens's Huckleberry Finn. The reader learns little about Nick's past; indeed, the common inference that Nick is recovering from the trauma of World War I is possible only when "Big Two-Hearted River" is read in light of other Nick Adams stories. Hemingway achieved a modernist perfection in this story by editing out expository passages and references to Nick's social relationships that would have interfered with what Harrison has called the "incorruptible purity of [Hemingway's] style, the splendor and clarity of the language as language" (*Just before Dark,* 236). The story impresses through inference and reduction, much in the manner of cubist painters. "Nick," Hemingway writes in one of the passages he edited out, "seeing how Cézanne would paint this stretch of river and the swamp, stood up and stepped down into the stream. The water was cold and actual" (248).

Despite his belief that "Big Two-Hearted River" would "be near the summit of any literature," Harrison is after quite a different effect in *Wolf* (*Just before Dark,* 237). Hemingway ends his story with Nick deciding not to enter a swamp, because "in the fast deep water, in the half light, the fishing would be tragic. In the swamp fishing was a tragic adventure" (202). Harrison, on the other hand, *begins* his novel with his protagonist plunging headlong into the very terrain, topographical and psychological, that Hemingway avoids. Through intriguing verbal shifts, flashbacks, and stream-of-consciousness asides, Swanson describes his aimless travel, sexual encounters, and work history with a self-effacing humor far removed from Hemingway's dignity and seriousness. As inept as Nick Adams is proficient at woodcraft, Swanson carries an old rifle with inaccurate sights and uses trotlines to catch fish instead of the casting rod so deftly handled by Nick. The compass reading he takes is "inaccurate and pointless as the ground in the area was full of varying amounts of iron ore." Proceeding anyway, he is soon "unfathomably lost," in which state he remains for the better part of the novel (19).

Nick Adams certainly approaches the woods and waters of northern Michigan with reverence and joy. But he is never lost, not even for a moment. Hemingway's pride as an outdoorsman would never have allowed it. Northern Michigan meant escape for Hemingway, as would Africa and the Gulf Stream in later years: escape from the bourgeois proprieties of Oak Park, Illinois, his childhood hometown, escape into the pine forests and wild rivers of summer, escape from women into a fantasy of male self-sufficiency. Harrison's protagonist, on the other hand, enters the woods at a loss. Missing his family and mourning the deaths of his father and sister, Swanson yearns for the domestic life, both remembered and anticipated, that Hemingway's heroes consistently avoid. "Being lost," Swanson decides, "somehow presupposes a distant location that you are trying to find, a warm center where a door will open, a screen door at that with a piece of cotton on it to keep off the flies, and into a yellow kitchen where a woman is cooking at the stove" (149–50). One explores wild nature, in other words, not out of rugged individualism, but as a ritual retreat from ego and ambition, from which one hopes to return chastened and better prepared to deal with social commitments. Harrison's perspective is rural, not suburban; his pastoral aspires not only to flight but also to return, to family and home.

Harrison's next pastoral novel, *Farmer* (1976), portrays his own people, Swedish Americans who "moved into Northern Michigan because it was a beautiful place" (126). *Farmer* is set in the 1950s, a period of school consolidation, migration to urban areas, and the industrialization of agriculture on ever-larger farms. The story concerns Joseph Lundgren, a "gimp forty-three year old schoolteacher farmer" torn between his love for one woman and sexual attraction to another (131). As the inevitable decision draws near, Joseph must face a larger issue: his prolonged inaction after the deaths of his father and best friend, Orin, a casualty of the Korean War. He has allowed grief and his physical limitations (a serious childhood injury left him with a permanent limp) to interfere with his passions and commitments: his love for Rosealee, widow of his best friend, and his long-deferred dream of traveling to see the ocean. The crisis, naturally, occurs in a setting of farms and semiwilderness where Joseph acquires greater consciousness and resolve.

Literary precedent plays an important role in *Farmer*. One of the first things we learn about Joseph is that he loves books and spends his free time "reading about the ocean, general works on marine biology, or popular history books dealing with war and the Orient" (3). These books stand in for the adventures he has missed, much as an inappropriate relationship with Catherine, one of his senior students, compensates for his mundane sexual history. Catherine "was from the outside world," having recently moved to the area from a city downstate, "and this clearly interested him no matter how dangerous the situation was" (10). After their first sexual encounter, Joseph goes hunting but is distracted by thoughts of his new lover. Sitting in "his favorite place, a hillock in a grove of oaks overlooking a creek," he contemplates the affair with difficulty because his only points of comparison are literary. Catherine "turned him into a lunatic making him think of the hundreds of novels he had read, written he always believed by liars because he had never until Catherine experienced anything remotely similar except in his imagination" (12).

Authors who have fired Joseph's imagination include Walt Whitman, William Faulkner, and D. H. Lawrence, among others. As in *Wolf,* Hemingway also makes an appearance. Late in the novel, while Joseph drives to Chicago with students on their senior trip, his thoughts briefly turn to Hemingway's *Green Hills of Africa* and then to *Farewell to Arms,* "the Hemingway novel about the love affair with the nurse named Catherine who was so unlike the Catherine he had dallied with. The book had upset him terribly and the night he had finished it he had had trouble sleeping" (151). The allusion simultaneously invites and negates comparison of Hemingway, Harrison, and their fictional characters. Harrison's Catherine resembles Hemingway's in name only, just as his fiction shares little with Hemingway's beyond northern Michigan settings and scenes of fishing and hunting. His view of nature is more "humane," in Thoreau's sense, more concerned with social "affections" than solitary adventurousness.

Catherine's name, however, may evoke a more accurate association among midwestern modernists: Cather. It is Cather, not Hemingway, who provided Harrison with the type and pattern of his novel. *Farmer* closely resembles Cather's *O Pioneers!* in many aspects of characterization and pastoral convention. Both novels portray Swedish American farm families on the margins of the Midwest: Harrison's Lundgrens reside in Michigan, just north of the transition between eastern hardwood and pine-oak forest, Cather's Bergsons in south-central Nebraska, just east of the ninety-eighth meridian and the Great Plains. Both protagonists cope with the narrow-mindedness of some in the provinces. Each misses someone who has moved to the city; Joseph's twin sister Arlice and Alexandra's friend and future husband Carl represent, as Harrison writes of Arlice, "both the treachery and glory of what [Joseph] thought of as the outside world" (133). Joseph and Alexandra both face the death of a parent, after which they must make crucial decisions regarding the disposition of the land they have inherited. Joseph's closest friend is Dr. Evans, a Welsh immigrant many years his senior who provides him with sage advice and company on fishing trips; Alexandra relies on Ivar, the old Norwegian, to speak frankly about family problems as well as livestock. Both novels pivot on stories of troubled love: Joseph's destructive triangle with Rosealee and Catherine, and Marie's with Emil Bergson and her husband, Frank, in *O Pioneers!* In its Virgilian concern with love, aging, and death; desire for wider knowledge; and intense awareness of local geography, *Farmer* adapts Catherian pastoral to a northern Michigan setting. It reads as an homage to Cather and to the farm community of Harrison's youth.

Place, as in earlier pastoral novels, is the unifying theme of *Farmer*. Joseph's challenge is to live authentically where he is, to center himself within the wider world. The pastoral convention of rural-urban contrast is operative here, with Joseph's twin sister Arlice providing a foil for Joseph with her sophisticated life in New York. Joseph might have followed her advice simply to leave. The benefits of city life are obvious: employment, access to cultural resources, and a general sense of novelty and adventure. Further incentive to move is provided by the limitations of rural society: the casual racism and xenophobia that sometimes make Joseph feel "that all country people were essentially hillbillies, no matter the distance to the Mason-Dixon line" (91). Rosealee, who also teaches, deals with bigotry by "accepting [people] as they were and [making] great efforts to register some change, however small." Since he lacks such patience, "Joseph's tactic was merely to stare with unconcealed contempt." But he is very much of the place; the locals "all knew Joseph was somehow one of them, no matter how strange and removed his behavior. They knew his parents and sisters, the dimensions of the family farm, who his relations were, how the family fared during the Depression and the war" (29). Despite his irritation at provincial intolerance and his yearning to see something of the world, Joseph belongs where he is. What he needs is not to leave but to face the past and make basic decisions about his future. Otherwise he will feel not at home in the country he loves, but trapped. As Dr. Evans tells him, "you have to act some other way than sitting here thinking that life has jilted you. That's what I mean. If you want to marry, marry, and if not say Rosealee I can't marry you. Just do something other than walking around this place pissing your life away brooding" (137).

The doctor, it is important to note, is not advising flight or that Joseph stop walking in the woods thinking things over. Hunting and fishing are more than pastimes for Joseph; being outdoors, occasionally pausing in special locations, constitutes his spiritual life. Joseph's attempt to sight a coyote, like Swanson's search in *Wolf* for that other wild canine, allows

him to transcend his obsessiveness and self-absorption: "Joseph could almost see through the coyote's eyes as he laughed with the embarrassment
of an amateur: the man sits there restless and stares for four afternoons.
He leaves some meat which is not eaten because I'm not hungry. He
leaves a lovely white chicken. He runs and waves at hawks and I circle
around the clearing. As he walks back to his hiding place I run out and
steal the chicken" (24). The idea of a "hiding place" is key here. Joseph's
surroundings are full of places that encourage self-transcendence and
reassessment. The "safe place of his youth" was "a corner of the mow in
the barn [where] he had made a rude house. . . . When he was unhappy
he would hide there with his pile of rabbit and raccoon skins, two sets of
deer antlers, the dried head of a large pike he had tacked to a board, and
his favorite blanket from his early childhood" (98). Favorite places outdoors include the hillock he visits after beginning his affair with Catherine, "a small grassy clearing which was thought of as an Indian graveyard
by hearsay," and a "narrow valley at the end of which was the beaver
pond and the beginning of the marsh" (123–24). Joseph's motivation in visiting these places is not escapist, but aesthetic and philosophical. "An idea
that fixed him to one spot," Harrison writes, "was that life was a death
dance and that he had quickly passed through the spring and summer
of his life and was halfway through the fall. He had to do a better job
on the fall because everyone on earth knew what the winter was like"
(14–15).

Joseph's musings are not only personal but also social and ecological.
After shooting feral dogs that have been dragging down deer, he imagines "a time when Michigan wasn't a game farm for hunters, when the
natural predators, the puma, wolf, coyote, and lynx still lived there. And
the Indian. Not man hunting for sport and his house pets gone wild and
utterly destructive" (46). Recent experiences have changed Joseph's attitude about hunting; he no longer shoots deer, ducks, or woodcock, a small
game bird he has removed from the "food category and allowed . . . to
join the highest strata, that of the owls and hawks, the raptors, harriers,
and *Falconiformes*" (19). These distinctions arise from ethical and aesthetic
imperatives suggested by local geography. Joseph lives in a landscape
shaped by glaciers, a region "which after the first wave of lumbering that
scalped the land of its giant white pine had not been able to support
anything but poplar, scrub oak, mixed stunted conifers, except in the

richer swampy areas." Like the Upper Peninsula country featured in *Wolf*, the area varies in its utility (some parts, "nearly gutted with sand blowing through ferns and brake . . . never should have been farmed at all") and in aesthetic appeal to the average eye (142). Yet to those who know it best, the region offers a way of life, if an uncertain source of income:

> The good farms in the county tended to follow a rather narrow irregular strip the glaciers had missed and their woodlots were dotted with huge beech and maple and the soil was rich. Joseph's father had stupidly chosen a fringe because of its beauty; all the improvident farmers in the county held one thing in common— they squatted on the moraine like hopeless ducks trying to scratch a living off the few inches of top soil that hovered over the pecker sand and gravel like a thin lid. But the rivers that ran swift and clean through this hilly country and the swamps in the valleys promised wonderful trout fishing, and Joseph and the doctor both loved this land the agriculturalists thought of as useless. (94)

Joseph, then, owns not only land but also a land ethic and aesthetic. He is the very sort of amateur naturalist that Leopold corresponded with and occasionally visited to gather field data. Because of his injured leg, he went into teaching rather than full-time farming, preferring to lease his land to neighbors like the "pleasant though utterly venal man who worked his wife and sons to exhaustion farming five hundred acres" (4–5). Lacking venality, Joseph has continued in the manner of his Swedish ancestors, who "came up and bought a small farm for seven hundred dollars just after the century's turn, not to make money but to have a way to live." He is, as far as possible in a time when "farm life . . . was quickly dwindling into the past," an independent yeoman rather than an agriculturalist (126).

Joseph, however, has not been as decisive in his personal life as in his outdoor pursuits, and his wavering ultimately diminishes his relationship to nature. Riding on horseback to the valley beyond which begins the marsh, he discovers a change, not in the location but in himself: "This had always been Joseph's favorite place, even in his youth when it had provided the equivalent in the natural world of his fort in the hay mow. But now he was grasping hard for a peace that refused to arrive" (124).

Nostalgia is pulling him down, much as "his rock in the barnyard," which "had seemed so large when they were children and used it to climb onto the pony . . . had shriveled [and] was sinking into the ground" (7). Like so many other physical aspects of his environment, the rock reflects Joseph's situation: if he does not overcome his grief, it will pull him into the ground. "I have to . . . get [Rosealee] to forgive me," he muses, "or I'm sunk" (115).

When Joseph finally does take action it necessarily encompasses love and place. He takes the advice his mother gives him before she dies of cancer, to sell the farm, marry Rosealee, and honeymoon at the ocean, before returning to cultivate the land Rosealee inherited from Orin. After "nearly destroy[ing] their love like some madman burning a barn or shooting his animals," Joseph gets a second chance at happiness, which means domestic tranquility in a broad sense: faithfulness to both Rosealee and the land (8). The novel has two endings. One occurs in the novel's final pages, as Joseph sleeps with Catherine one last time during the senior trip to Chicago. Chicago, like Detroit, is to Joseph "not so much . . . squalid" as a place "where he just wouldn't fit in" (125). The same might be said of Joseph's affair with Catherine, which begins as "something as full and wonderful as anything the imagination can muster," but ends, predictably, with tears and a bad hangover (13). Harrison places the novel's second ending at the beginning, "a late June evening in 1956 in a seacoast town" as a couple enters a restaurant. It is Joseph and Rosealee on their honeymoon, very much in love: "*They laugh and are tentative with a plate of oysters. The man scratches his head, messing his hair. She smiles and reaches across the table, nervously brushing his hair back into place with her palm. He closely examines an oyster shell, rubbing its rough outside surface with curiosity*" (1; emphasis Harrison's). Like Cather's Alexandra on her projected honeymoon in Alaska, Joseph has reconciled with his home and his past by traveling, not to escape but to explore and then return with a more open heart. As the other diners notice, Joseph and Rosealee belong together, and in their place: "The prescient ones in the restaurant who have eaten much more slowly than the couple have made up their minds. It is a farmer and his wife. And likely from the midwest, as the farmers from the west, ranchers, tend to dress more extravagantly, and those from the east with enough money to travel wear more fashionable clothes" (1–2).

Other than *Farmer,* Harrison's fiction in the 1970s tended to experimentalism. *A Good Day to Die* (1973) anticipated the premise of Edward Abbey's ecofable *The Monkey Wrench Gang* (1975): hard-drinking environmentalists decide to free a western river by blowing up an offending dam. *Legends of the Fall* (1978) is a collection of three novellas "comprised of adventure, violence, romantic obsession, and death" (Roberson, 234). Only one, "The Man Who Gave Up His Name," is partly set in the Midwest; the others take place in Mexico and in Montana. Although the book earned Harrison a wider audience and reviews comparing him to Faulkner and Melville, it also gave critics a chance to tag him as a "macho" writer. This, as William H. Roberson convincingly argues, is a "particularly myopic critical perception of [Harrison's] fiction":

> Although all of his stories may be marked with what some may narrowly and traditionally perceive to be the ancient rituals of masculinity—drinking, fishing, hunting, and sex—Harrison consistently deflates the super male animal. . . . If they are seen as macho, it must be as a macho pose, and that pose is ultimately sentimental and thus self-destructive. . . . [They] do not represent the epitome of manliness and virtue. They are not leaders; they are lost. . . . Their inability to commit themselves successfully to women or families is not a strength but a failure of the characters, a point Harrison makes clear in the relationships that evolve in his other works. (236)

In *Legends of the Fall,* as Roberson points out, machismo leads to "emptiness or exhaustion . . . loss, pity, and isolation" (235). Harrison's other fictions deal with the issue comically, from Swanson's bumbling through the woods in *Wolf* to the "goofiness" exhibited by several of his narrators, including Lundgren in *Warlock* (1981), "Jim Harrison" in *Sundog,* and Michael in *Dalva.* These characters all reflect aspects of their author at his imagined worst: impulsive, overindulgent, and prone to getting lost in the woods. Roberson sums up these characters well: "Any pretense at macho is more an example of their own narcissism, vanity, and false pride than any reflection of male dominance" (241).

The three works last mentioned undercut male vanity with strong comedic elements adapted, in part, from detective fiction. *Warlock* involves

"a goofy fop" hired by a mysterious and wealthy landowner to investigate violations of his property rights in northern Michigan. *Sundog* is
narrated by a version of Harrison as a dissipated journalist who embarks
on "a long journey back toward Earth" by investigating a retired engineer named Strang (xi). Humor in *Sundog* derives from the discrepancy
between "Harrison's" tough attitude and his dread of confrontation. At
times he sounds like a character from the fiction of John D. MacDon-
ald, a detective writer Harrison praises in *Sundog* and elsewhere for evoking "the riper colors of evil, sex, utter mayhem" (209): "You could enter
schizoid Michigan in the Detroit metropolitan area, where the old West
replays itself with over six hundred murders a year, the new mythology,
not the quick-draw face-off, but the squalor of anonymous slaughter;
then out Michigan's nether end, the U.P., as it's called, you enter a timbered-
over, rock-strewn waste, a land so dense and desolate it became obvious
to me that the most redoubtable survivalist couldn't survive" (14). Harrison's description of Detroit also brings to mind detective writers Elmore
Leonard and Loren Estleman, who have written extensively about the
Motor City's underworld and have created characters not unlike Strang's
brother Karl, a violent and implacable man. Harrison, however, uses detective convention, particularly the genre's wry and skeptical tone, with
self-effacing hyperbole. When, for example, Strang's ex-wife accurately
dismisses the narrator as "drunk on novelty, not reality," he begins to "to
strangle and hyperventilate at the same time," then falls "facedown in
[his] pear sorbet and chèvre cheese" (4).

As the narrator of *Sundog* says, however, "the [detective] genre was
limited and, finally, tended to attach itself to an excitement with a rather
low metaphysical lid" (210). The heart of the novel is Strang's own narrative, edited from "a thousand or so pages of transcribed tape" (x). His
story, "immersed in love, work, and death," is a pastoral invocation of
"the mystery of personality, of life itself" (210). Images of immersion,
particularly in rivers and lakes, dominate Strang's life as he tells it, beginning with his near drowning at age seven. Thrown from a boat one
night by a lightning strike, Strang survived because of his ability to swim
at night. The accident, however, brought on petit mal epilepsy, a lifelong affliction that almost killed him years later when a seizure caused
him to fall from a dam he was helping to construct in Venezuela. Strang
has returned to the region of his childhood, where he tries to recover

from his injuries by crawling through the woods and wading up rivers at night.

At the journalist's request, Strang also reviews his life as the son of an evangelical minister and as a construction foreman on irrigation projects around the world. Strang differs from Harrison's typical male character in his "capacity to be all of one piece at any given time" (167). The central conflict in Strang's life has been between spirituality and action, "the call to commit an act of daring that will lift him out of the commonplace in the eyes of others" (56). As a child, he plans either to follow his father into the ministry or to become a great engineer. Although he does preach for a time, Strang is ineluctably drawn to a life of passion, hard work, and travel. His call to adventure takes the form of the Mackinac Bridge, a landmark project to span the straits dividing Michigan's two peninsulas. This great bridge "represented the slowly building path to the outside world," which Strang explored for thirty years working on similarly grand constructions in Africa and South America (147). Having grown up in poverty, Strang is compelled by the social utility of his work. "Those triumphs of technology and engineering," he tells the narrator, "are questioned the most by the people who have the most," not by people in places "where the drilling of one first-rate well with pure water could save hundreds of lives from fatal cholera, not to speak of any number of slower deaths from other diseases" (154).

There is something of the midwestern tinkerer in Strang's makeup, in his practical bent and faith in applied science. Yet, as Roberson points out, "his is a triumph of spirit not physicality" (239). A life spent diverting rivers has given Strang cause to ponder the correspondence of human life with the rhythms of nature. His meditation on water, spiritual and scientific, culminates in "The Theory and Practice of Rivers," the title under which Strang has collected his thoughts about hydrology. In his *Paris Review* interview with Jim Fergus, Harrison explains the underlying metaphor: "In a life properly lived, you're a river. You touch things lightly or deeply; you move along because life herself moves, and you can't stop it; you can't figure out a banal game plan applicable to all situations; you just have to go with the 'beingness of life,' as Rilke would have it. In *Sundog,* Strang says a dam doesn't stop a river, it just controls the flow. Technically speaking, you can't stop one at all" (57). Strang's life and his narration of it has this kind of flow, as in a "speech, almost oracular, with some of the rhythms of an evangelist" that he delivers one day. This "odd disquisition" begins with memories of his sister "bathing him in a creek as an infant" and ends "with the nature of the great ocean currents and rivers such as the Humboldt, the Gulf Stream, and others." The point is "that water never stops: it is always in movement up into the air, or down into the earth where there are, of all things, underground rivers" (166). Despite his psychological and physical afflictions, Strang still seeks the center of streams, literally and figuratively. He allows his consciousness to flow backward in time, downward into the mysteries of his own identity and forward into an uncertain future.

The autobiographical dimension of *Sundog* is not limited to the journalist, who shares a name and part of his life history with the author. Strang himself is an alter ego for Harrison, who also suffered a life-altering accident at age seven, dabbled in theology, read adventure books by Richard Halliburton, and favored night walking along rivers as a form of meditation. In the novel, as it turns out, the relationship between Strang and the fictional Harrison may run thicker than water. Just when Strang's actual parentage has been clarified, the narrator learns that he and Strang may in fact be half brothers. Although the possibility that they share a father remains unconfirmed, it resonates as a final "mystery of personality" in this, the most philosophical of Harrison's novels. One of the author's most compelling characters, Strang figures as a model of consciousness and self-transcendence in relation to personal history and place. He is, in part, what Harrison would like to be. Strang remembers someone (psychologist James Hillman, actually) asking, "What have we done with the twin that was given us when we were given our soul?" (164). What Harrison has done is to personify his twin, soul, or anima as autobiographically inspired characters like Strang, whose private writings about water anticipate both the title and substance of Harrison's next book of poems, *The Theory and Practice of Rivers* (1985).

*Sundog* also anticipates Harrison's next novel, *Dalva* (1988), which resembles the earlier work in its use of multiple narration, characters representing contrary dimensions of the author's personality, and research into the family history of a well-traveled rural midwesterner. *Dalva* fulfills the epic ambitions of *Legends of the Fall* and *Sundog* by amplifying their historical as well as psychological concerns. It is an ambitious book and a landmark in midwestern pastoral.

The novel bears the name of its protagonist, a forty-five-year-old woman who returns to northwestern Nebraska after years spent elsewhere pursuing "a wonderfully undistinguished career, but an interesting enough life" (251). Most recently a social worker in Santa Monica, California, Dalva comes back to inherited wealth, a substantial ranch, and unresolved conflicts related to family history. On a personal level, she wishes to find the son she gave up at birth and to cope more effectively with the loss of her lover, the child's father, and with her father's death in the Korean War. The larger context of Dalva's return home is her family's role in plains history. She has agreed to let Michael, a historian and her current lover, read the diaries of her great-grandfather John Wesley Northridge, an agricultural missionary to the Sioux in the late nineteenth century. In return, Michael has agreed to help Dalva find her missing son. These stories converge in the novel's climax, when Dalva faces her own past and that of the nation by descending into the cellar of her home, which holds Northridge's secret collection of Indian artifacts.

The narrative strategies that Harrison employs in *Dalva* have occasioned most of the critical commentary, positive and negative, on the book. For the first time, Harrison narrates from a female point of view, speaking in Dalva's voice in the first and last of three sections. The middle section is told by Michael, the loutish historian who also quotes at length from Northridge's diaries. Their relationship reenacts the conventional pastoral contrast of urban and rural personalities, though in a comic fashion. Unlike the graceful and confident Dalva, Michael "seemed unaware that his head was connected in any meaningful way to his body" (84). He acts and speaks impulsively, drinking to excess and abusing Dalva's trust and that of her neighbors. His final irresponsibility is to have sex with an underage girl, whose father takes revenge by sending Michael to the hospital with a broken jaw and arm. Only then does Dalva reconsider her "involvement with the miserable son of a bitch," who "simply in some classic sense didn't know any better" (218).

While many reviewers agreed with Jonathan Yardley that "the book runs a bit off course while [Michael] is at center stage," most felt that Harrison had succeeded with the voice and character of Dalva (3). Perhaps the keenest assessment came from Louise Erdrich. Although she faults Harrison for excessive "descriptions of drinking ... sentimentalism, [and] a tendency to lecture," Erdrich praises his "fascinating mixture of voices that cut through time and cross the barriers of culture and gender to achieve a work in chorus." *Dalva,* Erdrich concludes, should be "celebrated, suspended in its own beauty, met halfway and read with trust and exuberance."

Coming from a major novelist and poet who has written extensively about the Great Plains, that is high praise indeed. As a pastoral novel, *Dalva* responds to Erdrich and other contemporary Native American authors who have caused Harrison to reconsider the relation of his own writing to history and landscape. In his essay "Poetry as Survival," Harrison observes that these writers are often "ignored by readers because they represent a ghost that is too utterly painful to be encountered":

> Actual readers of literature are people of conscience . . . but conscience can be delayed by malice, stereotypes, a natural aversion to the unpleasant. I'm old enough to remember when Langston Hughes and Richard Wright were considered the only black writers of interest. Publishers come largely from the East and anything between our two dream coasts tends to be considered an oblique imposition. There's also the notion that the predominantly white literary establishment idealizes a misty, ruined past when life held unity and grace. [For] Native American poets the past isn't misty, [and] the civilization that was destroyed was a living memory for their grandparents, and thus the Indian poet is a living paradigm of the modern condition. (*Just before Dark,* 300)

The idea of a "misty, ruined past" is of course one version of pastoral myth, best represented in midwestern fiction by Willa Cather. While she overcame the regional bias against writing from "between our two dream coasts," Cather did not transcend pastoral distortions of American history. However sensitive to the natural beauty of the prairie, her pioneer novels disregard Native Americans and the violence of their displacement. In *Dalva,* Harrison creates a version of Catherian pastoral, one modified by the lessons of Native American literature and history and motivated by his hope that "these people might clarify why I had spent over forty years wandering around in the natural world" and that "the two cultures had more to offer each other than their respective demons" (*Just before Dark,* 298).

*Dalva* resembles Cather's pioneer novels in its Nebraska setting and portrayal of an independent land-owning woman. Like Alexandra Bergson in O *Pioneers!* Dalva (who is partly of Swedish descent) is generous, imaginative, and sensitive to the subtle beauty of the prairie. Her relationship with Lundquist, an elderly Swedish American farmhand who also worked for her grandfather, is analogous to Alexandra's with Ivar, the old Norwegian who looks after the Bergson farm. Like Ivar, the eccentric Lundquist is protective of his employer, good with animals, and decidedly unorthodox in his religious beliefs. Dalva recalls his mystical behavior on a horse-buying trip to Montana, when Lundquist talked to "three ranch dogs about Nebraska, as if to explain why he was there." When asked why the normally unruly dogs had sat so quietly, Lundquist explained that he was being courteous and that "he had never met an animal that didn't know if your heart was in the right place. Humans could develop this ability with each other if they would only study the works of Emanual Swedenborg," the Swedish mystic who influenced Emerson (245). Lundquist's solicitude and propriety extend not only to the natural world, but also to social relations. The reluctance with which he enters Dalva's house demonstrates the same Old World decorum attributed by Cather to "Crazy Ivar," the barefoot mystic of the Divide.

Dalva also resembles Cather's Alexandra (and Ántonia) in her spirituality of place. Her landscape is storied, full of historical and personal resonances. At times she has felt as if "previous thoughts were hanging on the phone poles and power lines—even sexual fantasies from the distant past . . . lie in wait along creek bottoms and ditches, the village limits of no longer occupied crossroads, the name announcing nothing but itself and the memory of what you were doing and thinking other times you passed this way" (292). While significant locations sometimes disturb Dalva, they also reassure her and ease her sorrows. One such place is "the upper end of a small box canyon" across the Niobrara River from her grandfather's ranch. She first visited the place as a teenager, accompanied by her lover Duane, a half-Sioux boy who was trying to recover his heritage. Duane "announced that this was a holy place" and to "prove it he found several arrowheads, and sat on the flat rock for a full hour in silence, facing the east." The following year, after Duane's disappearance and the adoption of their child, Dalva returned to the spot, where she sat for a day meditating and watching animals. "Mostly," she remembers, "I had a very long and intensely restful 'nothing.' I had the odd sensation that I was understanding the earth. This is all very simple-minded and I mention it only because I still do much the same thing when troubled" (55–56).

Dalva's topophilia contrasts with Michael's placelessness. Having dissipated a "travel grant back to the Ohio Valley . . . on Chicago high life," Michael fabricated his first book, an ironically well-reviewed history of a steel town (127). His current research represents a chance to redeem himself personally and professionally. But Michael has never bothered to acquaint himself with living Indians or to explore the prairie with any care. "I am not by inclination a nature buff," he says, admitting to his "dislike of its tooth-and-claw world" (115). The idea of entering a river at night fills him with dread, and when he finds himself lost on his first morning in Nebraska, his accidental encounter with one of Dalva's sacred places (a group of Indian mounds in a thicket) only makes him feel "a helpless anger." Typically, he reassures himself with a historian's reliance on dates: "This is 1986—June 6, to be exact, and this fucking place is disturbing me" (117).

Michael's limited, intellectual response to landscape amounts to defensive rationalization. He claims, interrupting Dalva during a lunchtime talk, that he sees "human history with a dignity, albeit tentative," while her "vision is infected with a girlish infatuation with Wordsworth and Shelley." He dismisses her ideas as "Dalva's airplane theory":

> The upshot was that from an airliner the entirety of the United States, except for a few spotty wilderness areas, looked raked over, tracked up, skinned, scalped—in short, abused. . . . In out-of-the-way places there's still a certain spirit, I mean in gullies, off-the-road ditches, neglected creek banks and bottoms, places that have only been tilled once, then neglected, or not at all, like the Sand Hills, parts of northern Wisconsin, the Upper Peninsula of Michigan, or the untillable but grazed plains of Wyoming, Montana, Nevada, the desert, even the ocean in the middle of the night.

Dalva's thoughts are of course Harrison's own on the spirit of place. Michael's typically thoughtless response to her discourse emphasizes his doubtful academic authority: "Just where did you get your degrees?" When Dalva understandably walks out of the restaurant, even his manner of making up reflects his overreliance on intellectual authority. "I got down on my knees and begged her forgiveness," Michael says, "telling her the semi-fib that I had read something similar to her notion in Gaston Bachelard's *Poetics of Space*" (123).

The contrast between Michael and Dalva is consistent with Harrison's ongoing spiritual autobiography. Dalva represents Harrison's aspirations and Michael his fears, much as do Strang and the journalist-narrator, respectively, in *Sundog*. She is the answer to the question, borrowed from James Hillman, that Strang poses to "Harrison": "What have we done with the twin that was given us when we were given our soul?" James I. McClintock describes *Dalva* as "Harrison's experiment in developing his feminine side in the service of his art and his life, born of his sustained thinking about . . . James Hillman's post-Jungian ideas" ("Dalva," 327). Employing the categories of animus and anima, Hillman urges his readers toward "soul-making," a term borrowed from John Keats to signify the deepening of selfhood through sympathy and imagination. To cope with life and achieve fulfillment, one must work through suffering, listen to dreams, and integrate disparate parts of one's personality. Harrison does so by personifying his anima, or female principle, in Dalva, a fictional character whose dreams and sorrows closely match his own. By assuming the voice of a woman, McClintock finds, Harrison was able to find "the 'twin sister' he had lost . . . and extend in redemptive ways his understanding of masculinity" (328).

As an experiment in soul-making, *Dalva* should be understood in relation to place and history. Dalva's healing comes not only through dreams, but also through a confrontation of ghosts in her local landscape. Her grief, she concludes, is "too large to be understood" except in relation to the timelessness of the human condition in nature: "I was on the porch on a hot afternoon in June, and before me on hundreds of June afternoons Sioux girls looked for birds' eggs, buffalo whelped, prairie wolves roamed, and far before that—in prehistory we're told—condors with wingspreads of thirty feet coasted on dense thermals in the hills along the Niobrara" (281). While she may not be able to comprehend grief, Dalva must stop letting it hinder her from embracing life. "I'm forty-five," she realizes, "and there's still a weeping girl in my stomach.

I'm still in the arms of dead men—first Father then Duane. I may as well have burned down the goddamned house." This insight occurs to her on a road trip, during which she considers driving over to Fort Robinson, where the great warrior and holy man Crazy Horse was murdered. Dalva's anger at this moment over America's brutality toward its native people causes her to contemplate decisive action in her life. "What I'm trying to do," she decides, "is trade in a dead lover for a live son. I'll throw in a dead father with the dead lover and their souls I have kept in the basement perhaps. Even if I don't get to see the son I have to let the others go" (293).

The historical context of Dalva's self-transcendence encompasses literary precedent for Harrison's narrative strategies. In *My Ántonia,* Willa Cather assumes the voice of a male narrator, a character credited with a leading role in the development of former Indian lands in Nebraska. By speaking as Dalva, a woman of one-eighth Sioux descent, Harrison rectifies Cather's effacement of Native Americans from the plains. Furthermore, his pairing of Dalva and Michael as dual narrators serves more than the pastoral convention of paired rural and urban characters so often employed by Cather. Despite his limitations and faults, Michael represents historical consciousness and conscience. Harrison uses Michael to "poke fun at a tradition of scholarship," but stresses in the novel's acknowledgments "that without this tradition we are at the mercy of the renditions of political forces which are always self-serving and dead wrong" (n.p.). Likewise, while Dalva ultimately regrets her involvement with Michael, she recognizes that his research has helped her to overcome depression. "Perhaps unconsciously," Dalva thinks, "I had chosen Michael to rid myself of it" (292).

Dalva's grief, then, corresponds to the nation's troubled and violent history. Her healing, or soul-making, requires that she uncover not only her own past but also what Harrison elsewhere calls the "soul history" of America ( *Just before Dark,* 299). Harrison's belief that a nation, like an individual, possesses a soul concurs with Lawrence's commentary on "Spirit of Place" and remarks made by Snyder, Bly, and other writers. Yet "soul history" and "soul-making" in Harrison's vocabulary derive not only from Romantic, post-Romantic, and Jungian sources, but also from Christian teachings. Although he rejects the orthodoxy of "lunatic shit-brained fools" who deny soul to animals and landscape, Harrison's spirituality retains a strong Christian element (*Shape of the Journey,* 373). "I still seem to write totally within a Christian framework in an odd way," he admitted to interviewer Jim Fergus. "Never has it occurred to me not to believe in God and Jesus, and all that. I was quite a Bible student, pored over and over it, both the Old and New Testament in the King James Version" (79). Harrison does not identify as a Christian, just as he refuses to call himself a Buddhist despite his practice of Zen meditation (*Shape of the Journey,* 361). But Christianity colors his writing and his view of history and the current state of American society. "The way we killed [the Indians] is also what's killing us now," he told Fergus. "Greed. It's totally an Old Testament notion but absolutely true. Greed is killing the soul-life of the nation. You can see it all around you. It's destroying what's left of our physical beauty, it's polluting the country, it's making us more Germanic and warlike and stupid" (80–81).

In *Dalva,* Harrison personifies the ironies of religion in the first Northridge, who came to Nebraska in 1865. As his diaries reveal, Northridge intended to serve "as a Missionary and Botanist to help the native population, the Indians, to make the inevitable transition from warriors to tillers of the soil, an occupation toward which I am advised they have no predisposition" (115). During the Civil War, Northridge had been confined in the Confederate prison at Andersonville, where like Whitman he wrote letters for dying soldiers. The suffering he witnessed destroyed his faith, as well as his New Englander's taste for Emerson. Nevertheless, Northridge arrived on the Great Plains with optimism and determination to share the Gospel and horticulture with the Sioux. In this regard Michael cites fellow historian T. P. Thorton's argument that "the cultivation of fruit and other trees before the Civil War in New England and New York was considered to be morally uplifting, an antidote to the rapacity of greed that was consuming the nation" (125). Northridge's journal bears out Thorton's thesis; he writes in 1876, just before the nation's centennial celebration and the Battle of the Little Bighorn, that "the Anti-Christ is Greed" (198). In this way Northridge represents Jeffersonianism and Christianity at their best, as opposed to "the inanity of the 'Onward, Christian Soldiers' attitude that propelled millions of nitwits westward, utterly destroying much of the earth and all of the Native cultures" (*Road Home,* 107). As his son John Wesley Northridge II observes in *The Road Home* (1998), Harrison's sequel to *Dalva,* Northridge "was knowledgeable of the sound agricultural practices and the true Christian virtues that would have made the western movement other than the prolonged tragedy it became" (107). He is, in the best sense, a yeoman farmer.

Northridge, in this light, can also be described as a postbellum John Chapman. Better known as Johnny Appleseed, Chapman wandered Ohio and Indiana at the turn of the nineteenth century, when that region constituted the western frontier. Although Walt Disney has enfeebled our image of the man (just as he sanitized his hometown of Marcelline, Missouri, into Disneyland's Main Street, USA), Chapman did in fact plant apple trees and distribute seeds across the region. Contrary to the myth of a happy-go-lucky barefoot fool in rags, Chapman was a landowner, horticulturalist, and proselytizer of Swedenborgian gospel. He ranged the frontier in safety even during the Shawnee War because the Indians thought of him as a holy man. Similarly, Northridge owned nurseries in Illinois, Iowa, and New York and befriended the Sioux, who "thought of Northridge as a holy man in his many roles as one who fed them, who taught them to grow things no matter that they despised it, and who had become a capable if amateur doctor over the years" (*Dalva,* 314). Northridge, however, surpassed Chapman in sympathy for the native people of his region; he harbored warriors, participated in tribal rituals, and married Small Bird, the Sioux woman who became Dalva's great-grandmother. Perhaps Michael describes him best, in a letter to Dalva, as "a witness to the twilight of the gods," a man who "lived with people who talked to God and who thought 'God' talked back to them through the mouthpiece of earth herself" (276).

In John Wesley Northridge, Harrison embodies the moral dilemma at the heart of American pastoral ideology. The successful ranch that Northridge established near the Niobrara River, and that is passed down to Dalva, occupies former Indian land. The garden myth required the displacement of Native Americans. Yet as a local man wonders after Michael's speech to the Rotary Club (a situation recalling Sinclair Lewis's parodies of small-town booster groups), "What I don't get is, where was all those immigrants supposed to go?" Michael has no ready response; he can only admit that "this was a good question but I was describing what happened rather than what was supposed to happen" (202).

What was supposed to happen, at least according to well-meaning nineteenth-century Jeffersonians, was the assimilation of Indians into an

agrarian republic. While this project fell by the wayside with the rise of
Jacksonian democracy, it was revived by supporters of the Dawes Sever-
alty Act, passed by the U.S. Congress in 1887. Designed to end the tribal
structure of Indian society, the Dawes Act provided for the transfer of remaining tribal lands to individual Indians. In classic Jeffersonian fashion,
heads of families would be allotted 160 acres (a quarter section) of land,
individuals 80 acres. Remaining lands would be sold to white settlers.
Reformers hoped that through allotment Indians would learn to live as
did whites—as individualistic, property-owning yeoman farmers.

The Dawes Act pushed Northridge over the edge into rage and
madness. He ventured east to Albany, New York, in 1886, hoping to shoot
Senator Dawes at the Mohonk Conference on the "Indian Question."
Since Dawes was not present, Northridge settled for alienating the reformers at the conference with his "plan to create an entire Indian Nation" on the Great Plains. When the president of Amherst College spoke
on "the absolute need of awakening in the savage Indian broader desires
and ample wants," specifically a "desire for property of his own," Northridge assaulted the man and was subsequently thrown into jail (309–10).

History proved Northridge right about the Dawes Act, the enduring
legacy of which was not Indian assimilation and empowerment but a
staggering loss of land. In 1887, according to Wilcomb E. Washburn,
"the Indian land base amounted to 138,000,000 acres." By 1934, when
Congress repealed the Dawes Act, "about 60 percent [had] passed out of
Indian hands" (145). Even lands allotted to Indian families and individuals proved vulnerable, as land-grabbers leased, purchased, or stole Indian
allotments. Indian farming and ranching rarely succeeded, for several
reasons. Federal technical assistance was inadequate at best, and agricultural techniques from the East were ill suited to the semiarid plains. As
Dalva points out, the plains tribes had adapted perfectly to their environment; they were "nomadic hunters and gatherers, not farmers. The
Ponca and Shawnee were pretty good at crops, but not the Sioux" (128).

What happened, in Harrison's view as spoken by Michael, was "a
nasty pyramid scheme concocted by the robber barons of the railroads
and a vastly corrupt U.S. Congress. . . . The settlers came out and swindled and swiped the land treatied to the Indians, protected by a government drunk on power, money, and booze. When the settlers needed
more fuel for their greed they used Christianity, and the idea that the

Indians weren't using their land" (202). Michael goes further, comparing the American frontier to German expansionism in World War II. "History teaches us," he tells the Rotarians, "that your forefathers behaved like hundreds of thousands of pack-rat little Nazis sweeping across Europe" (204). His comparison extends to the Holocaust, which makes Northridge a nineteenth-century counterpart to German industrialist Oskar Schindler, who saved Jewish workers from the death camps. "Northridge is interesting," Michael concludes, "because of his consciousness and his conscience, just as Schindler alone is fascinating while millions of Germans who didn't give a fuck are lost to history" (147–48).

Harrison, however, avoids a sweeping condemnation of all settlers, immigrants, and their descendants. Near the end of his research, Michael has "extended his sympathies somewhat beyond the Indians to all those involved in the financial hoax of the westward movement. It was the unimaginable bleakness of being stranded in Cheyenne County during the drought of 1887 with a wife and children, the deaths by exhaustion and malnutrition" (266). A descendent of farmers, Harrison refuses to dismiss pastoralism, at its best, as a valid philosophy and way of life. His implicit notion is that history could have been otherwise if Americans and their government had actually lived up to Christian and republican ideals in dealing with the Indian nations. Harrison suggests as much on two occasions in *The Road Home*. During an argument between Dalva's son Nelse and a young girlfriend of Paul's, "Nelse rattled on rather listlessly about how the theology of land rape seemed to be a cornerstone of the Christian religion and she answered rather sharply that you couldn't blame that on Jesus" (351). On another occasion Dalva's half-Sioux grandfather observes that his "mother's people were sacrificed, in toto, for cows when they happily could have lived among them if the land had been shared rather than seized" (99–100).

Harrison's ultimate point is the relevance, too often ignored by Americans, of history to the living—a lesson conveyed by Dalva's quest for soul-making and Michael's research into soul history. Those parallel narratives converge in *Dalva*'s climactic moment, when Dalva enters the root cellar of her ancestral house for the first time. In accordance with her grandfather's wishes, she must dispose of Northridge's collection. Indian artifacts must be returned to their rightful owners; those that cannot be traced to particular tribes will be donated to museums. There are also skeletons to be buried: the remains of five Indian warriors who wished to have their remains hidden from grave robbers, and three soldiers killed by Northridge when they invaded his home. After meditating for an hour in the subterranean depths of her own past, her family's, and America's, Dalva feels her burden lifted. "My father and Duane seemed to be with me, then went away as did the weeping girl I had felt in my chest. She went out an upstairs window where she had sat watching the summer morning, the descent of the moon" (298).

Dalva's narration continues in *The Road Home*, along with that of four members of her family: her grandfather John Wesley Northridge II, who failed as an artist but managed to consolidate the estate; the geologist Paul, Northridge's second son and Dalva's uncle; Dalva's mother, Naomi, a schoolteacher and amateur naturalist; and Dalva's son Nelse, a wildlife biologist. Each narrator offers a perspective on the family homestead and the legacy of John Wesley Northridge. Northridge II speaks of his life on the edge between cultures, between the white world of buying cheap and selling dear and that of his mother's people, the Lakota Sioux. For him, life has been "a maddening struggle with ghosts," the most persistent of which are "the ghosts of my former selves that could not leave for more than a few months, excepting for the First World War, this trap my father had built, and I continued building, for body and spirit" (74). A difficult and not entirely likeable man, Northridge tries in his final years to propitiate his ghosts by following the advice of an old friend, a Sioux medicine man named Smith, to do his art and be good to people. In a demonstration of how Northridge can find freedom rather than entrapment on his ranch, Smith stands, after many years, in a favorite spot "that would be hard for anyone to detect . . . as it was a bit off center in the pasture and undifferentiated from its surroundings" (94).

In its multiple narration, historical allusiveness, and anthropological speculation, *The Road Home* is Harrison's most ambitious novel, and his most confident. Perhaps in response to Erdrich and other critics, he avoided the Falstaffian ribaldry of *Dalva,* only mentioning Michael and allowing no similar character to dominate the story. Driven by description and self-characterization rather than plot, the novel is less a sequel than an expansion of the earlier novel. We see Dalva from several points of view, concluding with her own, and we see how each character deals with Northridge II—or, in Nelse's case, with the old man's fateful decision to take him from Dalva at birth. Upon Dalva's death, Nelse will come into his legacy as John Wesley Northridge IV, an inheritance that includes the difficult fact of his parentage: though they did not know until it was too late, Dalva and Duane had the same father, Northridge III. It was out of shame that Northridge II arranged for Nelse's adoption, a loss that haunts Dalva until her son returns in 1986. Their reunion, seen through her eyes at the end of *Dalva* and through Nelse's at the end of his section in *The Road Home,* represents the healing of old wounds and the putting to rest of ghosts. Nelse helps Dalva bury the skeletons in the basement, and Dalva demonstrates for her son the patience and endurance he will need to succeed both as a husband and as a husbandman. A typical Northridge loner, claustrophobic and defiant of authority, Nelse is ready to overcome his tendency to retreat from responsibility. With his family's help he prepares to take the final step of their journey on the road home.

Harrison's most recent writing shares the assurance of *The Road Home. Just before Dark: Collected Nonfiction* (1991) showcases his distinctive talents as an essayist, as does *The Raw and the Cooked: Adventures of a Roving Gourmand* (2001). His latest novel, *True North* (2004), returns to the northern Michigan setting of his earlier fiction, following a young man researching the role of his family in the destruction of Michigan's forests. (Despite the reappearance of motifs from earlier writings, such as a white pine stump in which the protagonist seeks shelter, *True North* is less a pastoral than a tale of violence and retribution in the vein of *Legends of the Fall.*) Four more collections of novellas, *The Woman Lit by Fireflies* (1990), *Julip* (1994), *The Beast God Forgot to Invent* (2000), and *The Summer He Didn't Die* (2005), include two pastorals of retreat: the title story of the first book and "The Beige Dolorosa" from *Julip.* "The Beige Dolorosa" involves a college professor from Michigan who retires to the Arizona desert after being falsely accused of sexual harassment. While the novella's premise recalls Cather's *The Professor's House,* the professor in this case opens himself to the jubilance in nature rather than retreating behind the locked doors to his heart. "The Woman Lit by Fireflies" concerns a society woman from Grosse Pointe, Michigan, who leaves her husband, a former liberal activist who has become a materialistic and reactionary accountant. The novella features the same conflict as Lewis's *Main Street:* a utilitarian husband driving his wife to distraction by re-

ducing every aspect of life to economic matters. Clare, the woman of
the title, abandons her husband at a highway rest stop in Iowa, climbing over a fence into a cornfield where she spends the night talking
with loved ones, living and dead. What in clinical terms constitutes a
nervous breakdown actually figures as Clare's spiritual awakening, as another Harrison protagonist finds herself by getting lost in a midwestern
landscape.

The publication of Harrison's *The Shape of the Journey: New and Collected Poems* (1998) provided an opportunity to assess his accomplishment
as a poet. His best work begins with "The Theory and Practice of Rivers"
and continues to "Geo-Bestiary," a new series emphasizing animals and
wild places around North America. Other recent poems incorporate personal memories into a sweeping vision of geography and history. "The
Davenport Lunar Eclipse" finds him in a restaurant on the Mississippi
River, awaiting the celestial event while he contemplates time and

> the lovely way
> homely old men treat their homely old women
> in Nebraska and Iowa, the lunch time
> touch over green Jell-O with pineapple
> and fried "fish rectangles" for $2.95.

Humor and affection for midwestern people mix poignantly with "incom-
prehension" over Harrison's private sorrows and those of the nation, as he
talks with a waitress "home from wild Houston to nurse her sick dad":

> My grandma lived in Davenport in the 1890s
> just after Wounded Knee, a signal event,
> the beginning of America's *Sickness unto Death*.
> I'd like to nurse my father back to health
> he's been dead thirty years, I said
> to the waitress who agreed. That's why she
> came home, she said, you only got one.

The poem flows toward acquiescence and consolation in companionship
and the grandeur of creation. Back in his hotel room, Harrison cannot
"hear the river passing like time, / or the moon emerging from the shadow

of earth," but he perceives what Taoist philosophy describes as the flow of existence, "the water that never repeats itself." Granted a moment's contentment with life and the prospect of growing old, Harrison concludes the poem with a summation of the essential transcendentalism of his life's work: "It's very difficult to look at the World / and into your heart at the same time. / In between, a life has passed" (381–82).

Discussions, like the present one, of authors in relation to literary history tend to make them seem less than original, even derivative. Nothing could be further from the truth in Harrison's case. Indeed, his critical reputation and continued popularity originate in the distinctiveness and personality of his writing. Other dimensions of his work might be emphasized, such as the love of Keats and other British Romantics that almost constitutes a theme of his work. The influence of Faulkner deserves further consideration, and that of García Marquez and other Latin Americans who revere Faulkner, as does Harrison, as the crucial novelist of North American modernism. Harrison's differences from previous midwestern pastoralists should not be ignored, including his inclusion of Christian elements in Romantic spiritual eclecticism. Better traveled than were Cather, Leopold, Roethke, and Wright, Harrison also stresses to a greater degree the need to complement regional understandings with cosmopolitan breadth of vision. "Some people think you can extrapolate all life from one place," he has Strang say in *Sundog*. "That was Thoreau's mistake, though a very minor one. It's simply not true. The only way to extrapolate the spirit of Africa is to be in Africa" (160).

While Harrison's wider orbit has taken him around the Americas and beyond, it consistently brings him back to the Midwest. Unlike major writers of an earlier midwestern generation—Anderson, Cather, Hemingway, and Lewis, who left the region and created many fictional characters who do the same—Harrison emphasizes return rather than departure. The unity of person with place sought in his poetry and essays, and by characters in his fiction, involves "returning to earth" and "coming home," the titles, respectively, of one of his books of poetry and the last section of *Dalva*. Or, to invoke the titles of two recent volumes, we may say that "the shape of the journey" is that of "the road home." These phrases remind us of Harrison's midwestern predecessors: the first recalls Roethke's "journey to the interior," the second Cather's *My Ántonia*. In the concluding paragraphs of that novel, Cather describes a remnant of the pioneer road that brought Jim and Ántonia to the Divide, and that brings them together again late in life. On that road, Jim feels "the sense of coming home to myself, and of having found out what a little circle man's experience is" (937).

By the end of the twentieth century, however, authors have learned that the circle is wider than Cather supposed, and that the journey home is not only to self but also to community. While thoroughly Romantic in his mystical view of nature and concern for the formative influence of childhood, Harrison has worked hard to overcome the isolating tendencies of Romantic individualism. "The Romantic 'I,'" he writes in the introduction to *The Shape of the Journey*, "with all its inherent stormy bombast, its fungoid elevation of the most questionable aspects of personality, its totally self-referential regard of life, has tended to disappear" (1). Directly and in allusions, Harrison acknowledges many teachers of self-transcendence, whether American or foreign, Christian, Buddhist, Native American, or Romantic. In its inclusiveness, Harrison's writing represents the maturation of midwestern pastoral. Nostalgia in his vision does not mean a false idealization of the past or a denial of present realities but a yearning for wisdom, a backward glance before turning to face the future.[5] He finds this determination, of course, outdoors, as he reiterates in "Dream as a Metaphor of Survival," the last essay in *Just before Dark*. "When I walk several hours," he writes, "the earth becomes sufficient to my imagination, and the lesser self is lost or dissipates in the intricacies, both the beauty and the horror, of the natural world." While that sentiment hews closely to Romantic and pastoral traditions, Harrison follows it with an ecological and democratic declaration of interdependence: "I continue to dream myself back to what I lost, and continue to lose and regain, to an earth where I am a fellow creature and to a landscape I can call home. When I return I can offer my family, my writing, my friends, a portion of the gift I've been given by seeking it out, consciously or unconsciously. The mystery is still there" (317). Nature, place, and community: these are the values toward which midwestern pastoral has tended, and that converge in Harrison's best poems, essays, and fiction.

seven

# Further
# Views

> This is what, over all else, the prairie teaches us: there need
> be no contradiction between utility and beauty.
>
> —Paul Gruchow, *Grass Roots*

According to a well-established critical trope, the Midwest and its literature have passed into history, their best days having fled before the ho-
mogenizing effects of globalization and mass media. Ronald Weber suggests that these forces put "the Midwest as a place . . . more than ever in
danger of vanishing completely, erased as a fact by more pragmatic ways
of thinking" (224). Lisel Mueller likewise asserts that "when we speak of
Midwestern poetry, we speak of something that is passing out of existence" ("Midwestern," 69).

Many contemporary writers, however, beg to differ. While acknowledging the pervasive influence of mass culture, they continue the study
of place and culture begun by earlier midwesterners. One such writer is
Larry Woiwode (b. 1941). In his essay "The Spirit of Place" (1990), Woiwode cites lines from Roethke's "The Rose" in which the poet distances
himself from "those to whom place is unimportant." Having lived and
written fiction set in a number of places, including Michigan, Wisconsin,
and New York City, Woiwode has returned to his own place of origin,
North Dakota: "not a North Dakota of the mind, or a visitor's or East-
erner's misconception of it, nor one you may encounter in a general

book about the Great Plains, but a real place; a region, perhaps: now my home" (53). He defends regional and local awareness against distant market forces, rephrasing a familiar argument for the spiritual function of language and literature:

> I believe that American writing now stands at the threshold of being able to speak of the habitations of spirituality, or the lack of them, within the human heart as in no other period in history. And if those of us at the center of America can retain what we presently possess or, even better, turn farther inward toward what we've inherited, clearing away the falseness and superficiality that is constantly and electronically beamed into us from either coast, as if by its repetitiveness it could become the truth, and approach the land and the people who live on it as our ancestors did, with the cautious reverence of mutual regard, then I believe that a new form of expression, if not a new manner of literature, could, by the grace of God, be created for any generations who might come historically after us and wish to listen to our voices speak the truth to them about the places we have inhabited and that inhabit us through the unmerited gift of particular love. (65)

Woiwode lyrically recapitulates the same hope expressed by Roethke and others: that midwesterners will love and sustain the life around them and not unnecessarily elevate the pursuit of wealth, fashion, and technology. The difference between Woiwode and his predecessors is that he can refer to their work for examples and encouragement. Woiwode's reference to Roethke exemplifies a growing awareness among midwestern pastoral writers of belonging to a tradition. Metapastoral—a commentary on pastoral conventions running concurrent with an author's use of those conventions—has always characterized this literature, from Cather's allusions to Virgil and Whitman to those by Wright. References by Harrison to both Cather and Wright demonstrate how regional precursors have joined writers ancient and modern, national and international, in the contemporary frame of reference.

To reinforce my argument and to affirm the continuing presence of midwestern pastoral in American letters, this last chapter will discuss selected writings by three contemporaries: novelist Jane Smiley (b. 1949), poet Ted Kooser (b. 1939), and essayist Paul Gruchow (1947–2004). Treating midwestern rural landscapes with affection and a sensibility both historical and ecological, these writers carry on the critique of American culture initiated by earlier writers. They represent the continuing aesthetic and ideological development of midwestern pastoral in their respective genres.

Jane Smiley's best-known novel is the Pulitzer Prize–winning *A Thousand Acres* (1991). Set in Iowa during the late 1970s, *A Thousand Acres* depicts a farm family torn apart by its patriarch, a vain and autocratic man who has enlarged his operation to the size noted in the title through an industrial approach to agriculture, what Leopold disparaged as "clean farming." The farm, formerly a vast wetland, has been systematically drained and worked over with chemicals and heavy machinery to maximize production. Smiley's plot is classically simple: the farmer, Larry Cook, decides to retire, dividing his farm between his three daughters, Ginny, Rose, and Caroline. Because Caroline, the youngest, displeases her father at the time of the divestiture, he cuts her out of the inheritance and grants the farm to his two other daughters. If the story sounds familiar, it should; Smiley has transferred Shakespeare's *King Lear* to the cornfields of Iowa, modeling her novel after the play from its general premise to details of characterization and plot. The names of Smiley's characters alliterate with those of their counterparts Lear, Goneril, Regan, and Cordelia. Events in *A Thousand Acres* mirroring those in *King Lear* include a night in a thunderstorm, the blinding of the old man's closest friend, and murderous thoughts of one sister toward another. For readers fascinated by the artistic possibilities of intertextuality, the novel owns considerable formal charm.[1]

Smiley, however, subverts her Shakespearean premise. Whereas the villainous and paranoid Goneril and Regan persecute Lear, in *A Thousand Acres* the father is clearly the transgressor. Larry is not merely conceited, but abusive toward his daughters and his land. His reputation as a model farmer and family man belies a monstrous reality. His pursuit of maximum productivity has poisoned the groundwater, causing his wife and then his daughter Rose to develop fatal cancer. Ginny suffers several miscarriages as a result of drinking water from the well. Most shocking is the secret that emerges as Larry becomes mentally unhinged after dividing the farm: his repeated rape of Ginny and Rose as adolescents. By connecting utilitarian attitudes of domination over nature with unbridled male power over women, *A Thousand Acres* provides a powerful ecofeminist rereading of agrarian history in the Midwest. Smiley's, novel, as Sara Farris notes, "is the logical heir to *O Pioneers!*" but ironically so. "While Smiley flashes all the pastoral signs—the immigrant dream, inheritance of the farm sustaining subsequent generations, the farmer/father hero surrounded by his pleasantly subordinate family—she reveals each to be a lie" (34).

Smiley's revision of Cather encompasses her choice of literary models and allusions. Whereas Cather derives her pastoral sensibility from Virgil's *Eclogues* and *Georgics,* Smiley turns to Shakespeare, away from the bucolic to embrace tragedy. The title of Cather's *O Pioneers!* alludes to a lesser poem of Whitman's that extols an expansionist, domineering attitude toward nature. Smiley's title, however, references lines from the beginning of "Song of Myself" with a very different tone: "Have you reckoned a thousand acres much? Have you reckoned the earth much? / Have you practiced so long to learn to read? / Have you felt so proud to get at the meaning of poems?" The passage draws nature into semantic proximity with literature, challenging us to think of landscape as text, and of poetry as an approximation of place. Reading and inhabitation both require spiritual discipline and independence; one can "possess the origin of all poems" and "the good of the earth and sun," Whitman maintains, only by testing authority, tradition, and power against one's own experience (28). Through Ginny, the narrator of *A Thousand Acres,* Smiley accepts Whitman's challenge, reckoning the cost of agribusiness to humanity and nature on that thousand-acre Iowa farm. The price includes human health, both physical and psychological; it includes ownership of the land, assumed by a faceless corporation after the Cook family succumbs to acrimony and litigation; and it includes a spiritual connection to the land—Ginny's sacred place, a tiny area of native trees and prairie vegetation, serves as Larry's dump. Through Ginny, Smiley speaks truth to power, bearing witness to a history of violence against the false myth of pastoral innocence assumed by farmers like Larry and Ginny's husband Ty:

> You see this grand history, but I see blows. I see taking what
> you want because you want it, then making something up that

> justifies what you did. I see getting others to pay the price,
> then covering up and forgetting what the price was. Do I think
> Daddy came up with beating and fucking us on his own? . . .
> No, I think he had lessons, and those lessons were part of the
> package, along with the land and the lust to run things exactly
> the way he wanted to no matter what, poisoning the water
> and destroying the topsoil and buying bigger and bigger ma-
> chinery, and then feeling certain that all of it was "right."
> (342–43)

Having reckoned a thousand acres, as Whitman suggested, Smiley does in fact find that the microcosm matches the wider human relation to nature. A century and a half after Whitman, however, the inland plains constitute a text that reads less about democracy and nature than about sexism, oligarchy, and industrial monoculture.[2]

Smiley and Cather exemplify the vertical or lineal relationship of writers over time. Writers also dwell in a horizontal dimension created by awareness of their living peers. Although writing is a solitary activity, friendships among writers can result in supportive arrangements that deserve to be called communities. James Wright, as we have seen, benefited from the mutual aid of Robert Bly during a crucial period in his life and career. A more recent example is the poetic collaboration of Jim Harrison with Ted Kooser, his long-time friend and correspondent. The long foreground of that collaboration in Kooser's prolific poetic career suggests why Harrison and many other readers consider him to be one of the nation's finest poets.

Born in Ames, Iowa, and now retired from a career as an insurance executive, Kooser has spent most of his life in Nebraska, where he is often referred to as the unofficial state poet laureate. (The Library of Congress named him U.S. Poet Laureate in August 2004.) Like Harrison and Wright, Kooser writes poetry on rural themes in a manner reflecting long study of world literature, especially Asian and Latin American poetry. In *Official Entry Blank* (1969) and ten subsequent books of poetry, Kooser has elevated unassuming subjects, both people and places, usually by means of startling metaphors that heighten the sensual and associative power of his images. Among many typical passages is the first stanza of "So This Is Nebraska," which effortlessly transforms a

highway into a horse and the plumage of birds into combustible flashes
of color:

> The gravel road rides with a slow gallop
> over the fields, the telephone lines
> streaming behind, its billow of dust
> full of the sparks of redwing blackbirds.

The poem continues with the driver proceeding down the road, noting
barns, the thickness of air on a July afternoon, and an abandoned truck
surrounded by a lush growth of hollyhock. "You feel like that," Kooser
writes, establishing a greater intimacy by addressing the reader: "you feel
like letting / your tires go flat, like letting the mice / build a nest in your
muffler, like being no more than a truck in the weeds" (*Sure Signs,* 39).
Kooser's use of the second-person voice in "So This Is Nebraska" is consistent with his fundamentally communitarian outlook.[3] Even more than
Roethke, Wright, and Harrison in their poems, Kooser hews closely to
human associations, whether friends, family, neighbors, or even strangers,
whom he treats not as separate and unknowable others, but as kindred
beings whose concerns impinge on his consciousness. "It's never made
much sense to me to set poetry apart from its social context," he admits
in a short statement titled "Some of the Things I Think about When
Working on a Poem." He speaks of a desire to "honor my reader's patience and generosity by presenting what I have to say as clearly and
succinctly as possible" (439). Disdaining modernist elitism and alienation,
Kooser embraces Nebraska and its people, finding poignancy in the personal effects of people long dead, in animal signs like the shed skin of a
snake, or elements of local landscape like "an empty stone house alone
in a wheatfield" (*Sure Signs,* 78).

Kooser views landscape with an eye for social history, writing, for example, about small farms that failed, or were failed by the industrial
economy. In "Abandoned Farmhouse" he approaches an old homestead
in the manner of Leopold, interpreting visible signs of its former inhabitants much as one reads a written text.

> He was a big man, says the size of his shoes
> on a pile of broken dishes by the house . . .

> but not a man for farming, say the fields
> cluttered with boulders and the leaky barn.

A "bedroom wall / papered with lilacs" testifies to a woman's presence, and a "sandbox made from a tractor tire" tells of a child. A litany of absence and loss, the poem develops its sad cadence by the repetition of the verb "say" or "says," as in the line "It was lonely here, says the narrow country road." Every aspect of the place, whether stones in the field or jars of fruit, speaks of poverty, isolation, and failure. "Something went wrong, they say" (*Sure Signs*, 64). Kooser does not attribute that failure to the family that once lived in the house, blaming them in some hard utilitarian manner for their plight. Instead he leaves it to the reader to speculate about social trends that led to their difficulties. Whatever "went wrong" may have had as much to do with government agricultural policy and, more broadly, attitudes about land, as with the abilities of the farming couple. Something went wrong with pastoral ideology; the failure here is not merely personal but also cultural and political.

Like other midwestern pastoralists, Kooser is drawn to places of significance in what Harrison calls the "soul history" of the nation. In "Fort Robinson," he recalls a visit to the former military outpost in western Nebraska, where Lakota holy man and war leader Crazy Horse was assassinated in 1877 and where, as Kooser notes, "Dull Knife and his Northern Cheyenne / were held captive that terrible winter" of 1878–1879.[4] Typically, it is through personal narrative that Kooser evokes the site's significance. He and his young son never leave the car because "the grounds crew" at the historical site is "killing the magpies . . . going from tree to tree / with sticks and ladders" to knock down the nestlings and kill them on the ground. This violence by representatives of the state recalls Fort Robinson's mission as a staging platform for the subjugation of the Cheyenne, Lakota, and other western tribes during the Plains War. Rather than being didactic, Kooser simply and clearly describes the scene, letting the historical comparison form itself in the reader's mind. As his son weeps in the back seat, the speaker drives off "into those ragged buttes / the Cheyenne climbed that winter, fleeing" (*Sure Signs*, 40). The participle "fleeing" may refer either to the speaker and his son or to the Cheyenne, a grammatical ambiguity that implies rather than states the poet's empathy with Dull Knife's band. He creates a parallel rather than merging his identity with that of conquered people, as did Roethke in declaring "I'll be an Indian." However well meaning and multivalent, Roethke's assertion contains a certain arrogance. Like Harrison, who writes in *Just before Dark* that he "would not dream of trying to 'become'" an Indian (314), Kooser does not presume to speak for those who are capable of speaking for themselves. He exercises the same restraint in his unpublished long poem "Pursuing Black Hawk," a narrative of the Black Hawk War told not from a Sauk point of view, but in the voice of a young white militiaman. Like his Romantic predecessors, Kooser looks to midwestern landscape for a usable past. But he avoids Whitmanian panhumanism—famously phrased in "Song of Myself" in the line "I am the man. . . . I suffered. . . . I was there" (64)—in favor of narrative that reflects his own cultural background.

In addition to his empathy for rural midwesterners, Kooser's grounding in regional landscape, history, and ecology gives his collaboration with Harrison an air of inevitability. The two writers have corresponded for many years, their letters often taking the form of poems. Two books have resulted from this exchange: Kooser's *Winter Morning Walks: One Hundred Postcards to Jim Harrison* (2002) and *Braided Creek: A Conversation in Poetry* (2003), a collection of epigrammatic poems by Harrison and Kooser, addressed to one another. The poems in both books meditate on friendship, aging, and the consolation of beloved local landscapes, renewing these traditional pastoral themes by use of the epistolary mode. Reading the poems gives one the sense of having joined the writers' fellowship of outdoor words and walks.

Although published in book form a year later, the poems in *Braided Creek* predate those in *Winter Morning Walks*. For several years, Kooser and Harrison sent each other poems resembling haiku in their brevity, vivid imagery, and philosophical implications. Before Kooser edited the volume, he and Harrison agreed not to attribute particular poems to either writer, a decision that creates two distinct effects. First, readers familiar with the authors' earlier writings may take pleasure in discerning one poet's voice from the other's, according to a poem's diction, tone, figures of speech, and allusions. The last line, for example, of the following poem reveals it with near certainty to be Harrison's, since he used the phrase as the title of his first book of nonfiction: "At 62 I've outlived 95 percent / of the world. I'll be home / just before dark (33). In many cases, however, it is impossible to ascribe a poem with any degree of likelihood to either Harrison or Kooser. Far from being a source of frustration, the suspension of authorial credit creates a harmonic effect, a layering of two voices that emphasizes sounds, images, and ideas rather than the poets as individuals. It ultimately does not matter whether Harrison or Kooser wrote the following couplet: "On every topographic map, / the fingerprints of God" (7). What *is* important is that either poet *could* have written it, and that both believe the statement to be true. Taking pleasure in the poems' ambiguity of provenance requires of the reader the Romantic virtue of "negative capability," which John Keats famously defined in a letter to his brothers as the ability of "being in uncertainties, Mysteries, Doubts, without any irritable reaching after fact & reason" (1,209).

At the same time, however, Harrison's and Kooser's coauthorship challenges the Romantic emphasis on the individual artist, the "Romantic 'I'" that Harrison has said he wishes not to be confined by. "When asked about attributions for the individual poems," the book's dust jacket copy reads, "one of them replied 'Everyone gets tired of this continued cult of the personality. . . . This book is an assertion in favor of poetry and against credentials.'" The poetic creed asserted in *Braided Creek* is one of spirituality and place, a quiet wisdom conveyed in earthy, self-effacing humor and images of domestic life and rural midwestern landscape. The book's final poem illustrates the ecological principle of forest succession, while contrasting nature's mutability with its persistence—pastoral literature's perennial consolation for our mortality: "The pastures grow up / with red cedars / once the horses are gone" (85).

Images of midwestern landscape reflecting the theme of mortality also provide *Winter Morning Walks,* the other book resulting from Kooser's correspondence with Harrison, with its central motif. *Winter Morning Walks,* as Mary K. Stillwell notes in her study of the book, combines "the story of a middle-aged poet facing the aftermath of cancer surgery with the archetypal journey of Everyman summoned by Death" (399). In the summer of 1998, doctors removed a tumor from Kooser's tongue and discovered cancer in his lymph nodes. They prescribed radiation treatment, which along with the cancer itself sapped the poet's spirit and energy. He did not feel up to reading or writing until November, when his health had improved enough that he could take regular exercise. Under a doctor's orders to avoid sunlight for a year (as Kooser recounts in the book's preface), he "began taking a two-mile walk each morning . . . before dawn, hiking the isolated country roads near [Garland, Nebraska] where I live, sometimes with my wife but most often alone" (5). Following one such walk, he felt up to writing a poem. Before long he had made a ritual of writing every day, shaping what he had seen and thought about during or immediately after his walk into short poems. He decided to paste them on postcards to send to Harrison, who is never specifically addressed but is always present by implication as a sympathetic audience of one.

Following the same pastoral convention as *Walden* and *A Sand County Almanac,* the poems in *Winter Morning Walks* form a cycle structured on the changing seasons. From November 9 to March 20, Kooser notes the date and the weather, then describes one moment, one thought emerging from the discipline of his daily walk. On December 31 ("Cold and snowing") he speaks of the year that is ending as a book whose "opening pages" he cannot remember, followed by his "mother's death / in the cold, wet chapters of spring." Complicating the metaphor of nature as a book, earlier employed by Leopold, Kooser speaks of the year, rather than the landscape, as the figurative volume. Elements of landscape become the imagery, theme, and textual apparatus of this year-as-volume. Thus the initial chapters of spring give way to a "featureless text of summer / burning with illness" and "a conclusion" (by implication, the poems in *Winter Morning Walks* to date) narrating the year's "first hard frosts." The last of three stanzas concludes the extended metaphor with images summing up autumn, early winter, and that day's walk, the last of the year:

> A bibliography of falling leaves,
> an index of bare trees,
> and finally, a crow flying like a signature
> over the soft white endpapers of the year.
>
> (54)

The crow enters the poem as it did the poet's day, black against the snow and overcast sky, black as ink running across the whiteness of paper. The simile of the crow as a signature—an author's personalization of a book—implies a unity of identity and consciousness between place and person. By such figures of speech Kooser connects seasons of the year with the stages and transitions in human life.

Stillwell is exactly right when she describes these poems as "unified by time, threaded along the regularity of the month and date, repeated like a mantra—*I am here, I am here*" (409). Mantras, phrases repeated in the practice of Eastern meditation, help one focus on the moment and thereby transcend fear and desire. The poems in *Winter Morning Walks,* like those in *Braided Creek* and in fact like so much pastoral writing from Emerson to Kooser, constitute a kind of American Buddhist scripture, a spiritual literature in which human selfhood is characterized as one with place, inseparable from the characteristic seasons, plants, and animals of local landscape. Roethke writes that his "true self runs toward a Hill" (*Collected Poems,* 243). While the poet of *Winter Morning Walks* cannot run, he walks, if at times shakily, from sickness to health and from autumn to the spring equinox. By patterning his book on the seasons of the year, Kooser implies that health and happiness require that one walk—that is, live—as much as possible according to the rhythms of nature.

Kooser's recent writing is marked by the same understated virtuosity and attentiveness to people and place. *Delights and Shadows* (2004), for which Kooser received the Pulitzer Prize in poetry, features homely still lifes ("Casting Reels"), portraits of rural midwesterners ("Pearl"), and evocations of neglected landscapes ("Old Cemetery"). Kooser's facility with metaphor remains undiminished, as in "On the Road," in which "a pebble of quartz" picked up during a walk figures as "one drop of the earth's milk / dirty and cold" (77). He has also made his debut as a prose writer with two recent books. *The Poetry Home Repair Manual* (2005), a writing guide for beginning poets, champions intelligibility as a poetic virtue. Its humorous title subtly invokes the midwestern tinkerer archetype, emphasizing poetry as the result of work rather than of inspiration alone.[5] *Local Wonders: Seasons in the Bohemian Alps* (2002) is a book of nature writing arranged in four sections about spring, summer, autumn, and winter in the countryside around Garland, where Kooser has lived since the early 1980s. The Bohemian Alps of the title are glacial hills "which in the late 1870s began to be settled by Czech and German immigrants from that region of central Europe once known as Bohemia" (xi). Kooser focuses as much on the area's social dimensions—its history and the character of the living descendants of those original settlers—as on its physical landscape. One unifying motif in the book is Kooser's repeated citation of Bohemian proverbs, used to conclude passages of narration or description. An example appears after he laments the subdivision of previously open land into smaller lots for the construction of large, expensive homes. In building on hilltops (a placement that Frank Lloyd Wright warned against) the wealthy of Lincoln demonstrate an arrogant pastoralism that is ultimately self-defeating. The owners of a new hilltop house just north of Kooser's old farmstead may have anticipated "sunsets and sunrises, but soon their view to the east will be interrupted, because another family has bought a hilltop about a hundred yards away and will be building their own house there within the year." The families have urbanized the country to which they retreated; they "will have to draw their blinds at night and listen to each other's screen doors slam just as they did in the city." Kooser ends the passage with the homespun wisdom of the area's pioneers: "I trust in the Bohemian saying, 'He who places his ladder too steeply will easily fall backward'" (11).

Kooser's *Local Wonders* adds to an established tradition of midwestern nature writing, distinguished of course by Leopold but also by writers like the late Paul Gruchow, whose essays also challenge hidebound myths of progress and modernity while celebrating the particularities of landscape. In language equally polemical and poetic, Gruchow defends rural life and wild nature as seen from his home state of Minnesota.[6]

Like Leopold (and, in fact, all five writers to whom I devote chapters of this book), Gruchow often writes about wild places outside the Midwest (particularly in the West), on the region's periphery, or close to midwestern population centers but little known by the residents of those areas. *The Necessity of Empty Places* (1988) begins and concludes with essays about Minnesota; the rest of the book deals with Nebraska, Wyoming, and Montana. *Boundary Waters: The Grace of the Wild* (1997) focuses on the northern Minnesota preserve that many consider the greatest remaining wilderness in the Midwest. *Worlds within a World* (1999) collects Gruchow's essays on places protected under the State of Minnesota's Scientific and Natural Areas Program. These books portray wilderness areas not as sites for recreation or escape but as places one visits to be chastened and shaken from human arrogance. Wild places, Gruchow writes in *Necessity,* are nature's "basic documents. . . . And when we destroy some entire ecosystem, as we have nearly done with our prairies, for example, it is like eliminating whole sections of our libraries" (140). Putting a new spin on Leopold's metaphor of nature as text, he argues that the most important reason for preserving wilderness is the "wildly, hopefully unscientific" notion "that except by the measure of wildness, we shall never really know the nature of a place, and without a sense of place we shall never make a poem, and without a poem we shall never be fully human" (*Necessity*, 128–29).

It is in two books about the Minnesota prairie, however, that Gruchow's defense of nature is most pointed. The first, *Journal of a Prairie Year* (1985) follows the same seasonal sequence as the first section of *A Sand County Almanac*, beginning with winter and ending in autumn. Meditating on the country around Worthington, Minnesota, where he owned a farm, Gruchow evokes the local landscape while providing a natural history of the tallgrass prairie. A trip to observe bison at an ecological preserve, for example, occasions a brief history of the species, from the era of the plains tribes to the bison's near extinction at the hands of hunters and collectors. Although Gruchow does not employ the metaphor of land as text in such passages, he does approach the prairie as a reader, in both the figurative and literal senses. Quotations from Leopold, O. E. Rolvaag, and Black Elk establish the regional tradition in which he works, as does an addendum of suggested readings in the small but growing literature of the tallgrass prairie. Gruchow aims these references at a local audience as well as a general readership within and beyond the Midwest. Parts of *Journal of a Prairie Year* originally appeared in Minnesota newspapers and magazines at which Gruchow was either an editor or a contributing writer. The book itself emerged from a class on prairie literature that he taught at Worthington Community College. Gruchow's message, like Leopold's or Kooser's, is both local and universal. While the immediate mission of *Journal* is to educate local people about the cultural and ecological uniqueness of their home terrain, the lesson applies by implication to people in other places.

That mission continues in *Grass Roots: The Universe of Home* (1995), in which Gruchow develops the story of his early life, while projecting the pastoral themes of the earlier book into the realms of economics and public policy. If *Journal* is Gruchow's "Almanac," *Grass Roots* is his "Upshot." Like Leopold in that final section of *A Sand County Almanac*, Gruchow argues in this book for a renewed land ethic and aesthetic, putting forth specific recommendations for land use, education, and community revitalization in the rural upper Midwest. The polemic and narrative aspects of *Grass Roots* make it Gruchow's most incisive as well as his most personal book.

Although literary critics often describe pastoral as a leisure-class pursuit, Gruchow's working-class background, like Scott Russell Sanders's and James Wright's, contradicts that assumption. During most of his early life, Gruchow's parents did not own the land they worked; he describes them as "part of the underclass of tenant-farmers in the larger underclass of rural society, at a time when farmers still thought of themselves as the salt of the earth but after the Jeffersonian ideal of the yeoman farmer had lost its savor" (13). Gruchow's family found much to savor, however, in their lives, despite their poverty. In the 1940s and 1950s, places like Rosewood Township of Minnesota's Chippewa County, where the Gruchows lived, were vibrant and relatively self-sustaining communities. Local stores, churches, schools, and community centers served as gathering places for farm families, who knew one another well and rendered assistance when their neighbors were in need. The Gruchows cut their own fuel and grew most of their own food, "and it is," Gruchow insists, "more than fancy that what we ate, because of this, had a special flavor and meaning" (19). The land they tended had not been worked to death like the thousand acres owned by Jane Smiley's Larry Cook. Most of the native prairie had been plowed under, but pockets of wildness remained, including a cattail marsh, "a piece of Rosewood Township as it had existed for thousands of years, a surviving testament to the tallgrass prairie, and the richest and most complex representative of it" (21). The marsh was Gruchow's sacred place; there he experienced "absorbedness," which he defines as the feeling one attains during "brief moments in life when one is so occupied as to forget time, when time has become a translucent pair of wings" (31). A better description of the Romantic epiphany could hardly be written.

Like many pastoral writers, however, Gruchow necessarily speaks of loss. The social and natural landscapes of his youth were swept away forever by industrial agriculture, which depopulated rural areas across the United States and consolidated small farms into large holdings. The process accelerated in the 1960s, when farmers abandoned the land by

the millions, driven off as a result of government policies designed to reduce the rural labor force. Agriculture gave way to agribusiness, which
replaced human and animal power with machines and petrochemicals.
According to Gruchow, the U.S. government, banks, academia, and mass
media developed an official narrative, one that told of "a modern miracle in the world's most efficient agriculture, a way of farming so slick and
fine that it didn't need people anymore, or soils, or birds, or schoolhouses,
or children. All the miracle required was more petroleum and bigger
tractors and more land" (87). The Gruchow family was fortunate in
being able to afford, finally, their own farm, where the writer's father
stubbornly bucked the trend toward monoculture, refusing to use herbicides, buy a huge tractor, or plow under every wild spot. He continued
to raise diverse crops and livestock even when his neighbors turned vast
acreages to single crop production. But the overall result of the move was
loneliness for the community they had lost back in Rosewood Township.
"We had improved our station but not . . . our lot in life," Gruchow remembers (84). If any one image in *Grass Roots* symbolizes the results of
agronomic dogma, it is what became of Gruchow's sacred place on his
family's first, rented farm:

> The marsh is gone. It was underlain with plastic drain tiles
> that now siphon its waters into a nearby drainage ditch, which
> carries them to the Minnesota River, which is connected to the
> Mississippi River, taking the fertile waters I once knew directly
> to the sea. . . . The waterfowl are gone, the raptors are gone, the
> burrowing animals are gone, the predators and herbivores are
> gone. . . . Last season, the whole 160 acres of what used to be
> our farm was planted with a single crop—corn.

Like the Cook farm at the end of Smiley's *A Thousand Acres,* the Gruchow
place is now bereft both of people and of native plant and animal life.
"There is," he concludes, "hardly a desert so barren" (38).

The passage, like so many in pastoral literature, laments the passing
of an earlier time and changes in a beloved place. The elegiac tone of
pastoral has often been attacked by those who, fancying themselves un-
sentimental realists, use the words "nostalgia" and "Romantic" as terms
of opprobrium. These detractors range across the ideological spectrum.

On the Right are those who extol the virtues of a supposedly "free" market (carefully avoiding mention of governmental servility to business), who repeat the word "efficiency" like a mantra. Gruchow personifies this tired utilitarianism in a geographer he heard lecturing rural schoolteachers about "the triumphal march of agriculture from its mean beginnings in Indian plots to its present glory" (91). Confronted by critics of industrial agriculture, such "pietists of change . . . say, 'Ah! There you go again, wallowing in the myths of the past!'" (98). Gruchow sometimes found himself accused of "perpetuating 'the myth of a golden age in agriculture,' the 'myth of the cheerful yeomanry,' 'a pastoral paradise.'" He responds sharply to these charges:

> I don't, in fact, believe in such myths, nor for that matter, do I
> know of anybody who does. These are not myths in any func-
> tional sense, but shibboleths. I keenly recall the tedium and
> drudgery of the life I knew as a child. But my own children,
> who have grown up in affluence, are also loudly cognizant of
> the tedium and drudgery in *their* lives. And I remember, as do
> they, many joys and satisfactions. I do not believe that the state
> of one's soul is in direct relation to the condition of one's bank
> balance. Wealth is as fully capable of corrupting the soul as
> poverty. (43)

Gruchow also challenges intellectuals on the Left who regard pastoral as irremediably reactionary and hegemonic. Ironically, such critics promote a kind of American exceptionalism that parallels the jingoist rhetoric of boosterism in curious ways. Both sides imagine Euro-American culture as a single, monolithic entity: either one that must be uncritically celebrated, and maintained through cultural assimilation, or one that ought to be exposed and assailed at every turn. "Manifest destiny and Western culture as the unique expression of patriarchal and racist rot," Gruchow argues, "are both readings of history from the same point of view; both assume that the Western story is in some unique way a radical departure from the human story" (89). Neither interpretation of American history does justice to local culture, history, and ecology, or to the role of social class in rural economies. Yet these voices dominate the discourse in our systems of education. As a grade school student, Gruchow

was taught "to suppose that ethnicity was, if was anything at all, a private matter of no consequence to the community" and that "there was
no such thing in America as social class" (88). Norwegian and German
were not taught, although both languages were still spoken in the area.
He learned nothing about the ecology, history, or literature of the
prairie. He was not introduced to writings by Black Elk, Robert Bly,
or other authors of the tallgrass region at school or "at the University of
Minnesota, either. I was left to unearth by my own devices, years later,
the whole fine literature of my place" (134). The absence of regional
literature from school and college curricula is as imperious, even imperialist, as the domination of university agricultural programs by petro-
chemical and biotechnology firms. "Our universities," having "recently
discovered the evils of colonialism . . . are everywhere rewriting curricu-
lum to include this discovery, while simultaneously aiding and abetting
the new colonialism of the countryside" (97).

Yet Gruchow assigns a measure of blame for the situation in rural
America to country people themselves. "We in rural America have a long
list of enemies . . . but we have had no agricultural policy that someone
in agriculture didn't press for, and no lousy piece of advice ever came to
fruition except when somebody agreed to take it" (53). Rural Americans,
Gruchow believes, have sold themselves short; they have followed the industrial model to the point of their own demise. They need to go beyond
jeremiads and make the "strongest moral argument against our present
system of agriculture . . . not that it hurts individual farmers—although it
does—but that it tends toward totalitarianism: the system concentrates
wealth and power to the disadvantage of most citizens, urban as well as
rural, and it does so at an accelerating pace" (107). The upshot of Gruchow's book comes in essays such as "What Time Is It?" and "Guerilla
Warfare," in which he specifies ways in which rural people can develop
their communities for the benefit of all rather than a few. Many of his
proposals, consistent with Jeffersonian tradition as well as contemporary
bioregionalism, involve education. "We could teach our children rural history and rural culture. We could . . . raise them to know the ecological and
geological history of the place to which they have been born." Other proposals, echoing conservationists like Leopold, involve ecological restoration: "Were we to make the countryside beautiful again and safe for wild
creatures, perhaps more people would want to join us in living there" (114).

Extending his proposals to encompass issues of social justice, Gruchow calls for new cooperative agreements among farmers, producers, and consumers, and the economic empowerment of women and ethnic minorities. Women should "join together in entrepreneurial partnerships . . . taking heart and instruction from the economic awakening that Third World women are beginning to experience" (113). Recognizing systemic links between rural impoverishment and urban homelessness, he recommends the concentration of "economic-development resources on finding entrepreneurial opportunities" for the urban poor. This would require small-town people to overcome xenophobia, which Gruchow, like Cather and Lewis before him, recognizes as a serious problem in the rural Midwest. Small towns have much to gain from a well-planned influx of urban migrants, "not only their economic skills but fresh points of view and a new enthusiasm for small-town life" (109). The way to begin is by recognizing those newcomers, different in color and language, who have already arrived in Wisconsin, Minnesota, and Iowa in great numbers—"the Latinos and Asians attracted by jobs in the food processing plants—as an asset rather than a problem. We could celebrate the cultural diversity that they bring to our communities" (113).

Gruchow's analysis in *Grass Roots* corresponds with conclusions drawn by Leo Marx, dean of American pastoral scholars. In "Pastoralism in America," a 1986 reassessment of *The Machine in the Garden,* Marx concludes that for progressive pastoralism to succeed politically, it must reach beyond its traditionally white, middle-class constituency. "To provide the basis for an effective ideology," he argues, "adherents of pastoralism would have to form alliances with . . . those for whom 'the recovery of the natural' as yet has, in itself, little or no appeal," namely working-class whites, people of color, and recent immigrants (66). In this way pastoral theory meets environmental justice, the contemporary coalition between economically disadvantaged people and environmental activists who recognize class structure and racism as sources of environmental degradation as well as poverty. Poor people, more often than not dark skinned and/or foreign born, tend to live in polluted environments, from urban neighborhoods adjoining industrial plants and refineries to rural districts in which the air, soil, and water are contaminated by pesticides, herbicides, and chemical fertilizers. This situation is not coincidental but systemic, resulting from years of governmental policies that favor large industrial and agricultural concerns and protect the residences and playgrounds of the wealthy, while treating the places where workers live as sacrifice zones.

Interconnected problems like poverty, racism, and environmental degradation demand political and scientific solutions. But the underlying issues are cultural; we must also examine the images, metaphors, and narratives underlying our assumptions and behavior, including those associated with pastoral myth. "Not until those paradigms are brought to conscious awareness," ecofeminist scholar Annette Kolodny has observed, "can we begin to pick and choose among them, letting go of those by which we would relentlessly destroy our surroundings and holding onto those by which we might protect and preserve the continent as a home for all its creatures" (xii). Neither outright rejection of pastoralism as a social ideology nor rigid adherence to outdated understandings of nature, self, and society will serve this end. But an informed love of place, one that identifies the useful and beautiful in cultural productions of the past while remaining receptive to the foreign and the new and attentive to ecology, can exert a positive influence in an increasingly fragmented world.

Writers, artists, and intellectuals in the Romantic and Jeffersonian tradition of midwestern pastoral continue to express love and understanding of, and commitment to, this continent and its inhabitants. That commitment is expressed locally, in a middle ground located geographically between the Ohio valley, the Great Plains, and the Great Lakes, and figuratively, between wildness and domesticity, aesthetics and practicality. The midwestern pastoral ideal is just that: an ideal, an abstraction by which writers evaluate the actual circumstances of people and place. Contemporaries like Smiley, Kooser, and Gruchow are not wistful for an Arcadia that never existed in the first place. Rather, they fulfill the terms of Leo Marx's complex pastoralism, which not only invokes "the image of a green landscape—a terrain either wild, or if cultivated, rural—as a symbolic repository of meaning and value" but also "acknowledges the reality of history" and "the forces which have stripped the old ideal of most, if not all, of its meaning" (*Machine in the Garden,* 163). These writers are realists as well as dreamers; if modern, materialistic society is ignorant of (or even antagonistic toward) regional landscapes and history, they present it as such. But in their love of land and lore, of place and people, midwestern writers in the lineage of Cather, Leopold, Roethke, Wright, and Harrison extend the optimistic, if pragmatic, pastoralism of Thomas Jefferson, whose "dialectical" politics, according to Marx, recognize "the constant need to redefine the 'middle landscape' ideal, pushing it ahead, so to speak, into an unknown future to adjust it to ever-changing cir- cumstances" (*Machine in the Garden,* 139). We have in the region's litera- ture a vision of a land full of natural resources—fields, forests, rivers, and lakes—which can bring people cultural as well as economic rewards if they learn, as have many writers and artists, to love midwestern places for their intrinsic beauty and spiritual worth.

# Notes

## Preface

1. John Elder, *Imagining the Earth: Poetry and the Vision of Nature* (Urbana: University of Illinois Press, 1985); Frederick Turner, *Spirit of Place: The Making of an American Literary Landscape* (New York: Sierra Club Books, 1989).

2. For more on this history, see my essay "Michigan's Pioneers and the Destruction of the Hardwood Forest," *Michigan Historical Review* 15, no. 2 (1989): 1–22.

3. Edmund G. Love, *The Situation in Flushing* (New York: Harper and Row, 1965).

4. Jim Harrison, "The Road: A Love Story," *Men's Journal,* May 2002, 91ff.

## Introduction

1. This study recognizes the Midwest as the area encompassed by the twelve-state definition of the U.S. Census: Ohio, Indiana, Michigan, Illinois, Wisconsin, Minnesota, Iowa, Missouri, Kansas, Nebraska, South Dakota, and North Dakota. A number of ecological zones fall within those political boundaries. Broadleaf deciduous forests dominate in the east, while piney north woods characterize the upper Great Lakes; the agricultural heartland or "corn belt" centered in Iowa, which occupies the former site of the American tallgrass prairie, gives way in the western parts of the Dakotas, Nebraska, and Kansas to the relatively arid shortgrass Great Plains. In addition to this geographical variety, major cities such as Detroit, Chicago, and Minneapolis, with their ethnic diversity and mixed economies, complicate definitions of midwestern cultural identity. They contradict the rural, Euro-American image of the Midwest, which has long been an oversimplification.

2. The term "topophilia" was given academic currency by University of Wisconsin geographer Yi-Fu Tuan, author of *Topophilia: A Study of Environmental Perception, Attitudes, and Values* (New York: Columbia University Press, 1974).

## Chapter I: Midwestern Pastoralism

1. I draw here on Lawrence B. Gamache's definition of modernism in "Toward a Definition of Modernism," in *The Modernists: Studies in a Literary Phenomenon,* ed. Lawrence B. Gamache and Ian S. Macniven (London: Associated University Presses, 1987), 32–45. Gamache associates the movement with disillusionment and a "sense of crisis in human existence reflected in many late nineteenth- and twentieth-century cultural products." He further characterizes modernism by its "preoccupation with the present, usually urban and technical rather than rural and agricultural in its sense of place and time . . . related to the loss of a meaningful context derived from the past, from its forms, styles, and traditions; this sense of loss gives rise to a search for a new context—cosmopolitan, not provincial, in scope—and for new techniques to evolve an acceptable perception of reality, often, paradoxically, in the form of an attempt to rediscover roots in the depths of the past" (33).

2. The phrase "poetry makes nothing happen" appears in Auden's poem "In Memory of W.B. Yeats," in *Collected Shorter Poems, 1927–1957* (New York: Random House, 1967), 141–43. Thomas Wolfe contributed a commonplace to the American vernacular with the title of his 1940 novel *You Can't Go Home Again* (New York: Harper and Row, 1973).

3. Among Jefferson's influences, Leo Marx lists "the continuing dialogue of the political philosophers [of the eighteenth century] about the condition of man in a 'state of nature'; and the simultaneous upsurge of radical primitivism (as expressed, for example, in the cult of the Noble Savage) on the one hand, and the doctrines of perfectibility and progress on the other" (*The Machine in the Garden,* 88). Jefferson's reading of English poetry and classical literature, including the pastorals of Virgil, also shaped his pastoral idealism.

4. On the early political history of the Northwest Territory, see Peter S. Onuf's *Statehood and Union: A History of the Northwest Ordinance* (Bloomington: Indiana University Press, 1987).

5. Despite the rhetoric of his public speeches, Jefferson's actual Indian policies as president were provocative and at times underhanded. He directed William Henry Harrison, for example, to go beyond law and ethics in securing land cessions in the Indiana Territory. While some of Harrison's purchases were aboveboard, he obtained others with the help of whiskey, bribery, and intimidation of minor chiefs who had no authority to act on behalf of the tribes at large. Such treaties were rushed to Washington for quick approval by Congress and the president. Lest Harrison's

Machiavellian tactics be taken as the actions of a frontier officer far from the supervision of his commander in chief, consider the cynicism evident in Jefferson's secret 1803 letter to Harrison:

> When [the Indians] withdraw themselves to the culture of a small piece of land, they will perceive how useless to them are their extensive forests, and will be willing to pare them off from time to time in exchange for necessaries for their farms and families. To promote this disposition to exchange lands . . . we shall push our trading houses, and be glad to see the good and influential among them run in debt, because we observe that when these debts get beyond what the individuals can pay, they become willing to lop them off by a cession of lands. (1,118)

6. Given the history of progressive as well as conservative politics in the Midwest, qualification is in order here. Hart characterizes the typical midwesterner as pecuniaristic, materialistic, self-assured, functionalist, technologic, competent, simplistic, present oriented, and xenophobic (280–81). Fellow geographer Raymond D. Gastil, however, suggests that "the 'values' Hart ascribes to the Middle West family farm ideology vary considerably from north to south." The central Midwest, he argues—Ohio, Indiana, Illinois, and Iowa—is more utilitarian than the upper Midwest of Michigan, Wisconsin, Minnesota, and the Dakotas. Pointing to movements like populism and La Follette progressivism, Gastil describes the upper Midwest as "an area remarkable in the United States for the extent of its social experimentation at voter request" (210). Stronger support for public education and recurring periods of governmental activism in the upper Midwest, Gastil believes, are "based on a relative absence of Southern culture and the pressure of liberal elements of the peoples who immigrated to the region" (212). These included New Englanders, who had a decisive influence on midwestern culture and landscape. In "The New England Presence on the Midwest Landscape," *The Old Northwest* 9, no. 2 (Summer 1983): 125–42, historian Thomas J. Schlereth speaks of a "New England presence on the Midwestern landscape," characterized by place names, Greek Revival architecture, and village plans, as well as an early "enthusiasm for higher learning, abolition, and moral reform" (131). This civic idealism sublimated utilitarian values into the rhetoric of republicanism. Material success, in other words, necessitated social duty and participation in democratic processes.

7. The version of Wood's *American Gothic* is *This Is Your Life* (1972) by Carl Owens, a black artist from Detroit. It was commissioned by the Gordy family. For a reproduction and analysis, see Wanda Corn's *Grant Wood: The Regionalist Vision* (New Haven, CT: Yale University Press, 1983), 139, 141.

8. On the Black Hawk War, consult *Black Hawk's Autobiography* (1833), edited by Roger L. Nicols (Ames: Iowa State University Press, 1999), and Nicols's biography *Black Hawk and the Warrior's Path* (Arlington Heights, IL: H. Davidson, 1992).

9. Consult *Walt Whitman: The Measure of His Song* (Minneapolis: Holy Cow! 1998), ed. Jim Perlman, Ed Folsom, and Dan Campion. The book collects essays and poems about Whitman by poets from around the world, from Emerson's famous 1855 letter to Whitman to writings from the 1990s. Contributions by midwesterners include an essay by James Wright, "The Delicacy of Walt Whitman," and another by Robert Bly, "My Doubts about Whitman."

10. In addition to Wik, consult Robert Lacey's *Ford: The Men and the Machine* (New York: Ballantine / Random House, 1986). Lacey's portrait of Henry Ford includes a discussion of Ford's utilitarian reading of Emerson and ideological kinship with the populist movement.

11. Turner's "The Significance of the Frontier in American History" (1893), probably the most influential essay by an American historian, bears the influence of the author's rural upbringing in pioneer-era Wisconsin. While the bibliography on the debate over Turner's "frontier thesis" is too large to approach here, it may be helpful to mention one recent selection of his work, *Reading Frederick Jackson Turner: "The Significance of the Frontier in American History" and Other Essays* (New York: Holt, 1995), with an introduction and afterword by John Mack Faragher, who reviews the debate and connects Turner's work to that of contemporary environmental historians.

Veblen, a Norwegian American from Minnesota, gained fame as the author of *The Theory of the Leisure Class* (1899), an incisive critique of materialism and class consciousness in the United States. His writing also includes long sections on "The Independent Farmer" and "The Country Town" in *Absentee Ownership and Business Enterprise in Recent Times* (1923), excerpted in *The Portable Veblen,* ed. Max Lerner (New York: Viking Press, 1948). Both essays reflect on midwestern culture; the second begins with allusions to Edgar Lee Masters and Sinclair Lewis.

Cronon, a Wisconsin native and a central figure in the recent development of environmental history as a distinct academic discipline, has written such books as *Nature's Metropolis: Chicago and the Great West* (New York: Norton, 1991). He also edited *Uncommon Ground: Toward Reinventing Nature* (New York: Norton, 1995), a collection of essays that caused considerable controversy among environmentalists, some of whom interpreted the contributors to the volume as advocating an anthropocentric or utilitarian view of nature. Cronon's own view is closer to a philosophy of stewardship that emphasizes the extent to which humans have altered even apparently wild, "untamed" landscapes. (The subtitle of the book was changed to *Rethinking the Human Place in Nature* for the 1996 paperback edition.) He has published several articles on Turner, as well as "Landscape and Home: Environmental Traditions in Wisconsin," *Wisconsin Magazine of History* 74, no. 2 (Winter 1990–1991): 83–105, which considers Turner, Leopold, and John Muir in relation to their experiences of Wisconsin landscape, and appears as a commentator in the film *Frank Lloyd Wright* (1998), directed by Ken Burns and Lynn Novick.

Freyfogle, a native of Illinois, proposes new understandings of private property based on a reevaluation of legal precedent in relation to ecological and aesthetic imperatives. He draws extensively on Leopold in his writings, which include *Bounded People, Boundless Lands* (Washington: Island Press, 1998) and *The Land We Share: Private Property and the Common Good* (Washington: Island Press, 2003). Freyfogle also edited *The New Agrarianism: Land, Culture, and the Community of Life* (Washington: Island Press, 2001) and coedited, with J. Baird Callicott, *For the Health of the Land,* a collection of writings by Aldo Leopold (see "Works Cited").

12. See Donald Worster's *Nature's Economy: A History of Ecological Ideas* (Cambridge: Cambridge University Press, 1977). Cowles, a scientist at the University of Chicago, based his theory of ecological succession on studies of Lake Michigan dunes. An 1899 paper he published on the topic was foundational to the subsequent development of ecological science. Worster refers to Cowles as "America's first professional ecologist" (208). Building on Cowles's insights, Clements, a professor at the University of Nebraska at the turn of the century, developed a theory of "climax communities." He based his conclusions on his studies of succession in prairie environments. On Clements also see Ronald Tobey's *Saving the Prairies: The Life Cycle of the Founding School of American Plant Ecology, 1895–1955* (Berkeley and Los Angeles: University of California Press, 1981).

Incidentally, Clements was an acquaintance of Willa Cather's; they had been classmates at the University of Nebraska. Susan Rosowski notes that fact as an example of how "ecology shaped Cather's conception of the world ... [she] witnessed the creation of the science of ecology" (103). Susan Rosowski, "The Comic Form of Willa Cather's Art: An Ecocritical Reading," in "Willa Cather's Ecological Imagination," ed. Susan Rosowski, special issue, *Cather Studies* 5 (2003):103–27.

13. Consult Robert Thacker, *The Great Prairie Fact and Literary Imagination* (Albuquerque: University of New Mexico Press, 1989); Diane Dufva Quantic, *The Nature of the Place: A Study of Great Plains Fiction* (Lincoln: University of Nebraska Press, 1995); and Edward Watts, *An American Colony: Regionalism and the Roots of Midwestern Culture* (Athens: Ohio University Press, 2002).

## Chapter 2: Willa Cather

1. I have in mind the kind of response to Cather encouraged by Joan Acocella in *Willa Cather and the Politics of Criticism* (Lincoln: University of Nebraska Press, 2000). "Though critics will always be affected by the political climate," she writes, "we can still hope for a criticism that, while indebted to a certain politics, balances that with a sustained attention to what the artist is saying" (72). Cather scholarship may in fact have reached that point, after years of attacks on Cather's portrayal of gender, race, and empire. Guy Reynolds, for example, describes Cather in *Willa Cather in Context: Progress, Race, and Empire* (New York: St. Martin's, 1996) as "a writer whose work, almost in spite of her own occasional lapses, manifested a breadth of sympathy and a genuine progressivism" (24).

2. The extent and character of Cather's environmental conscience is a key issue in the most recent scholarship. A number of perspectives, for example, appear in *Cather Studies* 5, a thematic issue, "Willa Cather's Ecological Imagination," edited by Rosowski and published in 2003. One contributor, the important ecocritic Joseph W. Meeker, is decidedly negative. "It is unlikely," Meeker argues, "that Willa Cather will find a place among the great literary examples of the environmental imagination. . . . There is no environmental ethic that emerges from her work, but rather an ethic of development that supposes that land fulfils its destiny when it is successfully farmed" (87–88). On the other side of the debate is Thomas J. Lyon, another major figure in ecocritical theory, who credits Cather with a "capacity to feel for places" that "is inherently ecological, and lets us see and feel the environment in a participative, intimate way. Willa Cather is one of our greatest nature writers—without even being a nature writer—because she had this living sense of the biotic community" (97).

## Chapter 3: Aldo Leopold

1. Because of his belief that controlled hunting plays an essential role in land management, Leopold is disliked by proponents of animal liberation/rights, an ideology inconsistent with the modern science of ecology. Animal rights philosophy focuses on the psychology and well-being of individual animals, while ecology is concerned with the survival of entire species and, especially, entire biotic communities. For the relation between Leopold and the humane movement, see Roderick Nash, "Aldo Leopold's Intellectual Heritage," Callicott, 63–88.

2. The relationship of Turner, Muir, and Leopold to Wisconsin's Sand Country was first developed in Susan Flader, with Charles Steinhacker, *The Sand Country of Aldo Leopold* (San Francisco: Sierra Club Books, 1973). See also William Cronon's "Landscape and Home: Environmental Traditions in Wisconsin," cited in note 11 for chapter 1.

3. Leopold's metaphor of nature as a book that can be read by a sensitive and informed observer harkens to the Romantics, particularly Thoreau and Muir. Muir often referred to landscape as holy scripture or as natural history text. The metaphor is frequently used by humanistic geographers like John Brinckerhoff Jackson and Donald W. Meinig, who treat landscapes, particularly developed ones, as "texts." Essential readings are John Brinckerhoff Jackson's *Discovering the Vernacular Landscape* (New Haven, CT: Yale University Press, 1984) and D. W. Meinig, ed., *The Interpretation of Ordinary Landscapes* (New York: Oxford University Press, 1979).

Tallmadge discusses the book metaphor at length, drawing a parallel between the "book of nature" and the "cultural harvest" of Leopold's land aesthetic. Certain figures of speech, such as Leopold's reference to "the olfactory poems" written by animals ("Great Possessions," 43), thus evoke the "literary" quality of landscape. More explicitly illustrative of the land aesthetic are related metaphors of nature as art or artist: "I know a painting. . . . It is a river who wields the brush" ("The Green Pasture," 51); as music or musician: "The wind that makes music in November corn is in a hurry" ("If I Were the Wind," 66); and as dance or choreographer: "The drama of the [woodcock] sky dance is enacted nightly on hundreds of farms, the owners of which sigh for entertainment, but harbor the illusion that it is to be sought in theatres" ("Sky Dance," 34). Since "literature" has arguments to make about ecology, history, and ethics, Leopold's "book of nature" metaphor also illustrates his land ethic.

4. My case for the regionalism of Leopold's metaphorical language is further supported by the first and central image of "The Round River,"

derived from the midwestern folklore of giant lumberman Paul Bunyan. The Round River, according to Leopold, was one "of the marvels of early Wisconsin . . . a river that flowed into itself, and thus sped around and around in a never-ending circuit" (*Round River,* 158). Leopold uses this image to illustrate the cyclicality of all ecosystems. Since Paul Bunyan represents the aggressive, conquering attitude toward nature that led to the deforestation of Wisconsin and other midwestern states with northern pine forests, Leopold's archetypal cooptation of this familiar folk hero is a particularly deft rhetorical strategy.

5. An excellent portrait of Jackson and the Land Institute can be found in Evan Eisenberg, "Back to Eden," *Atlantic,* November 1989, 57–89. Scott Russell Sanders includes "Learning from the Prairie," an account of a visit with Jackson at the institute, in *The Force of Spirit* (Boston: Beacon, 2000), 45–58.

## Chapter 4: Theodore Roethke

1. Unless otherwise noted, all quotations of Roethke's poetry are taken from Theodore Roethke, *The Collected Poems.*

2. Violet Mortensen, Charles Roethke's daughter, told Seager that in their family "the field" meant the area behind the greenhouse, where oats were grown for horse feed and where an acre of beautiful lilacs was tended. She, Theodore, and other children often played there (22).

3. See Seager, 278, 236, and 56, for the corresponding anecdotes.

4. Interestingly, half of the writers disparaged by Rahv as "redskins" are midwesterners: Lewis, Anderson, Sandburg, Hemingway, Theodore Dreiser, and James T. Farrell. That there is a regional bias at work is suggested by Rahv's assessment of the "redskin writer": "He is a self-made writer in the same way that Henry Ford was a self-made millionaire. On the one hand he is a crass materialist, a greedy consumer of experience, and on the other a sentimentalist, a half-baked mystic listening to inward voices and watching for signs and portents" (4–5). To compare these writers with Ford, whom New York radicals like Rahv disparaged as both a philistine and an untutored brute, diminishes all culture west of the Hudson River by means of stereotype.

5. Roethke taught briefly at Michigan State in 1935, but lost his job after suffering his first nervous breakdown. The chain of events has become legendary in East Lansing. While Roethke was hospitalized at Mercywood Sanitarium near Ann Arbor, his departmental chairman investigated his past with what Seager describes as "an electric energy," writing letters to "all the men who had recommended Ted, asking about insanity in the

family, other mental attacks Ted might have had, and his drinking" (97). One response from an anonymous source at the University of Michigan (Roethke's alma mater), quoted in full in *The Glass House,* slandered the poet, and misrepresented his academic record. Denied continued employment at Michigan State, Roethke was in no condition, physical or psychological, to contest his dismissal.

Roethke later applied to the University of Michigan, in 1946. Had he been accepted, *The Lost Son,* as well as his later books, would have been published while he taught at the state's most prestigious institution of higher learning. The English Department chair, however, had heard of his hospitalization "and thought him unstable. There was also a kind of institutional self-deprecation at work: since Ted was a Michigan man and they had known him, they did not believe he could possibly be as good as his reputation" (153). That Seager taught for many years at Michigan, until his death in 1968, lends unusual authority to his account.

6. See my essay "To Sustain the Bioregion: Michigan Poets of Place," *Midamerica* 17 (1990): 10–33, on Roethke, Harrison, Gerber, and Minty.

7. Philip Levine, *They Feed They Lion* (New York: Atheneum, 1972); Jim Daniels, *Places/Everyone* (Madison: University of Wisconsin Press, 1985).

## Chapter 5: James Wright

1. All quotations of Wright's poetry are from *Above the River: The Complete Poems.*

2. "A Blessing" resembles Robert Frost's most beloved poem, "Stopping by Woods on a Snowy Evening" in subject matter (travelers stopping on the road), imagery (horses and woods), and the final deferral of transcendence.

3. The image of seeds being released harkens back to another *Branch* poem, "In Memory of a Spanish Poet," about Miguel Hernández. Wright dreams of the poet's "slow voice, flying, / Planting the dark waters of the spirit / With lutes and seeds." Wright envisions such foreign poets as Hernández as literary pastoralists in an extended sense of the term. Planted as new stock in the fallow soil of American poetry in the 1950s and 1960s, their poems brought new music ("lutes") and new life ("seeds") to a literature in need of cross-fertilization. Thus Wright declaims,

> Here, in the American Midwest,
> Those seeds fly out of the field and across the strange heaven
> of my skull.

They scatter out of their wings a quiet farewell,
A greeting to my country.

(130)

Wright's similar release of seeds at the end of "Milkweed" represents his newfound poetic confidence: each of the poems in the book is a seed, scattered to grow in the heartland of America.

4. For a concise and well-narrated account of the Minnesota Sioux uprising, see chapter 2 of Ralph K. Andrist's *The Long Death: The Last Days of the Plains Indians* (New York: MacMillan, 1964). The rebellion stemmed from the murder of a group of settlers by four impetuous young braves returning from an unsuccessful summer hunting trip to the Big Woods of central Minnesota. At a council of tribal leaders, the party advocating war held sway, having argued, according to Andrist, "with any amount of historical precedent to back them up—that it would do no good to turn the four murderers over to the whites for punishment because all Indians would be punished indiscriminately anyway" (34). Little Crow, who had been working to adapt his people to agriculture, argued eloquently against attack, which would surely prove futile. But as Andrist relates, when the peaceful chief "found the Sioux meant to fight regardless of his warnings, he had decided that it was better to fight a lost cause than become a nobody" (36). The days that followed saw the brutal killing of hundreds of settlers, followed by an all-out engagement with the Minnesota Sixth Infantry and state militia. The Sioux lost this first installment of the Plains War; even those who had remained neutral or had assisted whites during the uprising were exiled to reservations in Dakota Territory. Thirty-eight Sioux men were hung on a single scaffold in the town of Mankato to satisfy the whites' desire for revenge (306 had been sentenced to death, but President Lincoln signed an order of executive clemency). Little Crow was shot to death one year later by a farmer near the town of Hutchinson. He had been picking berries with his son, who escaped. The chief's body, unidentified at the time, ended up in the offal pit of a slaughterhouse.

## Chapter 6: Jim Harrison

1. As inspired by Neruda, Rilke, and Rimbaud as by Whitman, Harrison responds to Neruda's call for an "impure poetry," described by the Chilean Nobel laureate "as impure as a suit or body . . . stained by food and shame, a poetry with wrinkles, observations, dreams, waking, prophe-

sies, declarations of love and hatred, beasts, blows, idylls, manifestos, denials, doubts, affirmations, taxes" (128). Each of these themes and approaches can be exemplified by passages from Harrison's poetry. Neruda's essay "Some Thoughts on Impure Poetry" may be found in *Passions and Impressions,* ed. Matilde Neruda and Miguel Otero Silva, trans. Margaret Sayers Peden (New York: Farrar, Straus and Giroux, 1983), 128–29.

2. All quotations of Harrison's poetry are from *The Shape of the Journey: New and Collected Poems.*

3. Jim Harrison, correspondence with author, September 29, 1989.

4. Roethke, "The Far Field," *Collected Poems,* 193.

5. I take the phrase "backward glance" from Harrison's "Small Poem," which includes the image of a "doe's backward / glance at the stillborn fawn" (355). The poem connects personal grief with an awareness of historical wrongs.

## Chapter 7: Further Views

1. On Smiley's adaptation of Shakespeare, see James A. Schiff's "Contemporary Retellings: *A Thousand Acres* as the Latest Lear," *Critique* 39, no. 4 (Summer 1998): 367–82.

2. Smiley's novel ought to be included in any study of pastoral writing by midwestern women, which often contrasts women's experiences of rural life with the pastoral myth of domestic tranquility and freedom on the farm. An insistent realism has marked this writing ever since nineteenth-century authors like Caroline Kirkland, Margaret Fuller, Eliza Farnham, Alice Cary, and Caroline Soule first dissected farm life on the midwestern frontier, which was often harsher, more difficult, and lonelier for women than for men. In *The Land before Her: Fantasy and Experience of the American Frontiers, 1630–1860* (Chapel Hill: University of North Carolina Press, 1984), Annette Kolodny finds that these writers challenge "male assertions of a rediscovered Eden" (and metaphors of a feminized American landscape), dreaming instead "of locating a home and a familial human community within a cultivated garden" (xiii). Twentieth-century novelists of midwestern rural life like Susan Glaspell and Jane Hamilton similarly portray women struggling to maintain cohesive households while dealing with changing economic realities (as well as gender roles) in modern society. Midwestern women poets (such as Lorine Niedecker and Judith Minty) and essayists (Josephine Johnson, Kathleen Norris, and Carol Bly, for example) are more likely than fiction writers to convey spiritual sensibilities about

place and landscape, even if they attend to issues of gender in relation to the human experience of nature.

3. I use the term "communitarian" in the sense meant by sociologists and public policy experts—of a progressive but decidedly moderate political persuasion—who are concerned by the excesses of individualism (particularly the utilitarian variety) in the United States. A document titled "The Communitarian Platform," signed by many notable public figures, includes the following statement:

> American men, women, and children are members of many communities—families; neighborhoods; innumerable social, religious, ethnic, work place, and professional associations; and the body politic itself. Neither human existence nor individual liberty can be sustained for long outside the interdependent and overlapping communities to which all of us belong. Nor can any community long survive unless its members dedicate some of their attention, energy, and resources to shared projects. The exclusive pursuit of private interest erodes the network of social environments on which we all depend, and is destructive to our shared experiment in democratic self-government. For these reasons, we hold that the rights of individuals cannot long be preserved without a communitarian perspective.
>
> A communitarian perspective recognizes both individual human dignity and the social dimension of human existence.
>
> A communitarian perspective recognizes that the preservation of individual liberty depends on the active maintenance of the institutions of civil society where citizens learn respect for others as well as self-respect; where we acquire a lively sense of our personal and civic responsibilities, along with an appreciation of our own rights and the rights of others; where we develop the skills of self-government as well as the habit of governing ourselves, and learn to serve others—not just self.

Sponsored by an organization called the Communitarian Network, "The Communitarian Platform" can be found on-line at http://www2 .gwu.edu/~ccps/rcplatform.html. Without being directly tied to this organization or the political philosophy it espouses, Kooser portrays selfhood in relation to social ties of community and responsibility far more than most contemporary poets. Community, as much as reflective solitude, is a theme and narrative circumstance in his work.

4. In September 1878, Dull Knife led his people out of Indian Territory (present-day Oklahoma, where they had been relocated by the U.S. government). Heading north with the intent of reaching their home in the Powder River country of southern Montana, they fought cavalry units of the U.S. Army along the way in Kansas and Nebraska. Young warriors, in defiance of their leaders, raped and killed white settlers during the exodus. The Cheyenne were eventually captured, with Dull Knife's group being confined at Fort Robinson. Wishing to avoid return to Indian Territory, Dull Knife and his people escaped on January 9, 1879, again pursued by the army, which inflicted terrible casualties. The survivors finally took refuge on the Pine Ridge Reservation in South Dakota.

For accounts of this history, see John H. Monnett's *Tell Them We Are Going Home: The Odyssey of the Northern Cheyennes* (Norman: University of Oklahoma Press, 2001) and Vernon Maddux's *In Dull Knife's Wake: The True Story of the Northern Exodus in 1878* (Norman, OK: Horse Creek Publications, 2003). A novelistic version of these events appears in Mari Sandoz's *Cheyenne Autumn* (New York: McGraw-Hill, 1953; Lincoln: University of Nebraska Press, 1992), which was made into a 1964 film by director John Ford. Also worthwhile is Alan's Boye's *Holding Stone Hands: On the Trail of the Cheyenne Exodus* (Lincoln: University of Nebraska Press, 1999), a nonfiction account of a thousand-mile walk tracing the route taken by the Cheyenne.

5. Also see Ted Kooser et al., "More Letters to a Young Poet," *Midwest Quarterly* 44, no. 4 (Summer 2003): 389–419, in which several contemporary poets pretend to continue Rainer Maria Rilke's famous early twentieth-century correspondence. In his letter, Kooser develops an extended comparison of writing poetry with invention: "For each invention that catches on with the public—each electric light bulb poem, each jet turbine poem, each *The Love Song of J. Alfred Prufrock*—there are hundreds of poems— poems that will automatically tip a gentleman's hat—that fail to engage their readers." Kooser, like Leopold before him, subversively invokes the midwestern tinkerer archetype to convey ideas transcending individualism: "A poet serves a community and each poem ought to be thought of as a gift to the reader. What kind of a gift to the world is a pedal-powered-ear-wax-remover poem?" (389–90)

A revised version of the passage comparing poetry to invention appears in Kooser's *The Poetry Home Repair Manual: Practical Advice for Beginning Poets* (Lincoln: University of Nebraska Press, 2005), 22.

6. Paul Gruchow died of an intentional drug overdose at his home in Duluth, Minnesota, on February 22, 2004, at age fifty-six. He had long suffered from clinical depression, the subject of his as-yet unpublished final manuscript.

# Works Cited

Atherton, Lewis. *Main Street on the Middle Border.* Bloomington: Indiana University Press, 1954.

Baker, Bruce P. "Nebraska's Cultural Desert: Willa Cather's Early Short Stories." *Midamerica* 15 (1987): 12–17.

Bellah, Robert, et al. *Habits of the Heart: Individualism and Commitment in American Life.* Updated ed. Berkeley and Los Angeles: University of California Press, 1996.

Belt, Don. "Sweden: In Search of a New Model." *National Geographic,* August 1993, 2–35.

Berry, Wendell. *A Continuous Harmony.* New York: Harcourt Brace Jovanovich, 1972.

———. *What Are People For?* San Francisco: North Point, 1990.

Bloom, Harold, ed. *Willa Cather's "My Ántonia."* New York: Chelsea House, 1987.

Bly, Robert. *American Poetry: Wildness and Domesticity.* New York: Harper and Row, 1990.

———. *The Light around the Body.* New York: Harper and Row, 1967.

———. *Remembering James Wright.* St. Paul, MN: Ally, 1991.

———. *Silence in the Snowy Fields.* Hanover, NH: University Press of New England / Wesleyan University Press, 1962.

———. *Talking All Morning.* Ann Arbor: University of Michigan Press, 1980.

———. *The Winged Life: The Poetic Voice of Henry David Thoreau.* New York: HarperCollins, 1992.

———. "The Work of James Wright." In Stitt and Graziano, *James Wright,* 94–116.

Bryant, William Cullen. "The Prairies." In *American Poetry: The Nineteenth Century,* vol. 1, *Freneau to Whitman,* ed. John Hollander, 162–65. New York: Library of America, 1993.

Buell, Lawrence. *The Environmental Imagination: Thoreau, Nature Writing, and the Formation of American Culture.* Cambridge, MA: Belknap / Harvard University Press, 1995.

Burke, Kenneth. "The Vegetal Radicalism of Theodore Roethke." *Sewanee Review* 58 (1950): 68–108.

Callaway, Kathy. "The Very Rich Hours of the Duke of Fano: James Wright's *This Journey.*" In Stitt and Graziano, *James Wright*, 390–405.

Callicott, J. Baird, ed. *Companion to "A Sand County Almanac": Interpretive and Critical Essays.* Madison: University of Wisconsin Press, 1987.

Campbell, Joseph. *The Hero with a Thousand Faces.* Princeton, NJ: Princeton University Press, 1949.

Cather, Willa. *Early Novels and Stories.* New York: Library of America, 1987.

———. "The Enchanted Bluff." In Cather, *Stories*, 64–73.

———. "Escapism" (letter to *Commonweal*, April 17, 1936). In Cather, *Stories*, 968–73.

———. *The Kingdom of Art: Willa Cather's First Principles and Critical Statements, 1893–1896.* Ed. Bernice Slote. Lincoln: University of Nebraska Press, 1966.

———. *A Lost Lady.* New York: Knopf, 1923.

———. *My Ántonia.* In Cather, *Early Novels*, 707–937.

———. "Nebraska: The End of the First Cycle." *Nation*, September 5, 1923, 236–38.

———. *O Pioneers!* In Cather, *Early Novels*, 133–290.

———. *Stories, Poems, and Other Writings.* New York: Library of America, 1992.

Catton, Bruce. *Waiting for the Morning Train.* 1972. Detroit: Wayne State University Press, 1987.

Cayton, Andrew R. L. and Peter S. Onuf. *The Midwest and the Nation: Rethinking the History of an American Region.* Bloomington: Indiana University Press, 1990.

Cooley, John. "Introduction: American Nature Writing and the Pastoral Tradition." In *Earthly Words: Essays on Contemporary American Nature Writing and Environmental Writers,* ed. John Cooley, 1–15. Ann Arbor: University of Michigan Press, 1994.

Dougherty, James C. *James Wright.* Boston: Twayne, 1987.

Eliot, T. S. *Collected Poems, 1909–1962.* San Diego: Harcourt Brace Jovanovich, 1963.

Emerson, Ralph Waldo. *Collected Poems and Translations.* New York: Library of America, 1994.

———. *Essays and Lectures.* New York: Library of America, 1983.

Erdrich, Louise. Review of *Dalva,* by Jim Harrison. In *Contemporary Literary Criticism* 66, ed. Roger Matuz, 164. Detroit: Gale, 1991. Originally published in *Chicago Tribune, Books,* March 20, 1988, 1.

Farris, Sara. "American Pastoral in the Twentieth Century: *O Pioneers!, A Thousand Acres,* and *Merry Men.*" *ISLE: Interdisciplinary Studies in Literature and Environment* 5, no. 1 (Winter 1998): 27–48.

Fischer, Mike. "Pastoralism and Its Discontents: Willa Cather and the Burden of Imperialism." *Mosaic* 23, no. 1 (Winter 1990): 31–47.

Flader, Susan. "Aldo Leopold's Sand Country." In Callicott, *Companion,* 40–62.

Ford, Henry. *My Life and Work.* Garden City, NY: Doubleday, Page, 1922.

Frazer, Timothy C., ed. *"Heartland" English: Variation and Transition in the American Midwest.* Tuscaloosa: University of Alabama Press, 1993.

Garland, Hamlin. *Main-Travelled Roads.* 1891. Lincoln: University of Nebraska Press, 1995.

Garland, John H., ed. *The North American Midwest: A Regional Geography.* New York: Wiley, 1955.

Gastil, Raymond D. *Cultural Regions of the United States.* Seattle: University of Washington Press, 1975.

Gelfant, Blanche H. "The Forgotten Reaping-Hook: Sex in *My Ántonia.*" In Bloom, *Willa Cather's "My Ántonia,"* 79–97.

Goetzmann, William. "Savage Enough to Prefer the Woods: The Cosmopolite and the West." In *Thomas Jefferson: The Man . . . His World . . . His Influence,* ed. Lally Weymouth, 107–27. New York: Putnam, 1973.

Gruchow, Paul. *Grass Roots: The Universe of Home.* Minneapolis: Milkweed Editions, 1995.

———. *The Necessity of Empty Places.* New York: St. Martin's, 1988.

Harrison, Jim. Correspondence with author, September 29, 1989.

———. *Dalva.* New York: Dutton / Seymour Lawrence, 1988.

———. *Farmer.* New York: Delta / Lawrence, 1976.

———. "Jim Harrison" (prefatory remarks preceding two essays by Harrison). In *Silent Seasons,* ed. Russell Chatham, 145. Livingston, MT: Clark City, 1988.

———. "Jim Harrison: The Art of Fiction CIV." Interview by Jim Fergus. *Paris Review* 30, no. 107 (1988): 52–97.

———. *Just before Dark: Collected Nonfiction.* Livingston, MT: Clark City, 1991.

———. *The Road Home.* New York: Atlantic Monthly Press, 1998.

———. *The Shape of the Journey: New and Collected Poems.* Port Townsend, WA: Copper Canyon, 1998.

———. *Sundog.* New York: Dutton / Lawrence, 1984.

———. *Wolf.* New York: Simon and Schuster, 1971.

Harrison, Jim, and Ted Kooser. *Braided Creek: A Conversation in Poetry.* Port Townsend, WA: Copper Canyon Press, 2003.

Hart, John Frazier. "The Middle West." *Annals of the Association of American Geographers* 62, no. 2 (June 1972): 258–82.

Hemingway, Ernest. *The Nick Adams Stories.* New York: Scribner's, 1972.

Heyden, William. "Inward to the World: The Poetry of Robert Bly." In Peseroff, *Robert Bly,* 13–22.

Hicks, Granville. "The Case against Willa Cather." 1933. In *Willa Cather and Her Critics,* ed. James Schroeter, 139–47. Ithaca: Cornell University Press, 1967. Originally appeared in *English Journal* 22 (November 1933): 703–10.

Hofstadter, Richard. *The Age of Reform.* London: Jonathan Cape, 1962.

Horsman, Reginald. *Expansion and American Indian Policy, 1783–1812.* East Lansing: Michigan State University Press, 1967.

Jackson, Wes. *Becoming Native to This Place.* Lexington: University Press of Kentucky, 1994.

Janssens, G. A. M. "The Present State of American Poetry: Robert Bly and James Wright." In Stitt and Graziano, *James Wright,* 191–220.

Jeffers, Robinson. *The Collected Poetry of Robinson Jeffers.* Vol. 2. Stanford, CA: Stanford University Press, 1989.

Jefferson, Thomas. *Writings.* New York: Library of America, 1984.

Johnson, Hildegard Binder. *Order upon the Land: The U.S. Rectangular Survey and the Upper Mississippi Country.* New York: Oxford University Press, 1976.

Kalaidjian, Walter B. *Understanding Theodore Roethke.* Columbia: University of South Carolina Press, 1987.

Keats, John. John Keats to George and Tom Keats, 1817. In Perkins, *English Romantic Writers,* 1,209–10.

———. "On Seeing the Elgin Marbles." In Perkins, *English Romantic Writers,* 1,135–36.

Kennedy, Roger G. *Hidden Cities: The Discovery and Loss of Ancient North American Civilization.* New York: Penguin, 1994.

Kolodny, Annette. *The Land before Her: Fantasy and Experience of the American Frontiers, 1630–1860.* Chapel Hill: University of North Carolina Press, 1984.

Kooser, Ted. *Delights and Shadows.* Port Townsend, WA: Copper Canyon Press.

———. *Local Wonders: Seasons in the Bohemian Alps.* Lincoln: University of Nebraska Press, 2002.

———. "Some of the Things I Think About When Working on a Poem." *Midwest Quarterly* 40, no. 4 (Summer 1999): 439.

————. *Sure Signs: New and Selected Poems.* Pittsburgh: University of Pittsburgh Press, 1980.

————. *Winter Morning Walks: One Hundred Postcards to Jim Harrison.* Pittsburgh: Carnegie Mellon Press, 2000.

Kusch, Robert. *"My Toughest Mentor": Theodore Roethke and William Carlos Williams (1944–1948).* Cranbury, NJ: Associated University Presses, 1999.

Lambert, Deborah. "The Defeat of a Hero: Autonomy and Sexuality in *My Ántonia.*" In Bloom, *Willa Cather's "My Ántonia,"* 119–31.

Lawrence, D. H. *Studies in Classic American Literature.* Garden City, NY: Doubleday, 1951.

Leopold, Aldo. "A Criticism of the Booster Spirit." In Leopold, *River,* 98–105.

————. "The Farmer as a Conservationist." In Leopold, *For the Health,* 161–75.

————. Foreword to 1947 manuscript titled *Great Possessions.* In Callicott, *Companion,* 281–88.

————. *For the Health of the Land: Previously Unpublished Essays and Other Writings.* Ed. J. Baird Callicott and Eric T. Freyfogle. Washington, DC: Island / Shearwater, 1999.

————. *Game Management.* New York: Scribner's, 1933.

————. *Report on a Game Survey of the North Central States.* Madison, WI: Democrat Printing, for the Sporting Arms and Ammunition Manufacturers' Institute, 1931.

————. *The River of the Mother of God and Other Essays.* Ed. Susan L. Flader and J. Baird Callicott. Madison: University of Wisconsin Press, 1991.

————. *Round River.* 1953. Oxford: Oxford University Press, 1993.

————. "The Round River." In *A Sand County Almanac with Essays on Conservation from Round River.* New York: Ballantine, 1970.

————. *A Sand County Almanac.* New York: Oxford University Press, 1949.

Lewis, Sinclair. *Babbitt.* New York: Harcourt, Brace, 1922.

————. *Main Street.* New York: Harcourt, 1920.

Love, Glen A. "*Et in Arcadia Ego:* Pastoral Theory Meets Ecocriticism." *Western American Literature* 27, no. 3 (Fall 1992): 195–207.

Lutwack, Leonard. *The Role of Place in Literature.* Syracuse, NY: Syracuse University Press, 1984.

Lynch, Thomas. "Learning Gravity." In *Skating with Heather Grace,* 27–34. New York: Knopf, 1986.

Madison, John, ed. *Heartland: Comparative Histories of the Midwestern States.* Bloomington: Indiana University Press, 1988.

Martone, Michael, ed. *Townships.* Iowa City: University of Iowa Press, 1992.

Marx, Leo. *The Machine in the Garden: Technology and the Pastoral Ideal in America.* New York: Oxford University Press, 1964.

———. "Pastoralism in America." In *Ideology and Classic American Literature,* ed. Sacvan Berkovitch and Myra Jehlen, 36–69. Cambridge: Cambridge University Press, 1986.

McClintock, James I. "Dalva: Jim Harrison's 'Twin Sister.'" *Journal of Men's Studies* 6, no. 3 (Spring 1998): 319–30.

———. *Nature's Kindred Spirits: Aldo Leopold, Joseph Wood Krutch, Edward Abbey, Annie Dillard, and Gary Snyder.* Madison: University of Wisconsin Press, 1994.

Meine, Curt. *Aldo Leopold: His Life and Work.* Madison: University of Wisconsin Press, 1988.

Mellencamp, John. "Jack and Diane." *American Fool.* LP. Polygram, 1982.

Mersmann, James F. "Robert Bly: Watering the Rocks." In Peseroff, *Robert Bly,* 54–100.

Miller, James E. "*My Ántonia* and the American Dream." In Bloom, *Willa Cather's "My Ántonia,"* 99–108.

Mills, Stephanie. *In Service of the Wild: Restoring and Reinhabiting Damaged Land.* Boston: Beacon, 1995.

Mueller, Lisel. "Midwestern Poetry: Goodbye to All That." In *In the Middle: Ten Midwestern Women Poets,* ed. Sylvia Griffith Wheeler, 69–72. Kansas City: BkMk / University of Missouri–Kansas City, 1985.

———. "Versions of Reality." Review of *Locations,* by Jim Harrison, and books by seven other poets. *Poetry* 117 (February 1971): 322–30.

Narveson, Robert. "*Spoon River Anthology:* An Introduction." *Midamerica* 7 (1980): 52–72.

Nash, Roderick. *Wilderness and the American Mind.* 3rd ed. New Haven, CT: Yale University Press, 1982.

Nelson, Howard. *Robert Bly: An Introduction to the Poetry.* New York: Columbia University Press, 1984.

Niatum, Duane. "Lines for Roethke Twenty Years after His Death." In *Drawings of the Song Animals: New and Selected Poems,* 139–40. Duluth, MN: Holy Cow! 1991.

Nims, John Frederick. "Midwest." In Stryk, *Heartland,* 150.

Nordström, Lars. *Theodore Roethke, William Stafford, and Gary Snyder: The Ecological Metaphor as Transformed Regionalism.* Upsala, Sweden: Upsala University, 1989.

O'Brien, Sharon. *Willa Cather: The Emerging Voice*. New York: Oxford University Press, 1987.

O'Gorman, James F. *Three American Architects: Richardson, Sullivan, and Wright, 1865–1915*. Chicago: University of Chicago Press, 1991.

Opie, John. *The Law of the Land: Two Hundred Years of American Farmland Policy*. Lincoln: University of Nebraska Press, 1994.

Parini, Jay. *Theodore Roethke: An American Romantic*. Amherst: University of Massachusetts Press, 1979.

Perkins, David, ed. *English Romantic Writers*. San Diego: Harcount Brace Jovanovich, 1967.

Peseroff, Joyce, ed. *Robert Bly: When Sleepers Awake*. Ann Arbor: University of Michigan Press, 1984.

Peterson, Walter Scott. *An Approach to Paterson*. New Haven, CT: Yale University Press, 1967.

Pinchot, Gifford. *The Fight for Conservation*. 1910. Reprint, Seattle: University of Washington Press, 1967.

Polley, Jane, ed. *American Folklore and Legend*. Pleasantville, NY: Reader's Digest Association, 1978.

Rahv, Philip. "Paleface and Redskin." In *Image and Idea: Twenty Essays on Literary Themes*. Norfolk, CT: New Directions, 1957.

Ramsey, Jarold. *Reading the Fire: Essays in the Traditional Indian Literatures of the Far West*. Lincoln: University of Nebraska Press, 1983.

Randall, John H. "Willa Cather and the Pastoral Tradition." In *Five Essays on Willa Cather*, ed. John J. Murphy, 75–96. North Andover, MA: Merrimack College, 1974.

Richardson, Robert D. *Emerson: The Mind on Fire*. Berkeley and Los Angeles: University of California Press, 1995.

Roberson, William H. "'Macho Mistake': The Misrepresentation of Jim Harrison's Fiction." *Critique* 29, no. 4 (Summer 1988): 233–44.

Robinett, Jane. "Two Poems and Two Poets." In Stitt and Graziano, *James Wright*, 49–55.

Roethke, Theodore. *The Collected Poems of Theodore Roethke*. Garden City, NY: Anchor / Doubleday, 1975.

———. *On the Poet and His Craft: Selected Prose of Theodore Roethke*. Ed. Ralph J. Mills Jr. Seattle: University of Washington Press, 1965.

———. *The Selected Letters of Theodore Roethke*. Ed. Ralph J. Mills Jr. Seattle: University of Washington Press, 1968.

———. *Straw for the Fire: From the Notebooks of Theodore Roethke, 1943–1963*. Ed. David Wagoner. New York: Doubleday, 1972.

Rosowski, Susan. *The Voyage Perilous: Willa Cather's Romanticism*. Lincoln: University of Nebraska Press, 1986.

———. "Willa Cather and the Fatality of Place: *O Pioneers!*, *My Ántonia*, and *A Lost Lady*." In *Geography and Literature: A Meeting of the Disciplines*, ed. William E. Mallory and Paul Simpson-Housley, 80–94. Syracuse, NY: Syracuse University Press, 1987.

———, ed. "Willa Cather's Ecological Imagination." Special issue, *Cather Studies* 5 (2003).

Sanders, Mark, and J. V. Brummels, eds. *On Common Ground: The Poetry of William Kloefkorn, Ted Kooser, Greg Kuzma, and Don Welch*. Ord, NE: Sandhills, 1983.

Sanders, Scott Russell. Foreword to Leopold, *For the Health*.

———. *Secrets of the Universe: Scenes from the Journey Home*. Boston: Beacon, 1991.

———. *Staying Put: Making A Home in a Restless World*. Boston: Beacon, 1993.

———. *Writing from the Center*. Bloomington: Indiana University Press, 1995.

Seager, Allan. *The Glass House: The Life of Theodore Roethke*. New York: McGraw-Hill, 1968.

Sergeant, Elizabeth Shipley. *Willa Cather: A Memoir*. Lincoln: University of Nebraska Press, 1953.

Shepard, Paul. *Man in the Landscape: A Historic View of the Esthetics of Nature*. New York: Knopf, 1967.

Shortridge, James. *The Midwest in American Culture*. Lawrence: University Press of Kansas, 1989.

Smiley, Jane. *A Thousand Acres*. New York: Ballantine, 1991.

Smith, Henry Nash. *Virgin Land: The American West as Symbol and Myth*. New York: Vintage / Random House, 1950.

Snyder, Gary. *Earth House Hold*. New York: New Directions, 1969.

———. *The Real Work: Interviews and Talks, 1964–1979*. New York: New Directions, 1980.

Stillwell, Mary K. "When a Walk Is a Poem: *Winter Morning Walks*, A Chronicle of Survival, by Ted Kooser." *Midwest Quarterly* 45 no. 4 (Summer 2004): 399–414.

Stitt, Peter. Introduction to *James Wright: A Profile*. Ed. Frank Graziano and Peter Stitt, 7–20. Durango, CO: Logbridge-Rhodes, 1988.

———. *The World's Hieroglyphic Beauty: Five American Poets*. Athens: University of Georgia Press, 1985.

Stitt, Peter, and Frank Graziano, eds. *James Wright: The Heart of the Light.* Ann Arbor: University of Michigan Press, 1990.

Stouck, David. *Willa Cather's Imagination.* Lincoln: University of Nebraska Press, 1975.

Stryk, Lucien, ed. *Heartland: Poets of the Midwest.* De Kalb: Northern Illinois University Press, 1967.

Sullivan, Rosemary. *The Garden Master: Style and Identity in the Poetry of Theodore Roethke.* Seattle: University of Washington Press, 1987.

Tallmadge, John. "Anatomy of a Classic." In Callicott, *Companion,* 110–27.

Teaford, Jon C. *Cities of the Heartland: The Rise and Fall of the Industrial Midwest.* Bloomington: Indiana University Press, 1993.

Thoreau, Henry David. *A Week on the Concord and Merrimack Rivers, Walden; or, Life in the Woods, The Maine Woods, Cape Cod.* New York: Library of America, 1985.

Tocqueville, Alexis de. *Democracy in America.* Ed. J. P. Mayer. Trans. George Lawrence. New York: HarperPerennial, 1988.

———. *Journey to America.* Ed. J. P. Mayer. Trans. George Lawrence. Rev. ed. Garden City, NY: Doubleday, 1971.

Vanderbilt, Kermit. "Theodore Roethke as a Northwest Poet." In *Northwest Perspectives: Essays on the Culture of the Pacific Northwest,* ed. Edwin R. Bingham and Glen A. Love, 186–216. Seattle: University of Washington Press, 1979.

Washburn, Wilcomb E. *Red Man's Land / White Man's Law: A Study of the Past and Present Status of the American Indian.* New York: Scribner's, 1971.

Weber, Ronald. *The Midwestern Ascendancy in American Writing.* Bloomington: Indiana University Press, 1992.

Weinberg, Albert K. *Manifest Destiny: A Study of Nationalist Expansionism in American History.* Baltimore: John Hopkins Press, 1935.

White, Lynn, Jr. "The Historical Roots of Our Ecologic Crisis." *Science* 155 (March 10, 1967): 1,203–7.

White, Richard. *The Middle Ground: Indians, Empires, and Republics in the Great Lakes Region, 1650–1815.* New York: Cambridge University Press, 1991.

Whitman, Walt. *Poetry and Prose.* New York: Library of America, 1982.

Wik, Reynold M. *Henry Ford and Grass-Roots America.* Ann Arbor: University of Michigan Press, 1972.

Williams, Harry. *"The Edge Is What I Have": Theodore Roethke and After.* Cranbury, NJ: Associated University Presses, 1977.

Williams, William Carlos. *Paterson.* Rev. ed. New York: New Directions, 1991.

Woiwode, Larry. "The Spirit of Place." In *Inheriting the Land: Contemporary Voices from the Midwest,* ed. Mark Vinz and Thom Tammaro, 51–65. Minneapolis: University of Minnesota Press, 1993.

Woodress, James. *Willa Cather: A Literary Life.* Lincoln: University of Nebraska Press, 1987.

Worster, Donald. *Nature's Economy: A History of Ecological Ideas.* Cambridge: Cambridge University Press, 1977.

Wright, Anne, ed. *The Delicacy and Strength of Lace: Letters between Leslie Marmon Silko and James Wright.* St. Paul, MN: Graywolf, 1986.

Wright, Frank Lloyd. "In the Cause of Architecture." 1908. In *Collected Writings, Volume 1 (1894–1930),* ed. Bruce Brooks Pfeiffer, 84–100. New York: Rizzoli, 1992. Originally appeared in *Architectural Record,* March 1908.

Wright, James. *Above the River: The Complete Poems.* New York: Noonday and University Press of New England, 1990.

———. *Collected Prose.* Ed. Anne Wright. Ann Arbor: University of Michigan Press, 1983.

Yardley, Jonathan. "A Lonely Heart in the Heartland." Review of *Dalva,* by Jim Harrison. In *Contemporary Literary Criticism* 66, ed. Roger Matuz, 163–64. Detroit, Gale, 1991. Originally published in *Washington Post, Book World,* March 6, 1988, 3.

# Index